OPERATIONAL REVIEW WORKBOOK

OPERATIONAL REVIEW WORKBOOK

Case Studies, Forms, and Exercises

Rob Reider

John Wiley & Sons, Inc.
New York • Chichester • Weinheim • Brisbane • Toronto • Singapore

For general information on our other products and services, or technical support, please contact our Customer Care Department within the United States at 800-762-2974, outside the United States at 317-572-3993 or fax 317-572-4002.

Wiley also publishes its books in a variety of electronic formats. Some content that appears in print may not be available in electronic books.

ISBN 0-471-22811-7

Printed in the United States of America.

10 9 8 7 6 5 4 3 2 1

About the Author

Rob Reider, CPA, MBA, PhD, is the President of Reider Associates, a management and organizational consulting firm located in Santa Fe, New Mexico, which he founded in 1976. Prior to starting Reider Associates, he was a manager in the Management Consulting Department of Peat, Marwick in Philadelphia. His area of expertise encompasses planning and budget systems, managerial and administrative systems, computer processing, financial and accounting procedures, organizational behavior and theory, management advisory services, large and small business consulting, management information and control techniques, and management training and staff development.

Rob has been a consultant to numerous large, medium, and small businesses of all types in the aforementioned areas (in both the private and public sectors). In addition, he has conducted many and varied operational reviews and benchmarking studies and has trained both internal staff and external consultants in these techniques.

He is the course author and nationally sought after discussion leader and presenter for more than 20 different seminars that are conducted nationally for various organizations and associations. He has conducted more than 1,000 such seminars throughout the country and has received the AICPA Outstanding Discussion Leader of the Year award.

Rob is considered a national expert in the areas of operational reviews and benchmarking strategies. He provides specific consultation in the areas of general business management, development of internal and external consulting practices, organizational and management systems, and the development and conducting of continuing professional education and other training programs.

Rob is the course author of nine Reider Associates self-study courses marketed nationally. He is also the author of the following books also published by John Wiley & Sons, Inc.

The Complete Guide to Operational Auditing

Operational Review: Maximum Results at Efficient Costs

Benchmarking Strategies: A Tool for Profit Improvement

Improving the Economy, Efficiency, and Effectiveness of Not-for-Profits

Rob has also been a presenter at numerous professional meetings and conferences around the country and has published numerous articles in professional journals. He has been a frequent commentator on the educational video programs produced by Primemedia Workplace Learning such as The CPA Report, The Governmental Update, and the Accounting and Financial Managers Network.

Rob has earned the degree of Bachelor of Science in Business Administration and Master of Science in Business from Drexel University as well as Doctor of Philosophy in Organizational and Management Psychology from Southwest University. He is currently listed in *Who's Who in the East and West, Who's Who in the World, Who's Who in Finance and Industry, Personalities in America, International Biography, Who's Who of Emerging Leaders in America,* and *Who's Who in Executives and Businesses.*

For more information about Rob Reider and Reider Associates, visit his web site at www.reiderassociates.com/otp/ or e-mail him at hrreider@reiderassociates.com.

It Is a Good Author
Who Knows His Own Material

Contents

Preface   xi

Introduction   xiii

Chapter 1:   Overview of Operational Reviews   1

Stakeholders   2
Why Businesses Are in Existence   3
Businesses a Company Is Not In   4
Some Basic Business Principles   5
Criteria for Organizational Growth   7
Mental Models and Belief Systems   7
Organizational Criteria Example   9
Economy, Efficiency, and Effectiveness   12
Specific Objectives   13
Specific Purposes   15
Benefits of Operational Reviews   16
Operational Review Phases   17
Operational Review Engagement Development   18
What Functions to Review   19
Initial Survey   22
Case Study: Joe Sorry, Inc.   22
Case Situation: Leasing Insurance Costs   48
Review Questions   55
Suggested Responses   55

Chapter 2:   Planning Phase   59

Information to Be Obtained   60
Sources of Information   60

Review of Organizational Planning and Budget Systems   61
Organizational Structure and the Role of Management   62
Planning Phase Work Program   63
Case Study: Joe Sorry, Inc., Planning Phase   63
Case Situation: Purchase Order Quantity Tolerances   88
Review Questions   96
Suggested Responses   100

Chapter 3:   Work Program Phase   102

Benefits of the Operational Review Work Program   103
Work Program Work Steps   103
Engagement Control   105
Case Study: Joe Sorry Company, Work Program Phase   123
Case Study Situation: Defective Merchandise Returns   124
Case Study Situation: Equipment Maintenance Review   130
Review Questions   132
Suggested Responses   133

Chapter 4:   Field Work Phase   135

Field Work Techniques   136
Specific Field Work Techniques   137
Work Papers   161
Case Study: Joe Sorry Company, Field Work Phase   162
Case Situation: Clerical Procedures   196
Review Questions   197
Suggested Responses   197

Chapter 5:   Development of Review Findings   200

Operational Review Finding Attributes   201
Operational Review Criteria Standards   202
Some Possible Types of Causes   203
Effects of Operational Review Findings: Possible Indicators   204
Review Findings Development Checklist   206
Case Study: Joe Sorry Company, Development of Findings   207
Case Study: Finished Goods Shipments   228
Case Situation: Shipping and Receiving Procedures   237
Case Situation: Accounts Receivable and Collections   238

Review Questions   240
Suggested Responses   240

Chapter 6: Reporting Phase   243

Characteristics of Good Reporting   244
Examples of Reporting Operational Review Results   244
ABCs of Effective Report Writing   247
Case Study: Joe Sorry Company, Reporting Phase   248
Review Questions   283
Suggested Responses   283

Preface

Welcome to the how-to workbook accompanying the book *Operational Review*. Both the book and this workbook were developed and written by Rob Reider, CPA, MBA, PhD, President of Reider Associates, a management and organizational consulting firm located in Santa Fe, New Mexico. Dr. Reider is a nationally known consultant and seminar conductor and is considered an expert in the field of performing operational reviews. He has provided such operational review consultations to numerous clients in both the private and public sectors and has trained many individuals and groups in these concepts.

The objective in this how-to workbook guide is to help the reviewer understand the basic principles involved in planning and conducting an operational review, and to provide what the reviewer needs to know to use operational review concepts effectively. The materials in the book cover the fundamentals that the reviewer needs to be aware of in order to understand operational review concepts. The materials in the workbook are intended to reinforce the concepts covered in the book through exercises, tasks, checklists, sample forms and examples, case studies and situations, and other explanatory and reinforcing materials. These materials are designed to meet the reviewer's needs, regardless of whether he or she has any prior experience in performing operational reviews. The book and workbook provide both basic knowledge for those with no previous hands-on experience, and reinforcement and additional learning for those who already have some prior operational review experience.

The book and workbook answers such questions as:

- What is an operational review?
- When should I perform an operational review?

- How can I perform an operational review effectively and efficiently?
- How can I effect positive change as a result of an operational review?
- How can I use operational review tools and techniques to maintain operations in an economic, efficient, and effective manner on an ongoing basis?

The materials presented in this workbook can be used by internal employees to perform effective operational reviews for their employers and by external consultants and others to serve their clients in the same manner. In addition, the tools and techniques presented in this workbook can be used by anyone to maintain their operations in the most economical, efficient, and effective manner. If the organization is thinking of starting or expanding the use of operational reviews, this workbook will assist the review team in the proper steps in performing results-oriented operational reviews.

Each chapter in this workbook reinforces the materials in the book and emphasizes an aspect of the operational review in which the reviewer should be knowledgeable. These chapters are as follows:

1. Overview of Operational Reviews
2. Planning Phase
3. Work Program Phase
4. Field Work Phase
5. Development of Review Findings
6. Reporting Phase

Review questions and operational review case studies and situations are included in each chapter for the reader to answer and then compare to the provided suggested answers. The purposes of the review questions are to reinforce the major points covered in the section and to assist the reader in retaining the relevant material. The purpose of the case studies and situations is to familiarize the reader with operational review examples and how to handle them in actual practice.

The forms, checklists, tools, and review aids are designed and presented in the workbook to be used by the reader in the performance of actual operational reviews. However, each such tool should be modified where necessary to fit the specific requirements of the reader's organization.

Introduction

PURPOSE AND OBJECTIVES

In today's many-faceted and multidisciplined economic environment, organizational management has placed ever more emphasis on increasing results with fewer resources through evaluation of the economy, efficiency, and effectiveness of the organization's operations. The operational review is the tool used to perform such an evaluation, either singularly or as part of another procedure such as benchmarking, activity-based management, total quality management, and reengineering. This workbook presents the basic principles of planning and conducting such an operational review, as well as the fundamentals of which the reviewer must be aware to understand operational review concepts.

The objectives of this workbook are:

- To increase understanding of operational review concepts and the ability to use them effectively
- To increase understanding of the purpose and mechanics of conducting operational reviews
- To help identify the relationship and differences between operational reviews and other procedures such as benchmarking, activity-based costing/management, and reengineering
- To increase the skills and abilities needed to conduct operational reviews
- To increase awareness of operational review opportunities and to help in their identification

- To improve the reviewer's capability to perform operational reviews in his or her present situation

> ### *Knowing the Purpose and Objectives*
> ### *Ensures Taking the Correct Path*

ORGANIZATIONAL SYSTEMS: HELPFUL OR DETRIMENTAL?

In many organizations today, top management is seeking ways to become competitive and maintain market position—or merely to survive. Managers have sensed that many of their organizational systems are detrimental to progress and have held them back from achieving organizational, departmental, and individual goals and objectives. These are the very systems that are supposed to be helpful; for example:

- Planning systems, long- and short-term, that resulted in documented plans but not in actual results
- Budget systems that became costly in terms of allocating resources effectively and controlling costs in relation to results
- Organizational structures that created unwieldy hierarchies, which produced systems of unnecessary policing and control
- Cost accounting structures that obscured true product costs and resulted in pricing that constrained competitiveness
- Management systems that produced elaborate computer systems and reporting without enhancing the effectiveness of operations
- Sales functions and forecasts that resulted in selling those products that maximized sales commissions but may not have been the products management desired to produce and sell
- Operating practices that perpetuated outmoded systems ("We've always done it that way.") rather than promoted best practices

Operational reviews, together with other techniques, are tools to make these systems helpful as intended and direct the organization toward its goals.

Reader: Document how these systems, and others, are intended to be helpful to the organization in achieving its goals. Document how these systems actually operate that make them detrimental to the organization's progress. What changes would you suggest to make these systems more helpful? What factors would retard making such changes?

WHO IS THE OPERATIONAL REVIEWER?

An operational review can be performed by anyone with the appropriate skills. The attributes of an effective operational reviewer include:

- Curiosity (imagination)
- Analytical ability
- Persuasiveness
- Good business judgment
- Common sense
- Objectivity
- Communication skills
- Initiative to develop techniques in such areas as work measurement, flowcharting, cost-benefit analysis, organizational analysis, and information technology
- Independence
- Confidence

Beyond those previously listed, the successful operational reviewer should possess the following attributes:

- The ability to spot the trouble areas—to look at a given situation and quickly determine what is getting in the way.
- The ability to identify the critical problem areas, so as to avoid "chasing mice when one should be chasing elephants." The application of the 80/20 rule states that operational reviews require 80 percent common sense and 20 percent technical expertise; and that 80 percent of operational activities cause 20 percent of the problems, and 20 percent of operational activities cause 80 percent of the problems.

- The ability to place oneself in management's position, to analyze the problem and ask questions from management's perspective. This is sometimes difficult, as often the reviewer has never been in an operations-related management position. Even when this is not true, the reviewer may have difficulty understanding the constraints under which the manager must work—in effect, what he or she can and cannot do.
- The skill to effectively communicate operational review results. The success of an operational review is measured by the degree to which recommendations are implemented, and implementation is a direct by-product of effective communication. A rule of thumb in operational reviews is that the reviewer has been successful if he or she can persuade management to adopt more than 50 percent of the recommendations.

An operational review also requires the reviewer to possess a number of varied tools and techniques, which include:

- Planning and budgeting processes
- Cost analysis, such as direct, standard, and activity-based costing methods
- Preparation and analysis of systems flowcharts
- Development and/or analysis of computer systems and programs
- Evaluation of computerized procedures and results
- Statistical sampling procedures
- Development and understanding of forecasts and projections
- Interviewing skills
- Organizational planning development and analysis
- Creation of goals and objectives and other performance standards of measurement
- Development and analysis of organizational structures
- Identification of best practices—both internal and external—and development of a program of continuous improvements
- Verification of the accuracy of data
- Determination of compliance with laws and regulations

- Use of sophisticated analytical techniques such as matrix analysis, linear regression correlation, and critical path method
- Cost versus benefit analysis
- Communication skills, both oral and written
- Knowledge of current thinking and procedures such as total quality management (TQM), benchmarking, reengineering, and complexity theory

Reader: Why are these attributes important to possess for the successful operational reviewer? Does one need to possess these attributes or can one be trained in these areas? How would you develop someone to become an operational reviewer? Document a possible training program to ensure that members of the operational review team possess these skills and attributes prior to starting an initial operational review.

OPERATIONAL AREAS TO BE ADDRESSED

The book discussed the conducting of operational reviews of any and all organizational functions and activities that hinder or help the effort to maintain the company in the most economical, efficient, and effective manner possible. In this regard, the operational review team must be aware of basic business principles that help to enhance the organization's success as well as those that the company should avoid. With these principles in mind, the review team analyzes operations to identify areas for improvement in which best practices can be implemented that maximize the chances of success and minimize the risk of failure. Although the primary focus of the operational review is on the manner in which scarce resources are used by the organization, considering the sources and uses of resources and the policies and procedures used to deal with over and under operational conditions based on expected results, there are specific operational areas that need to be addressed, including:

Sales of Products or Services
- Are sales made to quality customers with the right products at the right time?
- Does each sale make a contribution to profits?

- Are all costs compared to the sale, such as product costs (direct material and labor); assignment of product-related activity costs (e.g., manufacturing processes, quality control, shipping, and receiving); functional costs (e.g., purchasing, accounts payable, billing, and accounts receivable); and customer costs (e.g., marketing, selling, support services, and customer service)?
- Do sales relate to an agreed upon sales forecast? Is the company selling the right products to the right customers?
- Do sales integrate with an effective production scheduling and control system?

Manufacturing or Production of Services

- Are sales orders entered into an effective production control system, which ensures that all sales orders are entered into production in a timely manner to ensure on-time, quality deliveries?
- Is work-in-process kept to a minimum so that only real customer orders are being worked on rather than building up finished goods inventory?
- Are the most efficient and economical production methods used to ensure that the cost of the product is kept to its realizable minimum?
- Are direct materials and labor used most efficiently so that waste, reworks, and rejects are kept to a minimum?
- Are nondirect labor (and material) costs such as quality control, supervision and management, repairs and maintenance, and material handling, kept to a minimum?

Billing, Accounts Receivable, and Collections

- Are bills sent out in a timely manner—at the time of shipment or before?
- Are accounts receivable processing procedures the most efficient and economical?
- Is the cost of billing, accounts receivable processing, and collection efforts more costly than the amount of the receivable or the net profit on the sale?
- Is the number and amount of accounts receivable continually analyzed for minimization?

- Are any customers paying directly or through electronic funds transfer at the time of shipping or delivery?
- Are bills and accounts receivable in amounts exceeding the cost of processing excluded from the system?
- Has consideration been given to reducing or eliminating these functions?

Inventory: Raw Materials and Finished Goods

- Are raw material and finished goods inventories kept to a minimum?
- Are raw materials delivered into production on a just-in-time basis?
- Are finished goods completed in production just in time for customer delivery?
- Is the company working toward getting out of these inventory businesses?

Purchasing, Accounts Payable, and Payments

- Are all items that are less than the cost of purchasing excluding from the purchasing system (with an efficient system used for these items)?
- Are all repetitive high-volume and cost items (e.g., raw materials and manufacturing supplies) negotiated by purchasing with vendors as to price, quality, and timeliness?
- Does the production system automatically order repetitive items as an integrated part of the production control system?
- Has consideration been given to reduce these functions for low- and high-ticket items leading toward the possible elimination of these functions?
- Does the company consider paying any vendors on a shipment or delivery basis as part of its vendor negotiation procedures?

Other Costs and Expenses: General, Administrative, and Selling

- Are all other costs and expenses kept to a minimum? Remember, an unnecessary dollar not spent is a dollar directly to the bottom line.
- Are selling costs directed toward customer service and strategic plans rather than maximizing salespeople's compensation?

- Is there a system in effect that recognizes and rewards the reduction of expenses rather than the rewarding of budget increases?
- Are all non–value-added functions (e.g., management and supervision, office processing, and paperwork) evaluated as to reduction and elimination?

Reader: Review the specific operational areas in each of the functions in the preceding lists. How many of these practices exist and are used effectively in your organization? Are there other best practices that you can identify (in your organization or not) related to these functional areas? Develop similar lists for other critical functions within your organization.

1

Overview of Operational Reviews

The operational review process is most helpful and beneficial in the following instances:

- Identifying operational areas in need of positive improvement—looking for best practices as part of a program for continuous improvements
- Pinpointing the cause (not the symptom) of the problem—avoiding quick-fix, short-term solutions in favor of longer-term, elegant solutions
- Quantifying the effect of the present situation on operations—identifying the cost of present practices and the benefits to be derived through implementation of best practices
- Developing recommendations as to alternative courses of action to correct the situation—identifying best practices in a program of continuous improvements

This chapter will:

- Introduce operational review concepts and principles.
- Provide an update of the current status of operational reviews.
- Familiarize the reader with commonly used operational review definitions and terms.

- Identify the purposes and components of operational reviews.
- Increase understanding of the benefits of operational reviews.
- Introduce the phases in which a typical operational review is conducted.

> *Pinpoint the Cause, Not the Symptom,*
> *of the Problem*
> *to Identify the Best Practice*

STAKEHOLDERS

Operational review processes are directed toward the continuous pursuit of positive improvements, excellence in all activities, and the effective use of best practices. The focal point in achieving these goals is the customer or stakeholder—both internal and external—who establishes performance expectations and is the ultimate judge of resultant quality. A company customer is defined as anyone who has a stake or interest in the ongoing operations of the organization, anyone who is affected by its results (type, quality, and timeliness). Stakeholders include all those who are dependent on the survival of the organization, such as:

- Suppliers/vendors: external
- Owners/shareholders: internal/external
- Management/supervision: internal
- Employees/subcontractors: internal/external
- Customers/end users: external

> *Stakeholder Expectations*
> *Are the Key to Evaluating*
> *the Company's Performance*

Reader: Identify the stakeholders in your organization and what you believe each one desires from the organization. List the major players in each stakeholder category (e.g., 20 percent of vendors and customers who provide approximately 80 percent of total volume). How do these various stakeholders affect the focus of the organization?

WHY BUSINESSES ARE IN EXISTENCE

Before one even thinks about performing an operational review of an organization, it is necessary to determine why the organization is in existence. When clients are asked this question, invariably the answer is to make money. Although this is partly true, there are really only two reasons for a business entity to exist:

1. *The customer service business.* To provide goods and services to satisfy desired customers, so that they will continue to use the business's goods and services and refer it to others. An organizational philosophy that correlates with this goal that has been found to be successful is "To provide the highest quality products and service at the least possible cost."

2. *The cash conversion business.* To create desired goods and services so that the investment in the business is as quickly converted to cash as possible, with the resultant cash-in exceeding the cash-out (net profits or positive return on investment). The correlating philosophy to this goal can be stated as follows: "To achieve desired business results using the most efficient methods so that the organization can optimize the use of limited resources."

This means that we are in business to stay for the long term—to serve our customers and grow and prosper. A starting point for establishing operational review measurement criteria is to decide which businesses the organization is really in (such as the two listed) so that operational efficiencies and effectiveness can be compared to such overall organizational criteria.

Being in the Customer Service
and Cash Conversion Businesses
Enables the Company to Make Money
and to Survive

Reader: Document the practices that your organization uses with regard to the customer service and cash conversion businesses. Identify any effective best practices and practices that appear to be counter to effectiveness. Identify any performance gaps that need to be addressed in an operational review.

BUSINESSES A COMPANY IS NOT IN

Once short-term thinking is eliminated, managers realize they are not in the following businesses and decision making becomes simpler:

- *Sales business.* Making sales that cannot be collected profitably (sales are not profits until the cash is received and all the costs of the sale are less than the amount collected) creates only numerical growth.
- *Customer order backlog business.* Logging customer orders is a paperwork process to impress internal management and outside shareholders. Unless this backlog can be converted into a timely sale and collection, there is only a future promise, which may never materialize.
- *Accounts receivable business.* Get the cash as quickly as possible, not the promise to pay. But remember, customers are the company's business; keeping them in business is keeping the company in business. Normally, the company has already put out its cash to vendors and/or into inventory. It may even be desirable to get out of the accounts receivable business all together. This is particularly true for small sales where the amount of the sale is less than the cost of billing and collections or where major customers (e.g., 20 percent of all customers equal 80 percent of total sales) are willing to pay at the time of shipping or receipt as part of price negotiations.
- *Inventory business.* Inventory does not equal sales. Keep inventories to a minimum—zero if possible. Procure raw materials from vendors only as needed, produce for real customer orders based on agreed upon delivery dates, maximize work-in-process throughput, and ship directly from production when the customer needs the product. To accomplish these inventory goals, it is necessary to develop an effective organizational life stream that includes the company's vendors, employees, and customers.

- *Property, plant, and equipment business.* Maintain at a minimum: be efficient. Idle plant/equipment causes anxiety and results in inefficient use. If it is there, it will be used. Plan for the normal (or small valleys) not for the maximum (or large peaks); network to out-source for additional capacity and in-source for times of excess capacity.
- *Employment business.* Get by with the least number of employees as possible. Never hire an additional employee unless absolutely necessary; learn how to cross train and transfer good employees. Not only do people cost ongoing salaries and fringe benefits, but they also need to be paid attention, which results in organization building.
- *Management and administration business.* The more an organization has, the more difficult it becomes to manage its business. It is easier to work with less and be able to control operations than to spend time managing the managers. So much of management becomes getting in the way of those it is supposed to manage and meeting with other managers to discuss how to do this. Management becomes the promotion for doing.

> **Knowing the Businesses Not to Be in**
> **Keeps the Company in the Business**
> **It Should Be in—**
> **and Makes it Grow and Prosper**

Reader: Document the extent that your organization is in the aforementioned businesses. Identify related critical areas in each of these areas that should be addressed in an operational review. Document any immediate recommendations that can effectively reduce or eliminate the extent of being in these business. What are the organization's goals for each of these areas?

SOME BASIC BUSINESS PRINCIPLES

Each company must determine the basic principles that guide its operations. These principles become the foundation on which the company bases its desirable operational practices. Examples of such business principles include:

- Produce the best quality product at the least possible cost.
- Set selling prices realistically, so as to sell all the product that can be produced within the constraints of the production facilities.
- Build trusting relationships with critical vendors; keeping them in business is keeping the company in business.
- The company is in the customer service and cash conversion businesses.
- Do not spend a dollar that doesn't need to be spent; a dollar not spent is a dollar to the bottom line. Control costs effectively; there is more to be made here than increased sales.
- Manage the company; do not let it manage the managers. Provide guidance and direction, not crises.
- Identify the company's customers and develop marketing and sales plans with the customers in mind. Produce for the company's customers, not for inventory. Serve the customers by providing what they need, not by selling them what the company produces.
- Do not hire employees unless they are absolutely needed; and only when they multiple the company's effectiveness so that the company makes more from them than if they did it themselves without them.
- Keep property, plant, and equipment to the minimum necessary to maintain customer demand.
- Plan for the realistic, but develop contingency plans for the positive unexpected.

> ***Basic Business Principles***
> ***Guide the Company's Operations***

Reader: Which of these basic business principles does your organization embrace—not just philosophically—but in reality? Document other basic business principles that you believe your organization operates under. Which ones increase the organization's effectiveness and which ones are detrimental?

CRITERIA FOR ORGANIZATIONAL GROWTH

There are numerous criteria that the organization may choose to implement in its program of continuous improvements leading toward organizational growth. As part of conducting an operational review, the reviewer must be aware of these criteria to be successful in addressing the company's desired direction—in total or by business segment or function. Some of these criteria include:

- Cost reductions
- Price increases
- Sales volume increases
- New market expansion
- New distribution channels
- Market share increase in existing markets
- Selling or closing a losing operation or location
- Acquire another company, division, operation, or product
- Developing a new product or service
- Efficiency or productivity improvements
- Non–value-added activities eliminated
- Making employees responsible
- Organizational structure revisions

Reader: Document your organization's criteria for organizational growth in each of the listed areas. How do they affect your organization's present and future effectiveness? Are there are other areas for organizational growth in your organization? What are they?

MENTAL MODELS AND BELIEF SYSTEMS

Many organizations operate on the basis of prevalent mental models or belief systems—usually emanating from past and present top management—which have an overriding effect on the conditions with which operations within the company are carried out. They can help to produce a helpful working environment or atmosphere or a hindering one. In effect, such mental models become performance drivers—those elements within the organization that shape the direction of how employees will perform their functions. Examples of such mental models and belief systems include:

- Hard work and doing what you are told are the keys to success for the individual and the company.
- The obedient child in the company survives and is promoted, while the rebellious child is let go or leaves the company.
- Only managers can make decisions.
- Power rises to the top—and stays there.
- Employees need to be watched to do their jobs.
- Power and control over employees is necessary to get results.
- Managers are responsible; employees are basically irresponsible.
- Those at the top of the organization know what they are doing.
- All functions should be organized in the same manner.
- Higher levels of organization ensure that lower levels do their jobs.
- Policing and control over employees ensure their compliance.
- All employees are interchangeable.
- Doing the job right is more important than doing the right job.
- Control the people, control the results.
- Organizational position is more important than being right.
- Top management has the right to set all policies and procedures.
- Managers create results; employees do the job.
- Organizational hierarchies ensure that things get done.
- Employees cannot be trusted on their own.
- You can not run a business without the proper organization structure.
- Managers know more than employees.
- Managers have a right to be obnoxious.
- Management is the enemy.
- Each function needs its own organization structure.
- The more employees reporting to you (and the larger your budget), the more important you are within the organization.

Reader: Check off those mental models and belief systems from the preceding list that exist in your organization. Are there others that you can identify? What are they? Document how these mental models and belief systems affect performance within your organization—positively and negatively.

ORGANIZATIONAL CRITERIA EXAMPLE

The first step in successful operational review planning is to define the company's desired criteria for results as related to their reasons for existence, basic business principles, mental models, belief systems, performance drivers, and so on. These organizational criteria typically encompass the company as an entity as well as its major functions. An example of such an organizational results criteria structure is as follows:

Organization-Wide Criteria

- Operate all activities in the most economical, efficient, and effective manner as possible.
- Provide the highest quality products to our customers at the least possible cost.
- Satisfy our customers so that they will continue to use the company's products and refer the company to others.
- Convert the cash invested in the business as quickly as possible so that the resultant cash-in exceeds the cash-out to the greatest extent possible.
- Achieve desired results using the most efficient methods so that the company can optimize the use of limited resources.
- Maximize net profits without sacrificing quality of operations, customer service, or cash requirements.

Sales Function

- Make sales to the right customers that can be collected profitably.
- Develop realistic sales forecasts which result in a present or future real customer order.
- Sell those products as determined by management to the right customers, at the right time, in the right quantities.

- Actual customer sales should directly correlate with management's long- and short-term plans.
- Sales efforts, and corresponding compensation systems, should reinforce the goals of the company.
- Customer sales should be integrated with other functions of the company, such as manufacturing, engineering, accounting, and purchasing.

Manufacturing

- Operate in the most efficient manner with the most economical costs.
- Integrate manufacturing processes with sales efforts and customer requirements.
- Manufacture in the most timely manner considering processes such as customer order entry, timely throughput, and customer delivery.
- Increase productivity of all manufacturing operations on an ongoing basis.
- Eliminate, reduce, or improve all facets of the manufacturing operation including activities such as receiving, inventory control, production control, storeroom operations, quality control, supervision and management, packing and shipping, and maintenance.
- Minimize the amount of resources such as personnel, facilities, and equipment that are allocated to the manufacturing process.

Personnel

- Provide only those personnel functions which are absolutely required as value-added activities.
- Maintain the levels of personnel at the minimum required to achieve results in each functional area.
- Provide personnel functions such as hiring, training, evaluation, and firing in the most efficient and economical manner possible.
- Develop an organizational structure that organizes each function in the most efficient manner for their purposes.
- Minimize the hiring of new employees by such methods as cross training and interdepartmental transfers and other best practices.

- Implement compensation systems that provide for effective employee motivation and the achievement of company goals.

Purchasing

- Purchase only those items where economies can be gained through a system of central purchasing.
- Implement direct purchase systems for those items that the purchasing function does not need to process, such as low-dollar purchases and repetitive purchases.
- Simplify systems so that the cost of purchasing is the lowest possible.
- Effectively negotiate with vendors so that the company obtains the right materials at the right time at the right quality at the right price.
- Maintain a vendor analysis system so that vendor performance can be objectively evaluated.
- Develop effective computerized techniques for economic processing, adequate controls, and reliability.

Accounting

- Analyze the necessity of each of the accounting functions and related activities, such as accounts receivable, accounts payable, payroll, budgeting, and general ledger.
- Operate each of the accounting functions in the most economical manner.
- Implement effective procedures that result in the accounting functions becoming more analytical than mechanical.
- Develop computerized procedures that integrate accounting purposes with operating requirements.
- Develop reporting systems that provide management with the necessary operating data and indicators that can be generated from accounting data.
- Eliminate or reduce all unnecessary accounting operations that provide no value-added incentives.

Organizational Criteria
Focuses the Operational Review Criteria

Reader: Check off those organizational criteria from the lists preceding that pertain to your organization. For those items not checked off, which ones should be implemented in your organization? Document other organizational criteria that exist or should exist for your organization. What is the effectiveness of existing organizational criteria?

ECONOMY, EFFICIENCY, AND EFFECTIVENESS

Operational review procedures embrace the concept of conducting operations for economy, efficiency, and effectiveness. The following is a brief description of each of the three Es of operational reviews.

1. *Economy (or the cost of operations).* Is the organization carrying out its responsibilities in the most economical manner—that is, through due conservation of its resources? In appraising the economy of operations and related allocation and use of resources, the reviewer may consider whether the organization is:
   - Following sound purchasing practices
   - Overstaffed as related to performing necessary functions
   - Allowing excess materials to be on hand
   - Using equipment that is more expensive than necessary
   - Avoiding the waste of resources
2. *Efficiency (or methods of operations).* Is the organization carrying out its responsibilities with the minimum expenditure of effort? Examples of operational inefficiencies to be aware of include:
   - Improper use of manual and computerized procedures
   - Inefficient paperwork flow
   - Inefficient operating systems and procedures.
   - Cumbersome organizational hierarchy and/or communication patterns
   - Duplication of effort
   - Unnecessary work steps
3. *Effectiveness (or results of operations).* Is the organization achieving results or benefits based on stated goals and objectives or some other measurable criteria? The review of the results of operations includes:

- Appraisal of the organizational planning system as to its development of realistic goals, objectives, and detail plans
- Assessment of the adequacy of management's system for measuring effectiveness
- Determination of the extent to which results are achieved
- Identification of factors inhibiting satisfactory performance of results

Reader: Document areas of economy, efficiency, and effectiveness in your organization. Can these areas be improved upon? Are there critical areas of ineconomy, inefficency, and ineffectiveness that need to be addressed in an operational review?

SPECIFIC OBJECTIVES

There are many reasons why management might desire to have an operational review of their operations performed. Some of these reasons are given in the following list. Keep in mind that management may be looking for a single objective (e.g., operational efficiency), a combination of objectives (e.g., least cost but most efficient systems—best practices), or their own specific agenda (e.g., achievement of results on the basis of cost versus benefits).

Financial and Accounting

- Adherence to financial policy
- Performance of accounting procedures
- Procedures performed by individuals with no incompatible functions
- Adequateness of existing audit trail
- Observability of right procedures

Adequacy of Internal Controls

Accounting controls

- Safeguarding of assets
- Reliability of financial records
- System of authorizations and approvals

- Separation of duties
- Physical controls over assets

Administrative controls

- Operational efficiency
- Adherence to managerial policies
- Adequacy of management information and reporting
- Employee competency and training
- Quality controls

Procedural Compliance

- Laws and regulations: federal, state, and local
- Adherence to administrative policy
- Performance of authorization and approval
- Evidence of action to achieve stated goals and objectives
- Adherence to long-range/short-term plans
- Achievement of management objectives
- Effective recruiting and training
- Evaluation of organizational policies

Organizational Efficiency

- Clear understanding of responsibilities and authority
- Logical, nonconflicting reporting relationships
- Current job/functional descriptions
- Separation of duties
- Productivity maximization (internal benchmarking)
- Staffing levels compared with those of similar organizations (external benchmarking)
- Elimination of non–value-added functions and activities
- The right number of people to do the right job

Operational Results

- Organizational planning: goals, objectives, and detail plans
- Detail plan development and implementation; considering alternatives, constraints, cost/benefit, and resource allocation

Evaluation of operational results
- Appropriateness of measurement criteria
- Feedback on success or failure
- Adjustment of goals, objectives, strategies

Doing the right job, the right way, at the right time

Reader: What are the specific objectives for performing an operational review in your organization in total or by function as listed above? Are there other objectives for performing the operational review? Why do you think an operational review should be performed?

SPECIFIC PURPOSES

In conducting an operational review, the reviewer should be aware of the purpose for which the review is being performed. Prior to the start of the operational review, the reviewer should communicate clearly his or her understanding of the purpose(s) to appropriate management personnel. There should be a mutual agreement as to the purpose of the operational review in the beginning. For example, the purpose may be one or more of the following:

- To review and evaluate the adequacy of the accounting system and related internal accounting controls (including both accounting and administrative controls)
- To analyze systems and controls, as related to internal controls, functional operations, and legal compliance
- To analyze the capability to accomplish agreed upon stated goals, objectives, and results in management's approved plan
- To compare actual accomplishments/results with the goals and objectives established in management's plan for the period; and to determine reasons that established goals and objectives were not met
- To analyze and explain cost overruns or high unit costs for each function/activity for which such data can be quantified
- To assess and evaluate compliance with federal, state, and local laws and regulations; ensuring at least minimal compliance
- To identify and report deficiencies and areas for improvement and to provide technical assistance and follow-up where necessary

> *The Operation Review*
> *Ensures Doing*
> *the Right Job, the Right Way,*
> *in the Right Time*

Reader: Document the purposes for which an operational review should be performed in your organization. Is there an encompassing purpose for the organization in total and specific purposes for functional areas? What are they?

BENEFITS OF OPERATIONAL REVIEWS

Depending on its scope, an operational review can be of significant benefit to top management and staff, in some or all of the following ways:

- Identifying problem areas, related causes, and alternatives for improvement
- Locating opportunities for eliminating waste and inefficiency (i.e., cost reduction).
- Locating opportunities to increase revenues (i.e., income improvement).
- Identifying undefined organizational goals, objectives, policies, and procedures
- Identifying criteria for measuring the achievement of organizational goals
- Recommending improvement in policies, procedures, and organizational structure
- Providing checks on performance by individuals and by organizational units
- Reviewing compliance with legal requirements and organizational goals, objectives, policies, and procedures
- Testing for existence of unauthorized, fraudulent, or otherwise irregular acts
- Assessing management information and control systems

- Identifying possible trouble spots in future operations
- Providing an additional channel of communication between operating levels and top management
- Providing an independent, objective evaluation of operations

---

Operational Review Benefits
Help to Sell the Review

Reader: Check off the benefits from the preceding list that apply to your organization. Are there other benefits for your organization that can be realized from an operational review? What are they?

OPERATIONAL REVIEW PHASES

Operational reviews consist basically of gathering information, making evaluations, and developing recommendations where appropriate. An operational review is essentially the evaluation of an activity for potential improvement. In addition, the review includes analyzing results and being alert to problems. These also provide insights into the effectiveness of management and the potential for improvements.

The phases through which an operational review progresses are:

- Planning
- Work programs
- Field work
- Development of findings and recommendations
- Reporting

Operational Review Phases
Cover All of the Bases

Reader: Document how you would proceed in conducting your operational review based on the five-phase approach and the engagement development chart (see Exhibit 1.1) for an organization-wide and a specific functional review.

EXHIBIT 1.1   OPERATIONAL REVIEW ENGAGEMENT DEVELOPMENT

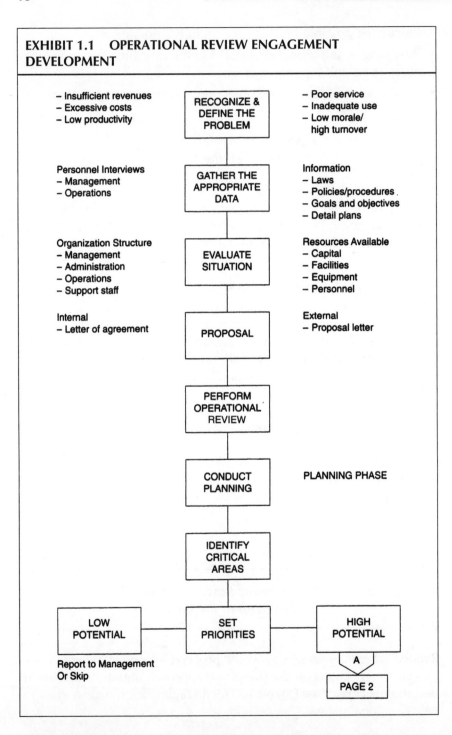

EXHIBIT 1.1   CONTINUED

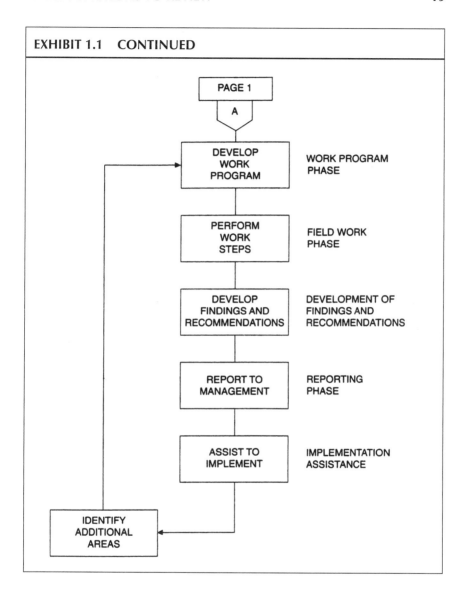

WHAT FUNCTIONS TO REVIEW

The most critical question for an organization to answer is what function or functions to include in the operational review. Where shall it
review? Does it perform the operational review for all functions of the

organization or for only selected areas? One way to decide which functions to review is to determine how critical each function is to the overall organizational operation. Criteria for determining a company's critical areas include:

- Areas with large numbers in relationship to other functions, such as revenues, costs, percentage of total assets, number of sales, units of production, and personnel.
- Areas where controls are weak; for instance, there may be a lack of an effective manufacturing control system, management reporting system, or organizational planning and control system.
- Areas subject to abuse or laxity; for example, there may be inventory and production controls that allow transactions to go unreported and undetected, uncontrollable time and cost reporting, and ineffective personnel evaluation procedures.
- Areas that are difficult to control; for example, there may be ineffective storeroom, shipping, or time recording procedures.
- Areas where functions are not performed efficiently or economically; for instance, there may be ineffective procedures, duplication of efforts, unnecessary work steps, inefficient use of resources such as computer equipment, overstaffing, and excess purchases.
- Areas indicated by ratio, change, or trend analysis, such as characterized by wide swings up or down when compared over a number of periods. Examples include sales changes by product line, costs by major category, number of personnel, and inventory levels.
- Areas where management has identified specific weaknesses or needs for improvement, such as personnel functions, manufacturing procedures, computer operations, and management reporting.

A list of major organizational functions is as follows:

Board of Directors
- Management
- Organizational
- Departmental
- Reporting and control

Planning Systems

- Organizational
- Departmental
- Detail planning

Personnel

- Hiring procedures
- Evaluation procedures
- Staffing levels
- Payroll procedures

Accounting

- Assets
- Liabilities
- Budget procedures
- Payroll and labor distribution
- Accounts payable
- Accounts receivable
- Billing and collections
- Financial reporting
- Cost accounting procedures
- Borrowing and debt outstanding
- General ledger and journal entry system

Computer Processing

- Systems design and analysis
- Programming and software development
- Equipment and hardware
- Operating procedures
- Data control
- Reporting

Operations

- Purchasing
- Personnel administration
- Plant and/or office operations
- Manufacturing and/or service delivery controls
- Production control
- Inventory control
- Marketing and sales
- Engineering
- Property, plant, and equipment
- Fixed assets
- Insurance and risk management

Reader: A good starting point is to list the organization's major functions, to check off those where operational review would be most helpful, and then to prioritize each function as to its criticalness and/or the desired order of review. Based on the criteria in the preceding list for determining criticalness, check off those functions from the list of organizational functions that should be included in your organization's operational review and document each one's degree of criticalness.

INITIAL SURVEY

A sample operational review initial survey form is shown in Exhibit 1.2. The purpose of the initial survey is to identify areas of major importance in the total organization or specific operations to be reviewed.

Reader: Review the initial survey form in Exhibit 1.2. Make any necessary additions, deletions, and changes to individualize the form for use in your organization.

CASE STUDY—JOE SORRY, INC.

If the basic purposes for being in business as described in this chapter (i.e., customer service and cash conversion) are understood, how

---

EXHIBIT 1.2   SAMPLE OPERATIONAL REVIEW INITIAL SURVEY FORM

Planning and Budgeting

1. How does the company plan? Describe the system of planning.
2. Does a long-range plan exist? Attach copy.
3. Do current short-term plans exist? Attach copy.
4. What are plans for expansion or improvement?
5. What are plans for physical plant development?
6. What are plans for future financing?
7. What are personnel plans?
8. How does the organization budget? Describe the budgeting system.
9. Does a current budget exist? Obtain or prepare copy.
10. Do budget versus actual statistics exist for the last five years of operations? Obtain or prepare copy.

Personnel and Staffing

1. Does an organizational chart exist? Obtain or prepare copy.
2. Do functional job descriptions exist for each block on the organization chart? Obtain or prepare copies.
3. Do staffing statistics by functional area exist? Obtain or prepare copy.
4. Is there a system of employee evaluations? Describe procedures.
5. How are employees recruited, hired, evaluated, and fired? Describe procedures.
6. How are new employees oriented and trained? Describe.
7. What are promotional policies? Describe.
8. How are raises and promotions determined? Describe.
9. Is there a grievance mechanism? Describe.
10. What type of personnel records are maintained? Obtain copies.

Management

1. Does a board of directors exist? Attach list of names and credentials.
2. Who is considered top management? Attach list of names and credentials.
3. Who is considered middle management? Attach list of names and credentials.
4. Who is considered lower management? Attach list of names and credentials.

EXHIBIT 1.2   CONTINUED

---

5. How adequate are existing reports in furnishing information for making management decisions? Describe.
6. Are there tools for internal downward communication to the staff? Attach copies.
7. Is authority effectively delegated to management and lower levels? Describe.

Policies and Procedures

1. Do written policies exist? Obtain copy.
2. Are written policies current?
3. Are systems and procedures documented? Obtain or provide copy.

Accounting System

1. What is the chart of accounts used? Obtain or prepare copy.
2. Is the accounting mechanized? Obtain documentation.
3. What financial reports are produced? Obtain documentation.
4. Is there an internal audit function? By and to whom?
5. Are internal operating reports produced? Obtain copies and determine uses.

Revenues

1. What are the sources of revenue for the last five years? Obtain or prepare statistics.
2. Have there been any substantial changes during this period? Document any that have been made.
3. Are actual versus budgeted data available? Obtain or prepare copy.

Expenses

1. What are the major expense accounts used? Obtain or prepare copy.
2. What are actual expenses for these accounts for the last five years? Obtain or prepare copy.
3. Have there been any substantial changes during this period? Document any that have been made.
4. Are actual versus budgeted data available? Obtain or prepare copy.

EXHIBIT 1.2 CONTINUED

Computer Processing

1. Where is computer processing presently located in the organization? Obtain or prepare copy of information technology organization.
2. What computer equipment is used? Obtain or prepare copy of equipment list and locations.
3. What is total cost of equipment rental or purchase price?
4. What are the major applications computerized? Obtain or prepare copy of list of applications, with general systems applications.
5. Are management, operational, control, and exception reports provided? Describe.

Purchasing

1. What is purchasing authority? Obtain or prepare copy of policy relative to purchasing authority.
2. Is purchasing centralized or decentralized? Describe operations.
3. How are purchase requisitions initiated? Describe general procedures.
4. Who determines quality and quantity desired?
5. Are purchase orders used? Describe procedure.
6. Are competitive bidding procedures used? Describe procedure.

Manufacturing Systems

1. Is a computerized manufacturing control system being used? Describe operation.
2. What type of manufacturing processes are being used? Describe processes.
3. How are jobs controlled in manufacturing? Describe procedures.
4. Is a manufacturing cost system used by job? Describe system.
5. Are operational and management reports provided to control manufacturing operations? Obtain or prepare copies.

Production Control

1. Is a manufacturing control system being used? Is it computerized? Obtain or prepare copy of general procedures.
2. What types of manufacturing processes are being used? Describe.
3. What is location(s) of manufacturing facilities? Document.

EXHIBIT 1.2   CONTINUED

---

4. Are production control cost centers used to control the routing of manufacturing orders? Obtain or prepare copy of cost centers.
5. Is a manufacturing cost system used? Obtain or prepare copy of cost accounting procedures.
6. Are operational and management reports provided to control manufacturing operations? Obtain copies.

Inventory Control

1. Is an inventory control system being used? Is it computerized? Obtain or prepare copy of general procedures.
2. What types of inventory control procedures are being used? Describe.
3. Where are inventory storeroom locations? Obtain or prepare copy of locations and describe storeroom procedures.
4. How are inventory records maintained? Describe procedures.
5. Are inventory statistics and data maintained? Obtain data as to items in inventory, dollar value, usage, on-hand balances, etc.
6. What is basis for reordering inventory items, and how are reorder quantities determined? Describe procedures.

Responsibility and Authority

1. Are responsibilities clearly defined and understood by managers and staff personnel? Describe procedures.
2. Has authority been delegated effectively to managers and lower levels within the organization? Describe process.

---

have so many businesses gone astray? To illustrate some of these principles and the application of operational review concepts, let me share the story of one of my consulting clients whom we'll call Joe Sorry. Joe was a professional friend of mine working for a large national electronics organization as a top middle manager, but who wanted to have his own business. He knew he could run a business better than his present employers. He decided he was ready and hired me to assist him in putting his business together.

Joe had been employed by ACE Electronics for nearly 20 years, serving in a number of engineering and manufacturing positions at various locations. Presently, Joe was assigned as plant engineer to a small division manufacturing specialty printed circuit boards for a select number of customers. The company had always looked at this division as a sharer of overhead, not as a growth profit center. In fact, the division shared manufacturing space with a larger division and was considered a divisional "stepchild." The company had recently been purchased in a leveraged buyout, and the new owners were going through a program of divestiture and selling off of various divisions and facilities, as well as a program of cost cutting and employee downsizing.

Joe's division was one that the new owners decided to put up for sale. Joe was eager to buy it, because he felt very strongly that with the sale of his division he would be let go. He also believed that he could do a better job of managing and running the division on a full time basis than was presently being done by the parent company on a "stepchild"-type basis. Joe saw good potential for additional sales as the present company mainly treated this division as a specialty house for their existing customers. He also foresaw numerous possibilities for cost savings through production efficiencies as presently production was accomplished by inefficiently sharing space and manufacturing processes with the main division. In addition, by breaking away from the company, he believed this division could be operated at much less administrative cost and would not have to share the inequitable share of overhead burden allocated to them. Joe had no doubt that he could improve operations dramatically within the first year, and growth possibilities were extremely attractive.

Fortunately, Joe chose to purchase and start a business in which he knew something about: He had been the plant engineer for his previous employers' electronics business. While he did not know everything there was to know about running a business—such as finance and accounting, sales and marketing, production and inventory control, and purchasing—he knew that in this business (at that time) it was fairly easy to produce a quality product for less than customers were willing to pay for it. He had seen his previous employer making bundles of money (in his terms) from this division in spite of themselves and their gross inefficiencies. He was certain that their internal reporting and allocation systems had made this division look worse than it was and a prime candidate for sale. Joe knew he could do better.

Financing the Business

Joe had acquired some financial backing (other than his and his wife's savings, and his children's college fund) from his in-laws. Although Joe had some basic accounting knowledge, he did not have strong financial and accounting skills, but he knew he had to present some kind of projected numbers to acquire the additional financial backing he needed from others. For this purpose, Joe developed the following income statement projection, comparing the last year of ACE Electronics operations (in millions of dollars) with the projected future goals of Joe Sorry Company's operations:

	ACE Electronics		Joe Sorry Company	
	12-31-X1 Actual		12-31-X2 Projected	
Sales	$4,200	100.0%	$6,300	100.0%
Cost of Goods Sold	2,940	70.0	3,900	61.9
Manufacturing Profit	1,260	30.0	2,400	38.1
Selling, General & Administrative Expenses	950	22.6	825	13.1
Operating Profit	310	7.4	1,575	25.0
Taxes	113	2.7	315	5.0
Net Income	$ 197	4.7%	$1,260	20.0%

Based on the above projection, which Joe believed was relatively realistic, Joe performed no further financial studies, and his financial backers requested no additional data. Joe believed that through his efforts he would be able to easily meet the targeted increase in sales, decreases in costs of manufacturing and selling and administration, and resultant improvements in profitability. The combination of these factors should be enough to avoid any financial difficulties.

Background of Situation

Unfortunately, Joe's projections proved inadequate. He had not taken into consideration three significant factors:

1. Investment of over $2 million in plant and equipment to gain all of his projected manufacturing efficiencies. Remember, the previous owners operated on a shared plant basis and Joe had to start from scratch.

2. Increase in sales to achieve his sales target from present customers and adding new customers would require increased sales efforts, possible lowering of prices, and more favorable credit terms. The previous owner did not actively look to increase this part of their business, as they saw it as a specialty service to their present customers.

3. It would take time (probably at least three years) to achieve the projected sales volume of over $500,000 monthly sales to attain the $6.3 million annual target.

ACE Electronics had enjoyed a unique position in its specialty circuit board division as demand for its products by existing customers exceeded its ability to supply the products. The division was able to sell all of its monthly allocated production quota of about $300,000 on a continuing basis with no real effort. Due to the nature of the specialty of the product to its customers, ACE could require in most cases cash payment at the time of delivery. ACE was also able to dictate delivery schedules, which allowed them to intersperse their specialty board manufacturing into idle production slots of the main division. This was basically the concept and philosophy of the specialty board division; to fill in production gaps and assume some of the overhead of the main division.

When Joe took over the specialty board division, the division had reached a plateau of about $300,00 in monthly sales, with operating profits in the 7 to 8 percent range. Joe set up an expansion program with a goal of increasing sales by at least 50 percent with an operating profit margin in the 20 to 25 percent range. Although Joe didn't achieve these goals the first year, by the third year his program was proving successful. His current monthly financial report showed that sales had increased to over $500,000 with over $100,000 in net income as shown below:

	Prior Month		Current Month		Next Month (Projected)	
Sales	$416,000	100%	$503,000	100%	$515,000	100%
Cost of Goods Sold	284,000	68%	335,000	67%	342,000	66%
Manufacturing Profit	132,000	32%	168,000	33%	173,000	34%
Other Expenses	58,000	14%	67,000	13%	70,000	14%
Operating Profit	$ 74,000	18%	$101,000	20%	$103,000	20%

Despite finally reaching his sales and profitability goals, Joe now found himself with an $85,000 cash flow deficit by the end of the current month. Joe had always assumed that a profitable operation would automatically provide for enough cash. Had Joe understood operations, financial reporting, and related cash flow management better, he would have been able to predict what was happening. His present cash flow situation looked like this:

Beginning Cash	$ 51,217
Collections	620,140
Inventory purchases	(248,386)
Payroll	(262,243)
Manufacturing Expenses	(86,667)
Selling General and Administrative	(112,834)
Equipment Purchases	(46,571)
Ending Cash	($ 85,344)

As Joe learned, even with the most successful businesses in terms of sales and net income, resources always have their limitations. Since Joe believed he understood the product side of the business, Joe hired us to conduct an operational review of his business to help put the business side together.

Educating the Client

The first thing Joe wanted explained to him was if he was making so much money, why didn't the business have any cash. Obviously, Joe's cash deficit wasn't due to anything magical, but developed predictably from his normal business operations. I explained a number of things to Joe about accrual accounting versus operational data, mainly:

- Sales are recorded when made (goods shipped to the customer) and set up as accounts receivable, with cash being received at the time of payment.

- Expenses are made on a different timing schedule from cash receipts. For example, payroll is paid when due, although you may not receive payback via customer sales until some time in the future (typically over 30 days hence). This is also true of manufacturing costs such as materials and supplies.

- Profits shown on the income statement are based on accrual accounting; that is, sales are recorded when made not when accounts receivable are collected, and expenses are recorded as incurred not when they are paid from accounts payable.

- Some expenses are handled via accounting entries such as depreciation and amortization, while prepaid items are recorded currently but they represent prior cash disbursements.

- Expenditures for fixed assets, inventory, and other deferred expenses are paid for currently but do not immediately appear on the income statement.

- Financial statements do not provide all of the necessary data needed to manage and operate effectively; for example, they do not provide the costs and profits generated for each manufacturing order, the number of on-time deliveries, the amount of returned merchandise, or the amount and cost of rework.

Based on the preceding items, Joe's profit for the current month of $101,000 turned into a cash deficit of $85,344. This exemplifies the difference between profitability and liquidity, and accrual versus operational reporting. Had Joe understood these principles, he could have avoided such operational problems. We agreed that we would look at the major aspects of Joe's operations during the course of our operational review.

Preliminary Survey

As part of the operational audit process, it is good practice to meet with the client initially and perform a preliminary review of their operations prior to submitting a proposal letter (or internal letter of understanding) as to the scope of the review and related fees. This preliminary review is normally performed at no cost to the client and takes from a half to a full day. It is your means to learn about the client and develop a proposal that incorporates the client's major critical operational areas into the operational review—so that you can provide the greatest benefit to their operations.

I started with Joe by explaining what I considered some basic business principles, such as:

- Produce the best quality product at the least possible cost.
- Set your selling prices realistically, so as to sell all the product that you can produce within the constraints of your production facilities (cost, pricing, volume analysis).
- Build trusting relationships with your critical vendors; keeping them in business is keeping you in business.
- You are in the customer service and cash conversion businesses.
- Don't spend a dollar you don't have to; a dollar not spent is a dollar to the bottom line. Control your costs effectively; there's more to be made here than increased sales.
- Manage your company; don't let it manage you. Provide guidance and direction, not crises.
- Identify your customers and develop marketing and sales plans with them in mind. Produce for your customers, not for inventory. Serve your customers, not sell them.
- Don't hire employees unless you absolutely need them; and only when they multiple your effectiveness so that you make more from them than if you could do it yourself.
- Keep property, plant, and equipment to the minimum necessary to maintain your customer demand.
- Plan for the realistic, but develop contingency plans for the positive unexpected.

Joe generally agreed with these principles, although he, like many new business owners, had visions of sugar plums in his head as to having an enormous physical plant and employees under his control. He wanted to be automatically large just like his previous employer, making the assumption that more was better. Joe wanted immediate gratification for being the boss and felt he should have the same perquisites as he had before. When I explained to him that when he worked for the large corporation he was spending other people's money, and now he was spending his money, he seemed to understand.

While he still wanted the big corporation comforts, he now wasn't willing to spend his money; for he realized that an unnecessary dollar spent in the business was a dollar out of his pocket. As part of the preliminary survey, I talked to Joe to acquire a background of his business and his present position. Joe told me that he initially started his business, after acquiring it from ACE Electronics, in a large garage (which used to be a bicycle repair shop) with low rent. At that time, he and his wife Flo were the only employees. Joe started with three small contracts for specialized printed circuit boards that Joe had developed while previously employed at ACE. He established relationships with four circuit board vendors (after over a dozen turned him down) to provide him with the product as needed. I took a quick look at what Joe was purchasing and realized rather quickly that he was ordering all customized boards. I suggested that Joe standardize his outside needs, and customize his product in-house, which would simplify his material purchasing for himself and his vendors as well as cut his material costs with no substantial increase in his manufacturing costs. Joe readily accepted this suggestion with the comment, "Why didn't I ever think of that?" This is what is known as a "free bone," providing something to the client either before you are engaged or in addition to contracted services. This approach also increases your professional credibility and enhances your image.

He and Flo initially set up the in-house production flow on large secondhand wooden tables. When they needed to meet customer delivery commitments, they would have the vendors deliver the boards and at the same time contract with just the number of individuals to customize the product. Flo would train the production staff; supervise production, packing, and shipping; and bill the customers. Joe was responsible for engineering, purchasing and vendor relations, and sales and marketing—working mainly out of his house and car. As Joe and Flo said in those days, "They were one big happy family."

As Joe was able to get more business, the cycle would continue. The first year, Joe worked to build the business, and sticking with specialty and custom circuit boards only, had over $3 million in sales with a reported net profit after Joe and Flo's salaries of about $440,000 (a net profit margin of over 13 percent—not bad for the first year of any business). He and Flo, of course, were working more than they had in their previous jobs. However, they now had one additional ingredient—ownership—and they were building appreciation in their own business.

Fairly quickly, the word spread that Joe was providing a proprietary quality product at reasonable cost. Joe was now able to bring in more business than his little garage shop and he and Flo could handle by themselves. With Joe's initial success, he now believed that he had the business acumen to run any business successfully. Nothing builds incompetence greater than success.

The company started to grow and grow and grow. During this period, I would see him every so often and he would tell me how well he was doing—in terms of square feet of production and office space, total sales, amount of backlog, number of employees and total payroll, and so on. I cautioned him not to grow too fast and lose control and those elements that had made him successful initially, but he didn't listen. He was becoming just like his previous employer. I asked Joe what he saw as the problems with his company. He started off telling me how well he was doing—again by the numbers. I stopped him and asked him specifically what was the trouble. After hesitating, he finally admitted that he was so successful, it was driving him crazy—and Flo was in therapy. They had become one big unhappy, dysfunctional family.

The Agreement

After talking with Joe, reviewing his operations, general analysis of the financial statements, review of internal reports, and so on, it was agreed that we would review the following functions of the Joe Sorry Company:

- *Personnel*: both manufacturing and general and administrative, as to number and types of personnel necessary.
- *Manufacturing operations*: production and inventory control methods and procedures.
- *Product line analysis*: sales, cost, and pricing considerations of the various products.
- *Profit center concepts*: looking at the various businesses such specialty boards, custom boards, defense business, and basic boards.

- *Operational reporting considerations*: such as key operating indicators, type of reporting, and use of reporting.
- *Planning and budget systems*: including strategic and long-term planning, organization and departmental short-term planning, detail planning, and effective budget techniques.

Proposal or Confirming Letter

Based on our agreement with Joe, we would submit either a confirming letter (where Joe has already agreed to have us perform the operational review) or a proposal letter (where Joe wants to review what we are proposing in writing prior to committing). In this case, as Joe agreed to our conducting the operational review, we submitted a confirming letter (see Exhibit 1.3). Note that if you are an internal auditor, it is still suggested that you submit either one of these documents as a letter of understanding to your internal client. Once agreed upon by the client, this becomes your contract.

THE INITIAL SURVEY

To achieve the greatest results from limited operational review resources (in this case about 200 budgeted hours of outside and inside assistance), the review team needs to identify the areas of major importance and those offering the greatest potential savings or benefits as quickly as possible. The identification of these areas is done as part of an initial survey, either prior to or as part of the planning phase of the operational review.

The initial survey form is a quick review tool to help identify critical areas for further review, where it is not feasible or is time or cost prohibitive to perform the more desirable (but time consuming) full planning phase. However, it is still the reviewer's responsibility to substantiate the identification of critical operational areas to be reviewed with adequate evidential matter. Improper identification results in spending unnecessary effort on less significant activities and insufficient effort on more important areas. The same questions and answers may also be reviewed with various personnel, such as departmental management, functional supervision, and operations and support personnel. The reviewer thus isolates patterns of agreement

EXHIBIT 1.3   SAMPLE CONFORMING LETTER

April 12

Mr. Joseph Sorry
President
Joseph Sorry, Inc.
#8 Lucky Chance Industrial Park
Broadacres, XX XXXXX

Dear Mr. Sorry

It was a pleasure meeting with you and Flo on April 4 to discuss how Reider Associates might assist you in the review and analysis of your operations. This letter confirms the arrangements agreed upon by us at this meeting.

Background

You are in the business of manufacturing various types of printed circuit boards for the electronics industry—such as specialty boards, custom boards, defense contractor requirements, and basic boards on a competitive basis. You bought the business from your previous employer, ACE Electronics, about three years ago and have had enormous success since then. In fact, recently you surpassed them both in sales volume and reported net income. However, with such growth, you have experienced many operational problems to the point that you are presently in a negative cash flow and short-term liquidity bind. In addition, the operation has grown so large that you can no longer exercise proper control, and your wife Flo, the titular Vice President of Operations, has opted for a less demanding role in the business. Due to these situations and others, you have asked Reider Associates to assist you in identifying workable solutions to these operational concerns.

Objectives of the Operational Review

Based on our preliminary review and our discussions with you and your personnel, we believe that the objectives of the operational review of your company would be to:

1. Determine the organization structure and the related number of personnel required to most effectively operate your company to meet your desired results.

EXHIBIT 1.3   CONTINUED

---

2. Determine which systems and procedures would be best to improve your manufacturing operations.
3. Determine which business or businesses—specialty, custom, defense, and basic—you should be in and which product lines you should be offering to whom and at what price.
4. Design operating systems and data processing procedures to enable all of your operating functions to assist in the effective management of the varied aspects of your business.
5. Identify opportunities for operational improvements within all functions of the Joe Sorry Company.
6. Develop effective planning and budget systems that will assist your providing effective direction and guidance for the company and its various departmental functions.

Identification of Major Areas

Based on our discussions with you and Flo and others in your organization, as well as our preliminary review of your operations, we have identified the following areas for concentration in the review of your operations:

- *Personnel*: including direct manufacturing and support functions, as well as selling, general, and administrative operations
- Manufacturing operations: including production and inventory control methods and procedures
- *Product line analysis*: reviewing the various product lines produced and sold including such aspects as sales, cost, and pricing considerations
- *Profit center concepts*: looking at the various businesses such as specialty boards, custom boards, defense business, and basic boards
- *Operational reporting considerations*: analyzing present reporting procedures and developing an effective operating reporting system that allows you to effectively manage all of the varied aspects of the business
- *Planning and budget systems*: assistance in developing effective planning techniques for your business, which would include strategic and long-term planning, organization and departmental short-term planning, ongoing detail planning, and effective budget techniques.

Our Approach

The work steps that we plan to follow to assist you in identifying and remediating those areas in need of positive improvement in your operations are:

EXHIBIT 1.3   CONTINUED

1. General review of existing operational methods and procedures to provide us with a clear understanding of your operating functions, so that we can provide effective consulting assistance in developing and implementing improved procedures. This would include a review of all operating systems and methods, as well as management and administrative practices.
2. Interview a number of management/supervisory and operating personnel so that we can assess individual needs and concerns as well as incorporate such concerns into overall considerations. We will attempt to interview each of your personnel assigned management/ supervisory responsibilities as well as a representative number of operations personnel in each function. We will also prepare an employee questionnaire for each employee's response. We will, of course, discuss the findings of our general review and interviews with you so that we can jointly agree as to the major issues for change to be included in our detailed review and analysis.
3. Detailed operational review and analysis of those critical areas identified in our preliminary review as previously described. We will perform sufficient analytical work to fully determine the present condition of each area, what it should be, the effect on operations, the cause of the condition, and practical recommendations for improvement.
4. Develop detailed findings and recommendations for improvement, which will be developed in a manner that will optimize each function's achievement of their individual goals and objectives. These findings and recommendations will be documented for your review in both an oral presentation and a written report.
5. Provide assistance to you and your staff in the implementation of recommendations that can be accomplished during the course of this operational review. Other longer-term recommendations will be reviewed with you at the oral presentation at the conclusion of our field work and subsequently documented in the final report summarizing the results of the operational review. We are available, of course, to provide the necessary assistance to you in the successful implementation of any of these longer-term recommendations.

Participation

Mr. Rob Reider, President of Reider Associates, will be personally responsible for the technical conduct and successful completion of this operational review of your company. We plan to assign two other members of

EXHIBIT 1.3   CONTINUED

our staff, Marlene Morris and Samuel Hornsworth, both of whom are qualified to perform the tasks required on this operational review. They would
be responsible for the performance of the work steps as described in the
Our Approach section.

As we discussed, we believe that it is essential for such an operational
review to be successful to have client participation. Accordingly, we are
recommending that your Vice President of Production, Ed Harrison, share
joint management responsibility, and that the Controller, Patricia Flood,
and one of the forepersons, Pedro (Pete) Herrara, work along with us. We
would expect these personnel to participate in the review as necessary, to
attend scheduled progress meetings, and to provide us with necessary
input. We do not expect them to be assigned tasks that would consume
more than two days per week during the course of the review or interfere
with their regular duties and functions.

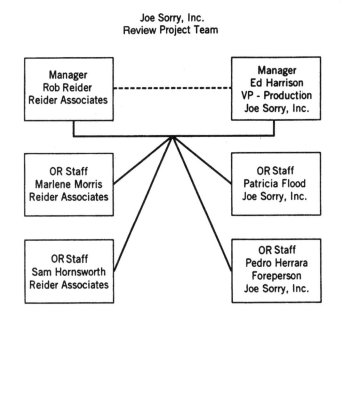

Joe Sorry, Inc.
Review Project Team

EXHIBIT 1.3   CONTINUED

Benefits to Be Provided

The benefits to be provided from the conducting of an operational review of the Joe Sorry Company are many and varied. However, you should expect at least the following:

1. Identification of operational areas in need of improvement, related causes, and recommendations for improvement.
2. Effective reduction of unnecessary costs through the identification of opportunities for eliminating waste and inefficiency.
3. Identification of undefined plans or desired results, goals, objectives, systems, and procedures.
4. Assessment of the existing management information and control system, together with recommendations for design of a more effective system that allows for appropriate management.
5. Development of meaningful operating systems and procedures that will enable you and your personnel to better control, monitor, and evaluate the results of operations.
6. Implementation of improved operating techniques that will enable all levels of your personnel to perform their current and proposed job responsibilities more effectively with a greater level of competency and understanding.
7. Provide for an independent, objective evaluation of your operations with practical recommendations for positive improvements.

Time and Cost

Based on our experience on similar operational reviews, our preliminary survey of your operations, and discussions with you, we estimate that our time participation should not exceed 140 hours at an estimated cost of $12,000 to $16,000 (see attached Confirming Letter Budget Estimate). We will, of course, bill you only for the time actually expended on this review. In addition we are to be reimbursed for out-of-pocket expenses.

We appreciate the opportunity to provide these important services to you and your company and look forward to working with you. If you have any further questions, please let me know. As we discussed, we are planning to begin the operational review next Monday. If the arrangements described above meet with your approval, you may indicate your acceptance by signing and returning the enclosed copy. We will then proceed as planned.

EXHIBIT 1.3   CONTINUED

Approved By: _____   Very truly yours,
                 Joe Sorry, President   _____
                 Joe Sorry, Inc.   Rob Reider, President
          Date: _____   REIDER ASSOCIATES

CONFIRMING LETTER BUDGET ESTIMATE

Joe Sorry Inc.
Confirming Letter Budget Estimate

	Manager	**Staff**	**Total**	**Client**
Review Area:				
1. Personnel				
—Manufacturing	4	16	20	8
—Selling, G&A	2	10	12	6
2. Manufacturing Operations				
—Production Functions	4	8	12	6
—Inventory Operations	2	4	6	2
3. Product Line Analysis	2	4	6	—
4. Profit Center Concepts	4	2	6	—
5. Operational Reporting	4	4	8	6
6. Planning and Budget Systems	4	4	8	6
Total Review Time	26	52	78	34
Other Functions:				
Prepare Work Program	4	6	10	6
Review Results	8	2	10	10
Develop Findings	4	8	12	8
Oral Reporting	4	4	8	4
Written Report	4	8	12	8
Total Other Time	24	28	52	36
Grand Total Time	50	80	130	70
Standard Billing Rates	$120	$ 80		
Total Estimated Fees	$6,000	$6,400	$12,400	
Contingency @ 10%			1,240	
Grand Total			$13,640	
Fee Quoted		$12,000 to $16,000		

and disagreement and various interpretations and perceptions that help reach the correct conclusions.

We asked Joe and Flo Sorry to respond to our initial survey prior to the start of our review. Our purpose was to increase our knowledge of their operations and gain some insight as to potential problem or critical areas. Their responses to our initial survey form are shown in Exhibit 1.4.

THE ENTRANCE CONFERENCE

Because many small (and large) businesses are skeptical or not knowledgeable about the operational review process, it is good practice to start the review with an entrance conference between the review team and the company's owners, management, and operations personnel. Based on the Joe Sorry situation, the purpose of the entrance conference would be to:

- Build initial rapport and a cooperative atmosphere between the review team members and operations personnel.
- Provide clear understanding to operations personnel as to the purpose, objectives, scope, approach, and expected results of the operational review.
- Clarify which tasks the review team will be performing on the operational review and what is expected of operations.
- Reduce operations personnel distrust as to why you are there and build confidence in what you are doing on the review.
- Communicate Joe and Flo's support of the review team's efforts, and that this review is something they want done.

The entrance conference at the Joe Sorry company was conducted by the review team, with Joe and Flo and the managers present, as well as affected operations personnel. This helped to prevent misunderstandings, which could be settled immediately prior to starting the operational review. The successful entrance conference served to create a favorable first impression and set a positive tone for the remainder of the review.

EXHIBIT 1.4   INITIAL SURVEY FORM

Joe Sorry, Inc.
Operational Review
Initial Survey Form

Planning and Budgeting

1. How does Joe Sorry, Inc. plan? Describe the system of planning.
   Response: Basically, day-to-day planning, with Joe making the decisions as to what needs to get out.

2. Does a long-range plan exist? If so, attach copy.
   Response: Joe's plan is to be the biggest he can, in terms of sales and income.

3. Do current short-term plans exist? If so, attach copy.
   Response: As mentioned, only Joe's day-to-day plans.

4. What are plans for expansion or improvement?
   Response: Recently expanded and already need more capacity. Talking to industrial park people as to additional available space.
   Systems need to be improved; that's why you're here.

5. What are plans for physical plant development?
   Response: Hoping you can tell us.

6. What are plans for future financing?
   Response: Present short-term line of credit of $3 million. Looking for long-term financing.

7. What are personnel plans?
   Response: Looking to increase management capability by adding Vice Presidents of Personnel, Purchasing, Sales (Marketing?), and Engineering. Also adding some middle-level management positions such as Plant Manager, Maintenance Manager, Shipping and Receiving Manager, and Production Expediters.

8. How does the organization budget? Describe the system.
   Response: Controller prepares annual budget and reviews with Joe and Flo each month.

9. Does a current budget exist? Provide copy.
   Response: Yes, copy attached.

EXHIBIT 1.4   CONTINUED

---

10. Do budget vs. actual statistics exist for the last two full years of operations?
    Response: No. Done on a month-to-month basis.

Personnel and Staffing

1. Does an organizational chart exist? If so, provide copy.
   Response: No.

2. Do functional job descriptions exist for each block on the organization chart? If so, provide copies.
   Response: No

3. Do staffing statistics by functional area exist? If so, provide copy.
   Response: Only via payroll records. Some departments may maintain their own, but don't know.

4. Is there a system of employee evaluations? Describe.
   Response: Joe evaluates all management personnel. Managers evaluate personnel reporting to them; Joe then makes final decisions.

5. How are employees recruited, hired, and fired?
   Response: Recruitment no problem—people want to work here—we're known for good pay in area. Hiring and firing done by department managers with Joe's review and approval.

6. How are employees oriented and trained?
   Response: Responsibility of each department.

7. What are promotional policies?
   Response: Recommendation of manager and Joe's approval.

8. How are raises determined?
   Response: For the two full years we have been in business, Joe has decided on across the board increases (6% and 8%) for nonmanagement employees and individual raises for managers.

9. Is there a grievance mechanism?
   Response: Departmental managers handle. May refer to Joe.

10. What type of personnel records are maintained?
    Response: Payroll records and time cards for nonmanagement.

EXHIBIT 1.4   CONTINUED

Management

1. Who is considered top management? Provide list of names.
   Response: Joe Sorry, President
   Flo Sorry, Vice President of Operations
   Ed Harrison, Vice President—Production

2. Who is considered middle management? Provide list of names.
   Response: Janet Birch, Personnel Manager
   Bill O'Hallaron, Quality Control Manager
   Russ Rogers, Purchasing Manager
   Todd Dailey, Engineering Director
   Patricia Flood, Controller
   Al Slap, Customer Service Manager

3. How adequate are existing reports in furnishing information for making management decisions?
   Response: Reports too late, have already taken action.

4. Are there internal downward communication tools to the staff?
   Response: By Joe, as necessary.

5. Is authority effectively delegated to management and lower levels?
   Response: Each department runs on its own; Joe oversees the overall operation.

Policies and Procedures

1. Do written policies exist? If so, provide copy.
   Response: No, Joe sets all policies.

2. Are systems and procedures documented? If so, provide copy.
   Response: If any, within each department.

Computer Processing

1. What computer equipment is used? Provide list and locations.
   Response: Each department has PCs networked to a central file server.
   No list is available.

EXHIBIT 1.4   CONTINUED

2. What major applications are computerized? Provide list.
   Response: Accounting Systems
             Manufacturing Systems
             Purchasing System
             Engineering—Computer-Assisted Design (CAD)

3. Are management, operational, control, and exception reports provided? Describe.
   Response: Lot of reports, mainly used by each department.

Manufacturing Systems

1. Is a computerized manufacturing control system being used?
   Response: Yes. Check with Ed Harrison.

2. What type of manufacturing processes are being used? Describe.
   Response: Six assembly tables with six positions each.

3. How are jobs controlled in manufacturing?
   Response: By customer and by demand.

4. Is a manufacturing cost system used by job?
   Response: No, only by total for the month.

5. Are operational and management reports provided to control manufacturing operations? If so, provide copies.
   Response: Not sure. Check with Ed Harrison.

6. Is an inventory control system being used? Computerized?
   Response: Yes, and it is computerized.

7. What type of inventory control procedures are being used?
   Response: Reorder points and reorder quantities.

8. Are inventory statistics and data maintained? Does it include data such as items in inventory, dollar value, usage, on hand balances, etc.
   Response: Yes, but can't be relied upon.

Responsibility and Authority

1. Are responsibilities clearly defined and understood by managers and staff personnel?
   Response: Joe defines responsibilities for managers, managers for their employees.

EXHIBIT 1.4 CONTINUED

2. Has authority been delegated effectively to managers and lower levels within the organization?

Response: Employees have authority to function on their own, come to Joe if there is a problem.

Joe Sorry, Inc.
Annual Budget
(in thousands of dollars)

	Dollars	%
Sales	$ 6,000	100%
Cost of Goods Sold	4,000	67%
Manufacturing Profit	$ 2,000	33%
Selling Expenses	550	9%
General & Administrative	350	6%
Operating Profit	$ 1,100	18%
Taxes	$ 300	5%
Net Income	$ 800	13%

Joe Sorry, Inc.
Monthly Budget Report—March

	Actual		Budget	
	Dollars	%	Dollars	%
Sales	$ 418	100%	$ 500	100%
Cost Of Goods Sold	295	71%	333	67%
Manufacturing Profit	$ 123	29%	$ 167	33%
Selling Expenses	54	13%	45	9%
General & Administrative	38	9%	30	6%
Operating Profit	$ 31	7%	$ 92	18%
Taxes	$ 10	2%	$ 25	5%
Net Income	$ 21	5%	$ 67	13%

At the conclusion of the entrance conference, all personnel were given the following two forms to fill out and return to the review team:

Violations of Principles of Good Business Practice (see Exhibit 1.5)

Job Responsibilities Questionnaire (see Exhibit 1.6)

CASE SITUATION: Leasing Insurance Costs

Reader: Review the case situation below and document your answers to the question presented. Then review the suggested responses.

During the course of your operational review procedures, you found that the company was paying for liability and property damage insurance as part of their lease agreement on 14 tractors and 19 trailers. The cost of the insurance was hidden in the fixed weekly/mileage rates billed by the lessor.

The company's policy is to self-insure or assume certain risks (such as auto collision and certain other property losses, and the front end of unknown claims such as liability claims) and to purchase protection for any other risks under a blanket policy.

Question for Consideration

1. What steps would you take to follow through on this operational practice?

Suggested Response

1. What steps would you take to follow through on this operational practice?

    a. Compare annual hidden insurance costs paid to the lessor as part of fixed weekly/mileage rates with what insurance would cost under the company's self-insurance and blanket insurance for major losses.

    b. Request insurance charges from lessor for preceding year.

    c. Determine insurance costs under company's blanket policy.

    d. Based on amount of savings (if any), decide what to recommend:

EXHIBIT 1.5   VIOLATIONS OF PRINCIPLES OF GOOD BUSINESS PRACTICE

Please review the following items representing violations of good business practices. Place a check mark next to those items that you believe Joe Sorry, Inc. or your department to be guilty of doing. Recording your name on this survey is optional. Please return your completed form to Rob Reider of Reider Associates.

A. *Planning*
    ___ 1. Not setting or updating organizational standards or goals
    ___ 2. Not establishing clear long-term or short-term objectives.
    ___ 3. Not developing detail plans as to how plans are to be carried out
    ___ 4. Not developing budgets that relate to short-term plans
    ___ 5. Not prescribing a system of review and replanning

B. *Organizing*
    ___ 1. Not hiring the right people for the job
    ___ 2. Not orienting, training, or instructing supervisees
    ___ 3. Not assigning work on an even distribution
    ___ 4. Not having the right number of personnel—more or less
    ___ 5. Not providing adequate resources, facilities, or equipment

C. *Scheduling*
    ___ 1. Not providing schedules and budgets for each job
    ___ 2. Not highlighting oldest, off-schedule, or over-budget jobs
    ___ 3. Not setting priorities for incoming work
    ___ 4. Not readjusting schedules when changes are necessary
    ___ 5. Not requiring approval for nonscheduled work

D. *Coordinating*
    ___ 1. Not providing for coordination of company goals and objectives with those of each department
    ___ 2. Not periodically reviewing the needs of all work units
    ___ 3. Not communicating organization policies and departmental procedures to personnel
    ___ 4. Not effectively communicating downward
    ___ 5. Not coordinating information relating to various departments

---

EXHIBIT 1.5   CONTINUED

E.   *Directing*
   ___ 1. Not providing clear expectations and instructions
   ___ 2. Not reviewing work and providing positive feedback so as to provide correction rather than ongoing criticism
   ___ 3. Not fixing the situation rather than fixing the blame
   ___ 4. Not providing a coaching or facilitative environment
   ___ 5. Not periodically reviewing work loads and priorities

F.   *Obtaining Feedback*
   ___ 1. Not providing feedback on the quality of work, so as to build on work done well and remediate work not done well
   ___ 2. Not comparing results with communicated expectations and investigating variances—both positive and negative
   ___ 3. Not effectively communicating to the worker where a job does not meet standards
   ___ 4. Not effectively inspecting ongoing processes at strategic points in the system (adequate quality control procedures)
   ___ 5. Not acting on customer complaints or returned work

G.   *Achieving Information*
   ___ 1. Not replacing ineffective standards, procedures, or systems
   ___ 2. Not establishing a program of positive improvement
   ___ 3. Not reviewing operations so as to be most economical, efficient, and effective
   ___ 4. Not encouraging (or coaching and facilitating) employees to upgrade their capabilities
   ___ 5. Not correcting or reporting variances promptly

Note: This form was sent to all 135 employees.

EXHIBIT 1.6   JOB RESPONSIBILITIES QUESTIONNAIRE

Instructions

The purpose of this form is to help you describe the duties and responsibilities of your job and the jobs of your supervisees. A separate questionnaire is to be completed for each employee under your supervision, as well as one for your own job. In the event that two or more employees perform identical duties, only one questionnaire need be completed. However, the names of all employees covered by the questionnaire should be included in the identification section. Please read the entire questionnaire carefully before answering any questions; type or print your answers clearly.

Please Return this Questionnaire to:
Mr. Cliff Chambers
By April 30, XXXX

Identification

Employee Name _____ Title _____

Division _____ Department _____

Name of Immediate Supervisor _____

Title of Immediate Supervisor _____

Your Name _____ Date _____

A. *Description of Regular Duties and Tasks.* Describe each of the duties and responsibilities in the employee's regular routine, in two or three sentences. The first sentence in each case might tell what the employee is supposed to do, and the next sentence might tell how it is done. Do not refer to previous job descriptions or attempt to describe what you think the job *should* be. Write what is *actually* done. In addition, enter the number of hours usually spent on each duty or responsibility under either the "Daily," "Weekly," or "Monthly" column.

   If you do not have enough room to describe the job duties and responsibilities, you can complete them on the back of Page 2 or on a blank piece of paper, which should then be attached.

EXHIBIT 1.6　CONTINUED

Duties and/or Responsibilities	Time		
	Daily	Weekly	Monthly
1. _____	___	___	___
_____	___	___	___
2. _____	___	___	___
_____	___	___	___
3. _____	___	___	___
_____	___	___	___
4. _____	___	___	___
_____	___	___	___
5. _____	___	___	___
_____	___	___	___

B. *Difficulty of the Job.* What, in your opinion, is the most difficult feature of the job, and why is this so?

C. *Description of Contacts.* List the persons (by general job title, not name) with whom the employee comes in contact in the performance of normal job duties. Contacts may be either (1) within the employee's own department or division or (2) within other divisions of the firm. Under the heading of "Frequency," indicate whether these contacts (conversations, correspondence, meetings, etc.) are made "not often," "moderately often," "very often," or "constantly."

EXHIBIT 1.6   CONTINUED

Contacts Within Your Own Department or Division	Reason for Contact	Frequency
_____	_____	_____
_____	_____	_____
_____	_____	_____
_____	_____	_____
_____	_____	_____

Contacts with Other Divisions of the Firm	Reason for Contact	Frequency
_____	_____	_____
_____	_____	_____
_____	_____	_____
_____	_____	_____
_____	_____	_____

D. *Work Flow.* The purpose of this question is to determine where the employee's work originates and where the results of employee's contributions to the work terminate; that is, where do the data for completing a form originate, and where copies of the form are sent.

Form Title	Data Source (No. Forms/Week)	Frequency
_____	_____	_____
_____	_____	_____
_____	_____	_____
_____	_____	_____

EXHIBIT 1.6   CONTINUED

| | Form Destination | | | | | |
Form Title	Copy A	Copy B	Copy C	Copy D	Copy E	Copy F

E. *Additional Remarks.* State additional information that you believe would help in describing or understanding the duties of this job.

F. *Types of Employees' Jobs Supervised.* List the job titles of employees supervised and the number in each classification.

If substantial savings, recommend insurance provided by the lessor to be dropped, and insurance to be provided under company's blanket policy.

If no savings or if savings are not substantial, recommend continuing present practice of lessor providing insurance (may also look into lessor reducing coverage and/or insurance premiums presently being carried).

If practice of obtaining insurance as part of the lease agreement is more economical than the policy of self-insurance, consider changing the self-insurance policy.

If the policy of self-insurance is the most economical route, review operations to determine to what extent the policy is being ignored and resultant cost.

Note: In a real-life version of this particular situation, it was found that lessor insurance costs totaled $39,000 for the year, and that the costs under the company's self-insurance and blanket policy would have been $6,000. Accordingly, an annual savings of $33,000 was realized by reverting back to the self-insurance policy. This situation would be reviewed periodically in the future to ensure that conditions hadn't changed or that other best practices had come into existence.

REVIEW QUESTIONS

Reader: Answer these questions as a review and reinforcement of areas presented in this chapter. Try to answer the questions for yourself prior to reviewing the suggested responses.

1. An operational review involves a systematic review of an organization's activities in relation to specified objectives. What are the three major purposes of such an operational review?
2. What are the major components of operational reviews?
3. List the benefits of an operational review to top management and staff.
4. What are the four major attributes that a successful operational reviewer should possess?
5. What are the five phases of an operational review?

SUGGESTED RESPONSES

1. An operational review involves a systematic review of an organization's activities in relation to specified objectives. What are the three major purposes of such an operational review?

Response

- *Assess Performance.* Compare the manner in which activities are conducted to established objectives or other appropriate measurement criteria.
- *Identify Opportunities for Improvement.* Through effective operational review techniques, identify those operational areas where increased economy, efficiency, or effectiveness would provide positive improvements.
- *Develop Recommendations for Improvement or Further Action.* Analyze the situation and determine the best alternatives and practices in the specific situation to effect positive improvements.

2. What are the major components of operational reviews?

Response

- *Financial.* Proper and adequate accounting and reporting procedures, basically the same as a conventional financial audit or review.
- *Compliance.* Adherence to rules expressed in applicable laws and regulations, and internal policies and procedures.
- *Economy and Efficiency.* Performance of operational activities economically and in an efficient manner. Is this the most economical and efficient way to get the right job done in the right manner.
- *Effectiveness.* Results and accomplishments achieved and benefits provided. Is activity achieving its ultimate intended purpose? Is the purpose the right one?

3. List the benefits of an operational review to top management and staff.

Response

- Identification of problem areas, related causes and alternatives for improvement
- Locating opportunities for eliminating waste and inefficiency—cost reduction
- Locating opportunities to increase revenues—revenue enhancement

- Locating opportunities to increase revenues and reduce costs—profit improvement
- Identification of undefined organizational goals, objectives, policies, and procedures
- Identification of criteria for measuring the achievement of organizational goals and objectives
- Recommending improvement in policies, procedures, and organizational structure
- Providing checks on performance by individuals, groups, work units and the organizational structure
- Reviewing compliance with legal requirements, organizational goals, objectives, policies, and procedures
- Testing for existence of unauthorized, fraudulent, or otherwise irregular acts
- Assessment of management information and control systems
- Identifying possible trouble spots in future operations
- Providing an additional channel of communication between operating levels and top management
- An independent, objective evaluation of operations

4. What are the four major attributes that a successful operational reviewer should possess?

Response

- Ability to spot the trouble areas.
- Common sense, to avoid milking mice when you should be chasing elephants.
- Ability to place yourself in the management position, analyze the problem, and ask the question from a management perspective.
- Effective communication skills relative to operational review results. The success of the operational review is measured by the degree with which your recommendations are implemented through your ability to convince and persuade management.

5. What are the five phases of an operational review?

Response

- The planning phase
- The work program phase
- The field work phase
- The development of findings and recommendations phase
- The reporting phase

2

Planning Phase

The proper steps to be taken in the planning phase to ensure successful results from an operational review are fully discussed in this chapter. This chapter will:

- Increase understanding of the purpose of the planning phase in an operational review.
- Introduce information that must be obtained during the planning phase and related sources of information.
- Increase knowledge of how to use planning phase information in the identification of critical operational areas.
- Increase understanding of planning and budget concepts and their expansion into operational areas and related principles of good operational controls.
- Introduce a sample operational review planning phase work program.

The starting point for the operational review is management's decision as to which operational area or areas are to be reviewed, and whether the operational review is to be preliminary or in-depth. Based on management's decision, the operational reviewer then starts the planning phase of the operational review. The primary purposes of the planning phase are to:

- Gather information about the operational area.
- Identify possible operational problem areas.
- Start to develop the basis for the operational review work program.

***Proper Planning
and the Planning Phase
Pays for Itself***

INFORMATION TO BE OBTAINED

The planning phase can be performed efficiently and systematically if the reviewer has a clear idea of what is needed. The records and information that could be required may include:

- Laws and regulations that apply to the activities being reviewed
- Material on the organization
- Financial information
- Operating methods and procedures
- Management information and reports
- Problem areas

***Chase the Elephants,
Not the Mice***

Reader: Document the information that you would obtain with regard to an operational review of your organization. How would you gather such information? What is the importance of each record and piece of information?

SOURCES OF INFORMATION

What are the sources of the information to be gathered in the planning phase? Such information could come from various sources; however, the following are the most usual sources:

- Effective interviewing
- Organizational data
- Financial data
- Policies and procedures
- Operating and management reports
- Physical inspection

Operational Information Comes from Many Sources

Reader: What are the sources of the records and information with regard to your operational review? How will you go about acquiring each record and piece of information?

REVIEW OF ORGANIZATIONAL PLANNING AND BUDGET SYSTEMS

A good starting point for the reviewer in the planning phase is to understand the organization, why it is in existence, and what it is trying to accomplish (i.e., its goals and objectives). To accomplish this, the reviewer needs to understand the organization's long-term and short-term planning methods and related budgeting and control processes. The planning process, if exercised effectively, forces the organization to:

- Review and analyze past accomplishments.
- Determine present and future needs.
- Recognize strengths and weaknesses.

It also enables the organization to:

- Identify future opportunities.
- Define constraints or threats that may get in the way.
- Establish organizational and departmental goals and objectives.
- Develop action plans based on the evaluation of alternatives.
- Prioritize the selection of action plans for implementation based on the most effective use of limited resources.

Reader: Document your organization's planning and budget systems. Would you consider it effective in achieving results—both long and short term—directed toward meeting desired goals. What are the system's major strengths and major weaknesses? What needs to be done to make it effective?

ORGANIZATIONAL STRUCTURE AND THE ROLE OF MANAGEMENT

Sample Planning Phase Organizational Work Program

The following are work steps that may be included in a planning phase operational review work program for the organization:

- Secure or prepare an organization chart with descriptions of each department's and work unit's specific functions.
- Determine formal and informal reporting relationships from top to bottom, bottom to top, and across functional lines.
- Analyze actual operations to determine whether such reporting is proper in relation to how the organization actually functions and whether it results in operational concerns and problems.
- Analyze each work unit's functions to determine whether they are appropriate.
- Document the duties and responsibilities of each employee. Obtain copies of existing job descriptions or prepare them through the use of user provided data such as a Job Responsibility Questionnaire.
- Interview the president, vice presidents, managers and supervisors, and each employee, to validate their functions.
- Observe actual work being performed to determine the necessity of all duties and responsibilities.
- Obtain or prepare company policies and procedures relating to each function under review.
- Determine that authority and responsibility relationships are clearly defined and understood by all personnel.
- Ascertain that all employees know their delegated authority and responsibilities; ensure that the responsibilities are proper for the function and do not overlap or duplicate another area.

- Look for functions and individuals that either are not providing value-added services or are not being cost effective. Examples may be isolates, dispatchers, controllers, unwieldy hierarchies typified by policing and control, and management/supervision that gets in the way.
- Review hiring, orientation, training, evaluation, promotion, and layoff/firing practices.
- Question inefficient practices such as management policing and controlling, reviewing and employee redoing, and inappropriate following of policies.
- Ascertain the level of self-motivated disciplined behavior.

Reader: From the sample Organizational Initial Survey Form (Exhibit 2.1) develop similar tools for your organization's operational review.

EXHIBIT 2.1   ORGANIZATIONAL INITIAL SURVEY FORM

Planning
1. How does the company plan? Describe the system of planning.
2. Does a long-range plan exist? If so, attach copy.
3. Do current short-term plans exist? If so, attach copy.
4. What are plans for expansion or improvement? How will they affect the organization?
5. What are plans for physical plant development? How will they affect the organization?
6. What are personnel plans?
   - Positions to be added
   - Positions to be eliminated
   - Functions to be changed
7. How does the organization budget? Does it encourage the increase of personnel costs and positions? Are personnel positions and costs part of the budget justification process?

Personnel and Staffing
1. Does an organization chart exist? If so, provide copy.
2. Do job descriptions exist for each block on the organizational chart? If so, provide copies.
3. Are job descriptions of a general nature by position, or specific functional descriptions for each employee?

EXHIBIT 2.1   (CONTINUED)

---

4. Do staffing statistics by functional area exist? If so, provide copy. Are there areas where such statistics do not exist?
5. How are employees recruited, screened, interviewed, and hired?
6. Is there a system of employee evaluations? Describe.
7. Is there a process of justifying a new position? Describe.
8. How are employees disciplined, laid off, and fired? Describe.
9. How are employees oriented and trained? Describe.
10. What are salary increase and promotion policies? Describe.
11. How are salary increases (and decreases) determined? Who makes these decisions?
12. Is there an employee personnel manual? Obtain copy.
13. Is there a wage and salary policy and adopted schedule? Is it shared with employees? Obtain copy.
14. Is there an employee grievance procedure? Describe.
15. What types of personnel records are maintained?
16. Are staffing patterns established based on operational requirements justified by the three Es or by some other means?
17. Are employees cross-trained, or do they remain in the same area throughout their employment with the company?
18. Are personnel adequately capable and competent for their jobs?

Management
1. Is there a board of directors? If so, provide list of names, addresses, and credentials.
2. What are the functions of the board? How often does it meet?
3. Who is considered top management? Provide list of names.
4. Who is considered middle management? Provide list of names.
5. Who is considered lower management (supervision)? Provide list of names.
6. How adequate are existing reports in furnishing information for making management decisions?
7. Are there internal downward communication tools for the staff?
8. Are authority and related responsibilities effectively delegated to management and lower levels?
9. Is there an effective mechanism for upward communication from the staff to levels of management? Describe.
10. Is management performing the functions of managing entrusted resources in the most economical, efficient, and effective manner? Describe how this is accomplished.
11. What are the criteria for management promotion? Describe system.

EXHIBIT 2.1 (CONTINUED)

Authority and Responsibility
1. Has authority been delegated effectively to managers and lower levels within the organization? Describe the process.
2. Are responsibilities clearly defined and understood by managers and staff personnel? Describe the process.
3. Are there written policies and procedures relating to personnel and other functions? If so, provide copies.
4. Do employees know clearly what is expected of them and exactly what authority and responsibility have been assigned to them?

Note: When completing this initial survey form or having client personnel provide the responses, make sure that answers encompass the entire organization, individual departments, specific job positions, and individuals performing each function. All exceptions to the norms should be noted.

PLANNING PHASE WORK PROGRAM

Reader: From the sample Planning Phase Work Program (Exhibit 2.2) develop a planning phase work program for your organization's operational review.

EXHIBIT 2.2 PLANNING PHASE WORK PROGRAM

---

1. *Goals and Objectives*
   a. Review legislative and internal materials that define the general goals and objectives of the area.
      Find out it auditee has elaborated on legislative goals and objectives. Does the area have a formal procedure for doing this?
   b. Planning Systems and Procedures
      • Document the planning procedure either with a narrative or with a flowchart plus narrative.
         Relate to copies of forms and reports.
         Note: Planning must be a coordinated effort between upper- and lower-level management—lower management levels incorporating broader objectives of upper management, as well as defining their own specific objectives.

EXHIBIT 2.2   PLANNING PHASE WORK PROGRAM

- Determine the extent of planning: use of short-term (current year) and long-term planning (five years forward).

  Do objectives and goals coordinate with those of other related and unrelated functions?

  Is there a formal procedure for identifying needs for operating improvements?

  Do planning procedures include a formal statement of justification and a statement of impact?

- Review present plans and related goals and objectives.

  Substantiate definition of needs incorporated in the planning process through a review of documentation, such as minutes of meetings and correspondence files.

  Note: Goals and objectives should be:

  clearly stated.

  communicated to various management levels.

- Review detail plans of action and procedures involved in administering the plan.

  Are the steps clearly outlined?

  Are the program responsibilities assigned?

  Are progress review dates established and slippages in schedules promptly reported and corrected?

  Are budget (plan) versus actual dollars controlled?

  Sometimes there are alternative courses to achieve program objectives. Have alternatives been analyzed in terms of effectiveness and cost?

2. *Budgets*

   a. Review budget process as related to planning procedures.

      - Are budget procedures integrated with the planning process?
      - Are budgets justified in terms of plan?

   b. Budget Justification Procedures

      - Review justification for all budget levels and measures these against actual conditions. Evaluate soundness of budget allocations.

      - Review justification and evaluate soundness for new and increased funding, and measure against actual conditions.

      - Relate one aspect of budget to another aspect. Some may be realized; others may not.

        Example: An expanded program requires:

        additional personnel.

        more equipment.

EXHIBIT 2.2   CONTINUED

---

   more furniture.
   more supplies.
The employees are not hired, but the department, meanwhile, has gone ahead and purchased the equipment, the furniture, and the supplies.
   Example of other areas where correlation is helpful:
      higher postage expenses with increased correspondence (e.g., billings).
      more equipment with increased supplies or paper.
      increased activities in one department matched by an increase in another department.
      request for fixed assets, if not for an expanded area, should alert the auditor to ask about asset retirement, scrap or surplus sales.
   c. Analyze budget reporting procedures and their effectiveness?
      • Budget versus actual reporting.
      • Use of flexible budgeting (relating budget to actual conditions).
      • Effective monitoring and control.
3. *Organization Chart and Procedures Manuals*
   a. Obtain copy or prepare organization chart, and analyze as to possible inefficiencies, such as:
      • One-on-one administration or supervision.
      • Span of administration much too wide for one person. This should be evaluated by competence of the administrator, capability of supervisees, complexity of functions performed.
      • Overlapping, so that personnel report to more than one person.
      • Apparent illogical placement of units within the organization.
      • Administrative positions that do not appear to be commensurate either with extend to responsibilities or with numbers supervised.
   b. Obtain copies of procedures manuals and review for:
      • Absence of definitions of jobs and responsibilities.
      • Existing but outdated or inadequate procedures.
4. *Flowcharts*
   a. Prepare for flowcharting by becoming familiar with the department and its operations.
      • Review the budget detail.
      • Review the procedures manual.
      • Review the organizational charts.
      • Review all reports.

EXHIBIT 2.2   CONTINUED

- Review analysis of expenditures and revenues.
- Obtain copies of all forms used.
- Discuss operations in a general way with auditee personnel.

   b. Prepare general systems flowcharts of major systems and procedures.

   c. Analyze flowcharts to identify such things as:
- Weaknesses in internal control.
- Work-flow bottlenecks or uneven distribution of work.
- Unnecessary handling of documents.
- Inefficient routing of documents.
- Unnecessary document copies or records or unused information.
- Duplication of efforts.
- Insufficient use of equipment.

5. *Reports*

   a. Obtain copies of management and operating reports.

   b. Discuss reports with appropriate personnel and prepare written description of contents and purpose of each report.
- Do reports provide usable information based on the auditor's understanding of the operation?
- Are users really using the reports? If not, discuss and document reasons.
- Prepare list of distribution of reports and frequency of their issuance.

   c. Review and analyze reports and related discussions with users to determine whether:
- There is adequate existing decision-making and performance information.
- There is adequate operating information to enable the department's activities and responsibilities to be performed efficiently.
- The information is timely. Are reports issued or prepared within acceptable schedules?
- Exception reporting is used. Has management defined levels of acceptance, with exceptions automatically brought to their attention?
- The information increases in detail as it is disseminated to each lower level of management and operations.

EXHIBIT 2.2 CONTINUED

- The information build-up at each level of management and operation is well integrated horizontally as well as vertically, or whether the various subunits function independently.
- The reports are accurate and reliable.

6. *Personnel*
   a. Obtain and review current job descriptions for the various positions within the department. Compare these with the current procedures manual.
   b. Review personnel folders and compare background with job descriptions.
   c. Analyze personnel functions within the department as to:
      - Determination of the experience and training requirements for each personnel position.
      - Subsequent review to determine that personnel levels are adequate.
      - Determination as to the number of personnel requested in its budget.
      - Existence of formal or informal staff training and how successful it is.
      - Employee evaluation procedures and their effectiveness.
   d. Prepare a summary of positions, the number of employees in those positions, and the salary range for each position.
      Compare this with:
      - Organization charts.
      - Budget requests.
      - Job descriptions.
   e. Observe employees at work; apply simple work-sampling techniques:
      - Start late?
      - Quit early?
      - Long lunches?
      - Long time away from desk?
      - Lengthy conversations?
      Minimum—one week's observations, daily for about one hour per day. Time all observations in order to arrive eventually at a cumulative time.
   f. Review employee statistics such as:

EXHIBIT 2.2   CONTINUED

- Employee turnover rates.
- Use and patterns of sick leave.
- Lateness: beginning of day, breaks, and lunchtime.
- Employee overtime rates.

7. *Facilities*

   a. Observe and analyze work layout and working conditions. Do they provide for:
      - Easy work flow?
      - Unencumbered access ways?
      - Sufficient space without extravagance?
      - Sufficient light?

   b. Prepare and analyze preliminary layout flow diagram.
      - A good technique is to obtain or prepare a sketch of various work areas in the department. Identify functions in each area and the number of personnel. Integrate this information with the general systems flowcharts and identify bottlenecks, uneven work distribution, etc.
      - Observe working conditions in each area. They reveal information about work attitudes, work load, employee performance, work layout, and work space. Look for such things as:
        - Papers stored on tops of desks
        - Computer reports stacked on tops of tables.
        - Lack of filing space.

   c. Review use of equipment. Look for equipment.
      - Not being used.
      - Not being used effectively.
      - Too sophisticated for needs.
      - Too costly for purposes.
      - Too primitive for purposes.

      Quantify exceptions on the basis of the amount of time used, and the salary levels of personnel using them.

   d. Analyze the department's general operating procedures. Are they:
      - Manual when automated would be better?
      - Automated when manual would be better?
      - Automated, but not fully utilized?

   e. Review fixed assets used in operations and related records. Some idea of the care the department lavishes or does not lavish on its fixed assets can be gleaned from these results.

CASE STUDY: JOE SORRY, INC.— PLANNING PHASE

The starting point for the operational review of Joe Sorry, Inc. is Joe and Flo's decision as to which operational area or areas to be reviewed. As was discussed and documented in the proposal letter, the general areas to be reviewed were agreed to be:

- Personnel: manufacturing, general and administrative
- Manufacturing operations
- Product line analysis
- Profit center concepts
- Operational reporting considerations
- Planning and budget systems

A planning phase work program for Joe Sorry, Inc. is shown in Exhibit 2.3. Note that the items included in the work program are based the agreed upon areas for review.

EXHIBIT 2.3   PLANNING PHASE WORK PROGRAM

JOE SORRY, INC.
PLANNING PHASE WORK PROGRAM

1. *Review of Gathered Data*
   Review and analyze the following materials gathered from management and employees:
   - Initial Survey Form
   - Violations of Good Business Practices
   - Job Responsibility Questionnaires
2. *Personnel and Organization*
   a. Obtain and review current job descriptions for the various positions within the company.
   b. Review personnel folders and compare backgrounds with job descriptions.
   c. Analyze personnel functions as to:
      - Determination of the experience and training requirements for each personnel position
      - Subsequent review to determine that personnel levels are adequate

---

EXHIBIT 2.3   CONTINUED

- Determination as to the number of personnel requested versus number necessary
- Existence/success of formal or informal staff training
- Employee evaluation procedures and their effectiveness

d. Prepare a summary of positions, the number of employees in those positions, and the salary range for each position.

e. Observe employees at work; apply simple work sampling techniques. Simple work sampling: Start late? Quit early? Long lunches? Long time away from desk? Lengthy conversations?

f. Review employee statistics such as:
- Employee turnover rates
- Use and patterns of sick leave
- Lateness; beginning of day, breaks, and lunches
- Employee overtime rates

g. Obtain copy or prepare organization chart, and analyze as to possible inefficiencies such as:
- One-on-one administration or supervision
- Span of administration much too wide for one person
- Apparent illogical placement of units within the organization
- Administrative positions that appear not commensurate either with extent of responsibilities or numbers supervised

3. *Manufacturing Operations*

a. Familiarize yourself with the department and its operations.
- Obtain copies of all forms and reports used
- Discuss operations in a general way with management and operations personnel

b. Review and observe manufacturing procedures as to:
- Specialty boards
- Custom boards
- Defense business
- Basic boards

c. Review related manufacturing functions such as:
- Production scheduling and control
- Inventory control: raw materials, work in process, and finished goods
- Shop floor control
- Quality control
- Packing and shipping

4. *Analysis of Financial Statements*

Analyze current year-ending financial statements as to:

EXHIBIT 2.3   CONTINUED

- Comparisons with prior years and common size
- Trend percentages
- Selected financial ratios related to operations

5. *Operational Reports*
   a. Obtain copies of management and operating reports.
   b. Discuss reports with appropriate personnel and prepare written description of contents and purpose of each report.
      - Do reports provide usable information based on your understanding of the operation?
      - Are users really using the reports? If not, discuss and document reasons.
      - Prepare list of distribution of reports and frequency of their issuance.
   c. Review and analyze reports and related discussions with users to determine:
      - If there is adequate existing decision-making and performance information.
      - If operating information is adequate for efficient performance of the department's activities and responsibilities.
      - If exception reporting is used. Has management defined levels of acceptance with exceptions automatically brought to their attention?

6. *Facilities and Equipment*
   a. Observe and analyze work layout and working conditions. Does it provide for:
      - Easy work flow?
      - Unencumbered access ways?
      - Sufficient space without extravagance?
   b. Observe working conditions in each area. They reveal things about work attitudes, work loads, employee performance, work layout, and work space.
   c. Review use of equipment. Look for equipment:
      - Not being used
      - Not being used effectively
      - Too sophisticated for needs
      - Too costly for purposes
      - Too primitive for purposes

      Quantify exceptions on the basis of the amount of time used and the salary levels of personnel using them.

EXHIBIT 2.3   CONTINUED

---

   d. Analyze the department's general operating procedures. Are
      they:
- Manual when automated would be better?
- Automated when manual would be better?
- Automated, but not fully utilized?

   e. Review fixed assets used in operations. Some idea of the care
      the department lavishes or does not lavish on its fixed assets
      can be gleaned from these results.

   f. Computer equipment:
- Prepare list of all computer equipment by location and use
- Prepare list of software being used by location or network
- Observe use of computer equipment
- Determine capability of software packages

Organizational Review

The original organization chart for Joe Sorry, Inc. is shown in Exhibit
2.4.

EXHIBIT 2.4   ORIGINAL ORGANIZATION CHART

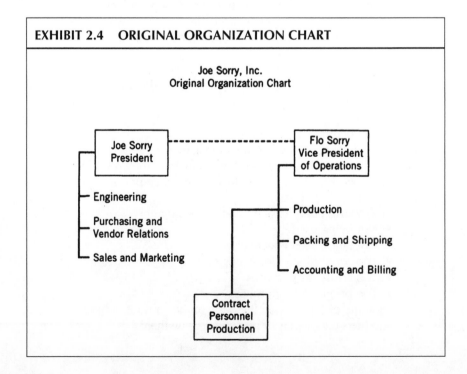

The organization structure while simple exemplifies many of the principles of proper organization such as:

- Clear lines of authority
- Proper division of duties and responsibilities
- Communication between functions, across functions, upward and downward
- Minimal use of personnel and then only as needed
- Proper delegation of responsibility and authority
- Management able to effectively control the sphere of their operations and results
- Management and other personnel clearly understanding what is expected of them and the results to be achieved
- Organization established based on the principles of the three Es— economy, efficiency, and effectiveness
- The right size organization for what needs to be accomplished
- Minimal levels of non–value-added employees and management
- Organization no larger than it has to be to accomplish results

The first thing I did upon arriving to conduct the planning phase of the operational review at Joe's business, which was now located in a fancy new industrial park in an upward mobile suburban area, was to take a tour of his operations. Joe took me around, proud of what he had accomplished—over 10,000 square feet of production space with 50 production employees, and 3,000 feet of office space with over 30 employees. I asked Joe to leave and let me mosey around the facilities, while he returned to the crisis of the day. This is what I found out by walking around and talking with the employees on my own:

> The 50 production employees were separated into six teams of seven employees each, with one team member assigned the role of team leader. Although the team leader received a minimal amount of additional pay, not one of them was comfortable exercising their team leader responsibility.

> Each of the six teams was assigned a foreperson, who was responsible for pushing and maximizing production. Only one of the forepersons was respected by their team, and that was only because she left them alone to do their jobs.

The production teams were divided into four groups by type of product. Joe had increased from strictly a producer of specialty boards to a diversified product line as follows:

- Specialty boards for a constant customer base: 1 team.
- Custom boards as requested by customers: 1 team.
- Defense contractors on a contract basis: 2 teams.
- Basic boards on a competitive basis to any and all customers: 2 teams. These basic boards were purchased from an off-shore producer, and Joe's employees checked them, and provided add-ons and Joe's identification materials.
- The other two production employees were a Vice President of Production responsible for Production Control and Scheduling and an Inventory Control Manager responsible for ensuring that sufficient materials were on-hand to meet production needs. There was to never be an idle team due to material stock-outs.

In addition, I found that there were also 12 additional employees which Joe considered indirect labor or overhead (neither plant nor office). These included:

- Five repair and maintenance employees who were responsible for maintaining equipment and cleaning the facilities in the plant and office. They appeared to be doing mainly busy work.
- Four packers and shippers, and three receivers. Both units appeared to work sporadically and at other times got in the way of the production people.

When I went to find Joe, he was in the midst of his next crisis, so I wandered around the office area and talked with those personnel I was able to catch in their offices. This is what I found out on my quick review tour of the office area:

The office and its 30 employees was divided into the following functions:

- Sales: 12 employees, with a sales manager for each product line. In effect Joe was in four businesses, with 8 salespeople assigned as follows: specialty boards: 2 salespeople; custom boards: 1 person; defense business: 2 salespeople; basic boards: 3 salespeople.

- Engineering Department: 9 employees—6 engineers (one head engineer) and 3 draftspeople—with Joe unofficially functioning as Engineering Manager.
- Accounting Department: 5 employees—a CFO/Controller; an employee each assigned to Accounts Receivable, Accounts Payable, Payroll, and General Ledger.
- Purchasing: 4 employees—a Purchasing Manager and 3 purchasing agents/buyers

Almost every employee in the office seemed to have their own PC networked into a central file server. Other than the accounting functions, I found three other PCs in the office area being used—two for word processing and one for a spreadsheet application.

In addition, I found the following functions, not included as production or office, but occupying office space:

- Quality Control (really a production function, but housed in the office area): 7 employees—a QC Manager and 6 QC inspectors, one assigned to each production team (whether they needed it or not).
- Customer Service: 3 employees—a manger and two others, who spent their day dealing with customer calls and complaints—mainly late deliveries and after sale issues.
- Personnel: 2 employees—a Personnel Manager and one assistant.
- Joe's Office: which included himself as President/CFO and 3 Assistants to the President (who turned out to be trouble-shooters for the crises that Joe couldn't handle).
- Vice President's Office: for Flo (who rarely appeared) and two assistants. Formal title: Vice President of Operations.
- Clerical Staff: 24 employees—4 each for Sales and Accounting, 3 each for Engineering and Purchasing, 2 each for Customer Service, Personnel, and Quality Control, 1 each for Joe and Flo, plus 2 receptionists.

Instead of the 80 or so employees Joe had claimed, there were actually over 130 (not including Joe and Flo); with many office personnel controlling and supporting production operations. It was apparent that Joe had created a corporate empire; almost rivaling his former employer. I compared the original organization chart for Joe's initial "garage shop" business to the one I prepared for the present organization. The differences were not only staggering; but Joe and the company were out of control. (See Exhibit 2.5.)

Joe's organization chart, after three years in business, now looked like a camel (i.e., a horse created by a committee). The organization had grown based on immediate crisis rather than on proper organizational principles. Quick review and analysis of the current organization showed some possible inefficiencies and organizational roadblocks, such as:

- Instead of Joe and Flo handling all of the major functions, they now had 135 employees.
- Gross payroll was now over $3,010,000 as shown on the summary of personnel positions (see Exhibit 2.6). Compared to the present level of $6,250,000 in gross sales, this represents over 48 percent of sales. Even at this relatively high level, the company was able to earn $830,000 or 13.3 percent of sales.
- Questionable staff personnel such as:
    - Three assistants to the president
    - Two assistants to the vice president of operations
    - Personnel Department: manager, assistant, and two clerical personnel
    - Six forepersons and production team leaders
    - Purchasing Department: manager, three buyers, and three clerical
    - Sales Department: four managers, eight sales staff, four clerical
    - Customer Service Department: manager, two staff, two clerical
- Overabundance of clerical personnel; 22 such individuals assigned to the following functions:
    - Secretary—President
    - Secretary—Vice President
    - Two clerical—Personnel Department
    - Two clerical—Quality Control
    - Three clerical—Purchasing Department

EXHIBIT 2.5   ORGANIZATIONAL CHART: PRESENT

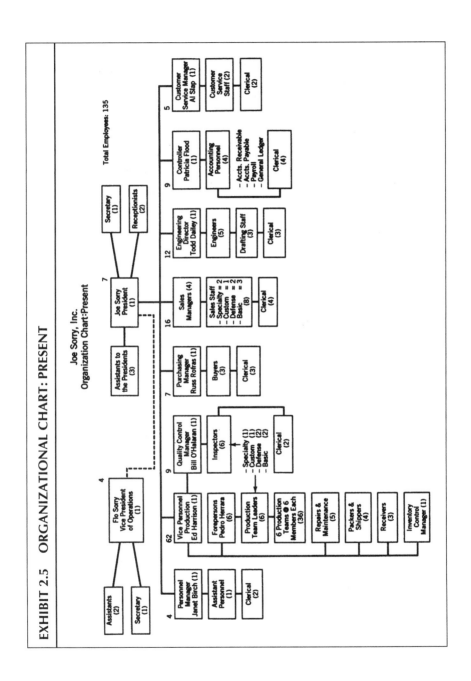

Joe Sorry, Inc.
Organization Chart:Present

Total Employees: 135

EXHIBIT 2.6   SUMMARY OF PERSONNEL POSITIONS

JOE SORRY, INC.
SUMMARY OF PERSONNEL POSITIONS

Position Description	# Employees	Salary Range
President	1	$140,000
Assistant to the President	3	$30 to $50,000
Vice President of Operations	1	$ 85,000
Assistant to the VP of Operations	2	$25 and 32,000
Secretary	2	$18 and 22,000
Receptionists	2	$ 15,000
Personnel Manager	1	$ 42,000
Assistant—Personnel	1	$ 28,000
Vice President—Production	1	$ 74,000
Forepersons	6	$22 to 26,000
Production Team Leaders	6	$20 to 24,000
Production Workers	36	$15 to 18,000
Repair and Maintenance	5	$ 24,000
Packers and Shippers	4	$12 to 15,000
Receivers	3	$10 to 12,000
Inventory Control Manager	1	$ 18,000
Quality Control Manager	1	$ 26,000
Inspectors	6	$20 to 24,000
Purchasing Manager	1	$ 28,000
Buyers	3	$20 to 22,000
Sales Managers	4	$32 to 36,000
Sales Staff	8	$22 to 28,000
Engineering Director	1	$ 38,000
Engineers	5	$28 to 34,000
Drafting Staff	3	$16 to 19,000
Controller	1	$ 34,000
Accounting Personnel	4	$18 to 22,000
Customer Service Manager	1	$ 28,000
Customer Service Staff	2	$22 and 24,000
Clerical	20	$14 to 18,000
Total number of employees	135	
Total Regular Gross Payroll		$3,010,000

- Four clerical—Sales Department
- Three clerical—Engineering Department
- Four clerical—Controller Department
- Two clerical—Customer Services
- A manager assigned to each functional area with undefined responsibilities and expectations such as personnel, production (vice president), quality control, purchasing, sales, engineering, controller, and customer services.
- Production, quality control, and sales functionally divided by type of product (specialty, custom, defense, and basic), which may result in improper division of duties and responsibilities, and an uneven distribution of work.
- Functions with possible overlapping or duplication, such as both forepersons and production team leaders, purchasing buyers and clerical staff, and sales managers and sales staff.
- Functions that seem superfluous with the presence of a computer system such as engineers and drafting staff, four accounting staff, and numerous clerical staff.

Analysis of Initial Survey Form

One of the first steps in the planning phase is to analyze the organization's responses to an initial survey form:

Planning and Budgeting. There are no real planning systems in place. The only defined goal is to be the biggest possible in terms of sales and income, which may create a conflict. In the absence of effective planning systems, the budget system does not integrate with the company's plans, but is merely a broad projection for the next year (based on Joe's wishes rather than any reality) compared on a monthly basis by the controller.

Personnel and Staffing. The organization is growing out of control. It appears that there are too many employees in almost every function, with a good possibility that instead of providing increased efficiency, they often get in everyone else's way. Many employees do not seem to know exactly what they should be doing; there is possibly more filling of time than achievement of desired results. Personnel hiring, orientation, training, supervision, evaluation, promotion, and firing practices have to be reviewed and greatly improved; there is too much control by Joe and the department managers.

Management. Top management is really Joe—not effectively delegating. Flo has almost disappeared from the operations of the company. Ed Harrison, although given authority over production, is continually being overridden by Joe. Middle management appears to be operating under similar conditions (i.e., controlled by Joe). An effective management and operating reporting system does not exist. There is a need for delegating down to the lowest possible levels and keeping Joe from interfering with everyone's operations.

Policies and Procedures. No formal policies or procedures exist. This is causing great confusion overall within the organization and within most of the departments. There is too much control by management, with capricious changes by management making it difficult for employees to sense any consistency.

Computer Processing. There are PCs in every department, one in almost every employee's workstation. Many are not being used at all; some are used minimally, others are used for packaged software applications. This area needs to be reviewing and analyzed to determine how an effective management and operating reporting system can be implemented.

Manufacturing Systems. Although there is a computerized manufacturing system for production and inventory control, it appears that it is being used ineffectively, mainly for routing customer orders through production and reporting inventory reorders (based on reorder points and reorder quantities) and on-hand inventory balances. The software is used to support ineffective manufacturing processes.

Responsibility and Authority. Responsibilities have not been clearly defined, so most employees do not know what they should be doing and what is expected of them. Although authority has been somewhat delegated to middle managers, Joe through his continual interference has sabotaged it. Review Exhibit 2.7, Violations of Principles of Good Business Practice—Summary of Employee Results.

Analysis of Financial Statements

We reviewed and analyzed the Joe Sorry, Inc. financial statements for the first three years of operations and then compared them with the

---

EXHIBIT 2.7   VIOLATIONS OF PRINCIPLES OF GOOD BUSINESS PRACTICE—SUMMARY OF EMPLOYEE RESULTS

Please review the following items representing violations of good business practices. Place a check mark next to those items you believe Joe Sorry, Inc., or your department to be guilty of doing. Recording your name on this survey is optional. Please return your completed form to Rob Reider of Reider Associates.

	Number of Responses
A. Planning	
1. Not setting or updating organizational standards or goals	118
2. Not establishing clear long-term or short-term objectives	114
3. Not developing detail plans as to how plans are to be carried out	122
4. Not developing budgets that relate to short-term plans	117
5. Not prescribing a system of review and replanning	108
B. Organizing	
1. Not hiring the right people for the job	96
2. Not orienting, training, or instructing supervisees	113
3. Not assigning work on an even distribution	83
4. Not having the right number of personnel—more or less	68
5. Not providing adequate resources, facilities, or equipment	49
C. Scheduling	
1. Not providing schedules and budgets for each job	117
2. Not highlighting oldest, off-schedule, or over budget jobs	105
3. Not setting priorities for incoming work	97
4. Not readjusting schedules when changes are necessary	116
5. Not requiring approval for nonschedules work	85
D. Coordinating	
1. Not providing for coordination of company goals and objectives with those of each department	128

EXHIBIT 2.7   CONTINUED

---

2. Not periodically reviewing the needs of all work units   93
3. Not communicating organization policies and
    departmental procedures to personnel   106
4. Not effectively communicating downward   127
5. Not coordinating information relating to various
    departments   96

E. Directing
    1. Not providing clear expectations and instructions   119
    2. Not reviewing work and providing positive feedback
        so as to provide correction rather than ongoing criticism 129
    3. Not fixing the situation rather than fixing the blame   126
    4. Not providing a coaching or facilitative environment   123
    5. Not periodically reviewing work loads and priorities   117

F. Obtaining Feedback
    1. Not providing feedback on the quality of work, so as to
        build on work done well and remediate work not
        done well   124
    2. Not comparing results with communicated expectations
        and investigating variances—both positive and negative   117
    3. Not effectively communicating to the worker where
        a job does not meet standards   106
    4. Not effectively inspecting ongoing processes at strategic
        points in the system (adequate quality control procedures) 109
    5. Not acting on customer complaints or returned work   114

G. Achieving Improvement
    1. Not replacing ineffective standards, procedures, or
        systems   105
    2. Not establishing a program of positive improvement   123
    3. Not reviewing operations so as to be most economical,
        efficient, and effective   127
    4. Not encouraging (or coaching and facilitating)
        employees to upgrade their capabilities   118
    5. Not correcting or reporting variances promptly   106

Note: This form was sent to all 135 employees, and the number of
check-offs was recorded by the review team in the planning phase.

final year of ACE Electronics' operations. As the financial statements were in the company's computer system, we were able to prepare:

- Comparative statements for the last three years
- Common-size statements for the last three years
- Comparison with ACE Electronics' last year of operations

We developed trend percentages and selected financial ratios for critical operational areas such as:

- Cash liquidity
- Accounts receivable
- Inventory
- Accounts payable
- Sales
- Cost of sales
- Selling expenses
- General and administrative expenses
- Profitability

We were not able to analyze the statements as to type of products (specialty, custom, defense, and basic), as such information is not available in the computer system. This analysis should be done in the field work phase.

The financial statements and our developed trends and ratios are shown in Exhibits 2.8 through 2.14.

Identification of Critical Areas for Review

A good method to use in identifying critical areas for review is to have the review team staff record each possible area as they work through the preliminary survey and the planning phase. At the end of the planning phase, the review team members critique the list accumulated and combine like items, eliminate unnecessary or less critical items, and then prioritize the remaining items. The original list and the final list are shown in Exhibits 2.15 and 2.16.

EXHIBIT 2.8   COMPARATIVE BALANCE SHEETS AS OF DECEMBER 31

JOE SORRY, INC.
COMPARATIVE BALANCE SHEETS AS OF DECEMBER 31

RENT	*20X1*	*20X2*	*CUR*
ASSETS			
CASH IN BANK	$ 300	$ 200	30
ACCOUNTS RECEIVABLE	600	1,080	1,860
INVENTORY	800	1,200	2,680
TOTAL CURRENT ASSETS	$1,700	$2,480	$4,570
PROPERTY, PLANT & EQUIPMENT	$2,200	$2,840	$3,790
LESS: DEPRECIATION	(600)	(770)	(1,080)
NET PROPERTY, PLANT & EQUIPMENT	$1,600	$2,070	$2,710
OTHER ASSETS	370	380	420
TOTAL ASSETS	$3,670	$4,930	$7,700
LIABILITIES AND STOCKHOLDERS' EQUITY			
ACCOUNTS PAYABLE	$ 250	$ 420	$ 980
NOTES PAYABLE	100	100	100
CURRENT PAYABLE:			
LONG-TERM DEBT	300	340	420
OTHER CURRENT LIABILITIES	180	220	280
TOTAL CURRENT LIABILITIES	$ 830	$1,080	$1,780
LONG-TERM DEBT	$2,200	$2,600	$3,840
TOTAL LIABILITIES	$3,030	$2,680	$5,620
COMMON STOCK (1,000 SHARES)	$ 100	100	100
ADDITIONAL PAID-IN CAPITAL	100	100	100
RETAINED EARNINGS	440	1,050	1,880
TOTAL STOCKHOLDERS' EQUITY	$ 640	$1,250	$2,080
TOTAL LIABILITIES & S/H EQUITY	$3,670	$4,930	$7,700

EXHIBIT 2.9   COMPARATIVE INCOME STATEMENTS FOR YEARS ENDED DECEMBER 31

JOE SORRY, INC.
COMPARATIVE INCOME STATEMENTS FOR YEARS ENDED DECEMBER 31

	20X1	20X2	CURRENT
NET SALES	$3,240	$4,680	$6,250
COST OF GOODS SOLD:			
MATERIAL	$ 480	$ 860	$1,130
LABOR	970	1,170	1,630
MANUFACTURING EXPENSES	640	860	1,040
TOTAL COST OF GOODS SOLD	$2,090	$2,890	$3,800
MANUFACTURING PROFIT	$1,150	$1,790	$2,450
SELLING EXPENSES	$ 260	$ 420	$ 560
GENERAL & ADMINISTRATIVE			
EXPENSES	270	520	740
TOTAL OPERATING EXPENSES	$ 530	$ 940	$1,300
OPERATING PROFIT	$ 620	$ 850	$1,150
PROVISION FOR INCOME TAXES	$ 180	$ 240	$ 320
NET INCOME	$ 440	$ 610	$ 830

EXHIBIT 2.10   COMMON-SIZE BALANCE SHEETS AS OF DECEMBER 31

JOE SORRY, INC.
COMMON-SIZE BALANCE SHEETS AS OF DECEMBER 31

	20X1	%	20X2	%	CURRENT	%
ASSETS						
CASH IN BANK	$ 300	8.2	$ 200	4.1	$ 30	.4
ACCOUNTS RECEIVABLE	600	16.3	1,080	21.9	1,860	24.2
INVENTORY	800	21.8	1,200	24.3	2,680	34.8
TOTAL CURRENT ASSETS	$1,700	46.3	$2,480	50.3	$4,570	59.4
PLANT & EQUIPMENT	$2,200	59.9	$2,840	57.6	$3,790	49.2
LESS: DEPRECIATION	600	16.3	770	15.6	1,080	14.0
NET PLANT—EQUIPMENT	$1,600	43.6	$2,070	42.0	$2,710	35.2
OTHER ASSETS	370	10.1	380	7.7	420	5.4
TOTAL ASSETS	$3,670	100%	$4,930	100%	$7,700	100%
LIABILITIES AND STOCKHOLDERS' EQUITY						
ACCOUNTS PAYABLE	$ 250	6.8	$ 420	8.5	$ 980	12.7
NOTES PAYABLE	100	2.7	100	2.0	100	1.3
CURRENT PAYABLE:						
LONG-TERM DEBT	300	8.2	340	6.9	420	5.5
OTHER CURRENT						
LIABILITIES	180	4.9	220	4.5	280	3.6
TOTAL CURRENT	$ 830	22.6	$1,080	21.9	$1,780	23.1
LONG-TERM DEBT	$2,200	59.9	$2,600	52.7	$3,840	49.9
TOTAL LIABILITIES	$3,030	82.5	$3,680	74.6	$5,620	73.0
COMMON STOCK	$ 100	2.7	100	2.0	100	1.3
PAID-IN CAPITAL	100	2.7	100	2.0	100	1.3
RETAINED EARNINGS	440	12.1	1,050	21.4	1,880	24.4
TOTAL EQUITY	$ 640	17.5	$1,250	25.4	$2,080	27.0
TOTAL LIABILITIES & S/H EQUITY	$3,670	100%	$4,930	100%	$7,700	100%

EXHIBIT 2.11   COMMON-SIZE INCOME STATEMENTS FOR YEARS ENDED DECEMBER 31

JOE SORRY INC.
COMMON-SIZE INCOME STATEMENTS FOR
YEARS ENDED DECEMBER 31

	20X1	%	20X2	%	CURRENT	%
NET SALES	$3,240	100	$4,680	100	$6,250	100
COST OF GOODS SOLD:						
MATERIAL	$ 480	14.8	$ 860	18.4	$1,130	18.1
LABOR	970	29.9	1,170	25.0	1,630	26.1
MANUFACTURING EXPENSES	640	19.8	860	18.4	1,040	16.6
TOTAL COST OF GOODS SOLD	$2,090	64.5	$2,890	61.8	$3,800	60.8
MANUFACTURING PROFIT	$1,150	35.5	$1,790	38.2	$2,450	39.2
SELLING EXPENSES	$ 260	8.0	$ 420	9.0	$ 560	9.0
GENERAL & ADMINISTRATIVE EXPENSES	270	8.3	520	11.1	740	11.8
TOTAL OPERATING EXPENSES	$ 530	16.3	$ 940	20.1	$1,300	20.8
OPERATING PROFIT	$ 620	19.2	$ 850	18.1	$1,150	18.4
PROVISION FOR INCOME TAXES	$ 180	5.5	$ 240	5.1	$ 320	5.1
NET INCOME	$ 440	13.7	$ 610	13.0	$ 830	13.3

EXHIBIT 2.12   COMPARATIVE INCOME STATEMENTS FOR YEARS
ENDED DECEMBER 31, WITH COMPARISON TO FINAL YEAR OF
ACE ELECTRONICS

JOE SORRY, INC.
COMPARATIVE INCOME STATEMENTS FOR YEARS ENDED
DECEMBER 31 WITH COMPARISON TO FINAL YEAR OF
ACE ELECTRONICS

	20X1	*20X2*	*CURRENT*	*ACE*	*%*
NET SALES	$3,240	$4,680	$6,250	$4,200	100
COST OF GOODS SOLD:					
MATERIAL	$ 480	$ 860	$1,130	$ 780	18.6
LABOR	970	1,170	1,630	1,180	28.1
MANUFACTURING					
EXPENSES	640	860	1,040	980	23.3
TOTAL COST OF					
GOODS SOLD	$2,090	$2,890	$3,800	$2,940	70.0
MANUFACTURING PROFIT	$1,150	$1,790	$2,450	$1,260	30.0
SELLING EXPENSES	$ 260	$ 420	$ 560	480	11.4
GENERAL &					
ADMINISTRATIVE					
EXPENSES	270	520	740	470	11./2
TOTAL OPERATING					
EXPENSES	$ 530	$ 940	$1,300	$ 950	22.6
OPERATING PROFIT	$ 620	$ 850	$1,150	$ 310	7.4
PROVISION FOR INCOME					
TAXES	$ 180	$ 240	$ 320	$ 113	2.7
NET INCOME	$ 440	$ 610	$ 830	$ 197	4.7

EXHIBIT 2.13   SELECTED TREND PERCENTAGES

JOE SORRY INC.
SELECTED TREND PERCENTAGES

20X1 - BASE YEAR	*20X1*	*%*	*20X2*	*%*	*Curr*	*%*
BALANCE SHEET						
1. Cash in Bank	300	100%	200	67%	30	10%
2. Accounts Receivable	600	100%	1080	180%	1860	310%
3. Inventory	800	100%	1200	150%	2580	335%
4. Total Current Assets	1700	100%	2480	146%	4570	256%
5. Property, Plant & Equipment	1600	100%	2070	129%	2710	169%
6. Accounts Payable	250	100%	420	168%	980	392%
7. Long-Term Debt	2200	100%	2600	118%	3840	175%
8. Retained Earnings	440	100%	1050	239%	1880	427%
INCOME STATEMENT						
1. Net Sales	3240	100%	4680	144%	6250	193%
2. Material Costs	480	100%	860	179%	1130	235%
3. Labor Costs	970	100%	1170	121%	1630	168%
4. Manufacturing Expenses	640	100%	860	134%	1040	163%
5. Total Cost of Goods Sold	2090	100%	2890	138%	3800	182%
6. Manufacturing Profit	1150	100%	1790	156%	2450	213%
7. Selling Expenses	260	100%	420	162%	560	215%
8. General & Administrative	270	100%	520	193%	740	274%
9. Operating Profit	620	100%	850	137%	1150	185%
10. Net Income	440	100%	610	139%	830	189%

EXHIBIT 2.14   SELECTED FINANCIAL RATIOS

JOE SORRY, INC
SELECTED FINANCIAL RATIOS

	20X1	20X2	CURRENT
LIQUIDITY RATIOS			
1. Working Capital			
Current Assets	1700	2480	4570
Current Liabilities	830	1080	1780
Working Capital	870	1400	2790
Increase (Decrease)			
2. Current Ratio			
Current Assets	1700	2480	4570
Current Liabilities	830	1080	1780
= Current Ratio	2.05	2.30	2.57
3. Quick (Acid-Test) Ratio			
Quick Assets (Cash & Recs.)	900	1280	1890
Current Liabilities	830	1080	1780
= Quick Ratio	1.08	1.19	1.06
PERFORMANCE RATIOS			
1. Accounts Receivable Turnover			
Total Sales	3240	4680	6250
Average Accounts Receivable	600	840	1470
= Accounts Receivable Turnover	5.4X	5.6X	4.3X
2. Accounts Receivable Collection			
Accounts Receivable	600	1080	1860
Average Daily Sales	3240/365	4680/365	6250/365
= Days Collection Period	67.6	84.2	108.6
SELECTED FINANCIAL RATIOS			
3. Inventory Turnover			
a. Total Sales	3240	4680	6250
Average Inventory	800	1000	1940
= Inventory Turnover	4.1X	4.7X	3.2X

EXHIBIT 2.14   SELECTED FINANCIAL RATIOS

	20X1	20X2	CURRENT
Days in the Year (365)	365	365	365
Inventory Turnover Rate	4.1	4.7	3.2
= Average Age of Inventory	89.0	77.7	114.1
b. Cost of Goods Sold	2090	2890	3800
Average Inventory	800	100	1940
= Inventory Turnover	2.6X	2.9X	2.0X
Days in the Year (365)	365	365	365
Inventory Turnover Rate	2.6	2.9	2.0
= Average Age of Inventory	140.4	125.9	182.5
PROFITABILITY RATIOS			
1. Net Profit Margin			
Net Income	440	610	830
Net Sales	3240	4680	6250
= Net Profit Margin	13.6%	13.0%	13.3%
2. Gross Profit Margin			
Gross (Manufacturing) Profit	1150	1790	2450
Net Sales	3240	4680	6250
= Gross Profit Margin	35.5%	38.2%	39.2%

EXHIBIT 2.15   INITIAL LIST OF POSSIBLE CRITICAL AREAS

1. Lack of mission statement and clear direction as to why Joe Sorry, Inc. is in business
   - No long-term planning and direction.
   - No short-term organizational and departmental plans.
   - No integrated budget (really no budget) with plans.
2. Operating different businesses within same structure
   - Four businesses: specialty, custom, defense, basic.
   - Creating internal chaos and crises.
   - Detracting from being a customer service business.
3. Cash flow problems and need for cash management review
   - Sales and net income emphasis.
   - Resulting in increases in backlog, accounts receivable, inventory, and payroll costs.
   - Short-term line of credit ($3 million).
4. Production scheduling and control
   - Scheduling by customer order
   - Controlling by exception (as customers scream).
   - Not maximizing production throughput.
5. Customer backlog growing
   - Inability to efficiently meet customer requirements.
   - Increase in late deliveries.
   - Inability to determine lost sales.
6. Sales efforts
   - Lack of effective sales forecast.
   - Lack of sales planning; what products to sell and to whom.
   - Lack of customer coordination.
   - Lack of internal coordination: engineering and manufacturing.
7. Selling to less than desirable customers
   - Increase in accounts receivable.
   - Laxity in credit checks, terms, and follow-up.
   - Ineffective collection procedures.
8. Inventory control problems
   - Increase in raw material inventories.
   - Inability to effectively control work in process.
   - Buildup of finished goods inventory.
   - Physical control problems.
9. Vendor relations
   - Increase in accounts payable.
   - Less reliance on critical vendors.
   - Increase in rejects and late deliveries.

EXHIBIT 2.15 CONTINUED

---

10. Property, plant, and equipment
    - Inefficiently operated manufacturing facility.
    - New facility already overcrowded.
    - Not getting effective return on investment.
11. Personnel
    - Managers for each function possibly unnecessary.
    - Unwieldly hierarchy; confusion as to authority relationships.
    - More staff than needed (e.g., manufacturing, quality control, sales, engineering, accounting, clerical).
    - Poor coordination and work cohesion.
    - Lack of proper hiring, orientation, training, and supervision.
12. Management
    - Too much control by Joe.
    - Titular delegation of authority, but really Joe decides.
    - Ineffective management at manager/supervisor level.
13. Operational reporting
    - Emphasis on growth in total as to sales and net income.
    - No control and exception reporting.
    - No definition as to key operating indicators, such as meeting production schedule, quality criteria, on-time deliveries, cost and profit criteria, rejects/rework, and productivity.
14. Cost, pricing, volume analysis
    - Lack of effective cost accounting system by product/job.
    - No pricing guidelines (presently based on historical and market conditions).
    - Market share erosion on high-profit specialty and custom.
    - No sales volume considerations: breakeven analysis, sales planning (what to sell and to whom), volume targets.
15. Cost control
    - No budget and profit plan tied to organizational plans.
    - Emphasis on sales, none on controlling costs.
    - Inefficiencies such as too much personnel, equipment (PCs), inventory; poor use of overtime, systems, and procedures.
16. Computer systems
    - Overkill on equipment: almost every employee has a PC or access to one (135 employees and 79 PCs).
    - Manufacturing software not being effectively used.
    - Lack of operating reports to manage business.
    - Needs equipment and systems specifications study.

EXHIBIT 2.15   CONTINUED

---

17. Manufacturing systems
    - Production scheduling and control by customer order.
    - Orders pushed through based on customer commitment or crisis, creating increased costs for all jobs.
    - Running four businesses (specialty, custom defense, basic) through same manufacturing system.
    - Use of personnel: forepersons, production team leaders, production teams, repair and maintenance, packers/shippers, receivers, inventory control manager.
    - Computerized manufacturing control system not being used effectively; reliance on manual reporting.
    - Data collection and accuracy as to costs and job control.
    - Inventory system ineffective.
18. Manufacturing layout
    - Manufacturing processes: six assembly areas with six positions each (specialty, custom, two defense, two basic).
    - Unequal distribution of work due to different demands of each type of business.
    - Productivity uneven between types of jobs.
    - Crowded conditions; workstation encroaching on each other.
    - Need most efficient manufacturing processes for each type of product.
    - Quality control housed in office area; should be integral part of production.
    - Overcrowding prevents on-line versus off-line testing.
    - Inventory spread around the production facility.
    - Receiving and packing/shipping areas forced together.
19. Analysis of financial statements
    - Financial reports (balance sheet and income statement) produced at end of month without any effective analysis or interpretation.
    - Statements not providing data as to product lines.
    - Need for systems specifications as to data and reporting needs.
    - Need to convert financial data into operating data such as cash liquidity, accounts receivable, inventory, and accounts payable problems.
    - Need to establish reporting criteria such as trends and ratio analysis
20. Computer systems
    - Equipment in place (79 PCs, 4 file servers, 23 laser printers) but not being used as intended.

EXHIBIT 2.15   CONTINUED

- Manufacturing system was to be networked, fully integrated MRP II system, but being used minimally.
- Network for Personnel, Purchasing, Sales, and Customer Service only being used by Purchasing to any extent.
- Engineering system (primarily for CAD applications) needs to be reviewed as to effective use.
- Accounting system operations need to be reviewed as to methods of operation, data and reporting requirements, etc.
- Clerical staff PCs need to be reviewed as to effective use and necessity.
- President (Joe) and Vice President of Operations (Flo) have 9 PCs between their functions: determine necessity and use.
- Joe intended to set up a fairly sophisticated computer network to manage and operate the business, but never did. Need to review and analyze how best to use these systems.

EXHIBIT 2.16   REVIEW TEAM FINAL LIST OF CRITICAL AREAS FOR REVIEW

*	1.	Planning and budget systems.
#	2.	Cash flow/cash management.
Now	3.	Four businesses: profit center/product line/separate businesses.
Now	4.	Manufacturing systems: operations, facilities, and personnel.
*	5.	Sales functions: forecasting, sales efforts, customer service.
*	6.	Customer service: quality, on-time deliveries, credit and collection practices, after-sale service.
Now	7.	Inventory control systems and procedures.
Now	8.	Personnel: number, responsibilities, hiring, training, etc.
Now	9.	Operational reporting: financial and operations.
#	10.	Cost, pricing, volume analysis.
*	11.	Computer systems: hardware and software.
Now	12.	Manufacturing: facility layout and production procedures.

These 12 areas were discussed by the review team with Joe and Flo, and it was jointly decided that the following items would be the priority items to be included in this operational review:

EXHIBIT 2.16   CONTINUED

1. Review of personnel (#8)—manufacturing and quality control. Other personnel areas were to be addressed by Joe and Flo and if necessary picked up later for operational review.
2. Manufacturing systems (#4 & #9): review of MRP II concepts and what to implement, as well as operational reporting requirements.
3. Manufacturing (#12)—facility layout and production procedures.
4. Inventory control systems and procedures (#7).
5. Four business concepts (#3): profit centers/product lines/separate businesses.

Other items marked * were to be considered for later review and those marked # were to be started internally, with the review team providing oversight-type assistance.

CASE SITUATION: Purchase Order Quantity Tolerances

Reader: Review the case situation below and document your answers to the questions presented. Then review the suggested responses.

During the planning phase of an operational review, the reviewer found in reviewing the Purchasing Department's methods and procedures that vendors could be allowed to ship the ordered quantity plus or minus 10 percent. However, this practice was approved only for certain commodities such as nuts, bolts, wire, and rope.

During physical inspection of the Purchasing Department and discussions with the manager of the Purchasing Department as part of the planning phase of the operational review, the reviewer found that:

The 10 percent quantity tolerance was being used for items that did not require a tolerance, such as office supplies, maintenance items, and cleaning supplies.

Most vendors took advantage of the tolerance terms and shipped the ordered quantity plus 10 percent.

Although procedures existed relative to such purchase order tolerances, each buyer was deciding what was appropriate based on personal knowledge of industry practice.

Questions for Consideration

1. What additional steps might the reviewer want to perform in the planning phase relative to this situation?
2. What could the reviewer suggest, if anything, to the Purchasing Department to correct the situation at this point?

Suggested Responses

1. What additional steps might the reviewer want to perform in the planning phase relative to this situation?

   Response: Time-consuming efforts to show the existence of significant deficiencies should not be undertaken. Accordingly, this situation should only be documented at this point, for consideration when deciding on areas for additional work.

2. What could the reviewer suggest, if anything, to the Purchasing Department to correct the situation at this point?

   Response: Written instructions should be prepared for each buyer stating the specific items that require tolerance and the level of tolerance to be used.

   Note that the institution of such written instructions, and exercise of granting such purchase tolerances only to those items requiring it, resulted in an net annual savings of approximately $320,000 for the Example Company.

REVIEW QUESTIONS

1. What are the primary purposes of the planning phase?
2. List the type of information that could be gathered during the planning phase.
3. What are some of the sources of information available to the operational reviewer in the planning phase?
4. What are some techniques by which the operational reviewer can identify critical problem areas?
5. What areas should be part of the successful operational reviewer's review of administrative controls?

SUGGESTED RESPONSES

1. What are the primary purposes of the planning phase?

Response

Gather information.

Identify possible problem areas.

Develop the operational review work program.

2. List the type of information that could be gathered during the planning phase.

Response

- Applicable laws
- Organization
    - Reporting relationships
    - Division of duties and responsibilities
    - Delegation of authority
    - Location, size, and nature of operating sites
    - Number of employees—by area
    - Location of physical assets and records

- Financial information
    - Cost of operations by periods
    - Revenues: year by year, by product line, product, and so on
    - Budget versus actual data: present and past periods
    - Cash flow analysis: sources and uses of cash
    - Cost accounting data: by product, function, customer, and so on
- General description of operating methods and procedures.
- Management information reports.
- Problem areas: identify and document areas of major deficiency.

3. What are some of the sources of information available to the operational reviewer in the planning phase?

Response

- Interviews with management
- Organization charts, functional job descriptions, and so on
- Financial records: statements, budgets, audit reports (internal and external)
- Policies, procedures, directives, relevant memos, and so on
- Reports: internal and external
- Internal audit reports and materials
- Physical inspection and observation

4. What are some techniques by which the operational reviewer can identify critical problem areas?

Response

- Identification of key activities
- Use of management reports
- Examination of audit reports
- Physical inspection of activities
- Discussion with responsible officials and personnel directly concerned with the activity

5. What areas should be part of the successful operational reviewer's review of administrative controls?

Response

- Organization
- Policies and procedures
- Accounting and other financial records
- Performance standards
- Information systems and related internal reports

3

Work Program Phase

The work program phase is the bridge between the planning phase and the field work phase. The operational review work program is, therefore, the plan of action for conducting the operational review. However, it is initially written for the preliminary review of those selected activities as determined in the planning phase. Accordingly, it is subject to change based on actual findings during the field work phase.

The following points are discussed in this chapter:

- Benefits of the operational review work program
- Standards by which operational review work programs are developed
- Who develops the work program
- Work program development procedures

In addition, a sample operational review work program and related work steps will be presented. By the end of this chapter, via the use of case study materials, an increased understanding of the development of an operational review work program for areas identified in the planning phase will have been obtained.

> **The Work Program**
> **Is the Key to a Successful**
> **Operational Review**

BENEFITS OF THE OPERATIONAL REVIEW WORK PROGRAM

A well-constructed operational review work program is essential to conducting the operational review in an efficient and effective manner. Operational review work programs are the key to successful operational reviews as they provide benefits such as:

- A systematic plan for the work to be performed in the operational review that can be communicated to all operational review staff.

- A systematic basis for assigning work to review staff members according to their specialized skills, technical competencies, and type of task

- A means by which operational review supervisors and other reviewers can compare performance with approved plans, review standards, and requirements

- Assistance in training inexperienced staff members and acquainting them with the scope, objectives, and work steps of the operational review

- The basis for a summary record of work actually performed in the operational review

- Aid in familiarizing successive review groups with the nature of the work performed in the present operational review

Reader: Document your reasons for using a work program for the conducting of an operational review. Add any additional benefits to the preceding list that a work program provides.

WORK PROGRAM WORK STEPS

After deciding on the functions to be included in the operational review, the next step is to develop the work steps to be performed for each of those areas identified as significant in the planning phase. To help in developing these work steps, the reviewer needs to be aware of some of the more common techniques that can be used in the performance of the operational review in the field work phase, such as:

- Review of existing documentation, such as policy and procedures manuals

- Preparation of organization charts and related functional job descriptions
- Analysis of personnel policies and procedures related to hiring, orientation, training, evaluation, promotion, and firing.
- Analysis of organizational policies and related systems and procedures—both administrative and operational
- Interviews with management and operations personnel
- Flowchart preparation
  - Systems flowcharts, showing the processes of a functional area
  - Layout flow diagrams, showing the physical layout of a work area and its related work flow
- Ratio, change, and trend analysis
- Questionnaires, for use by the reviewer or client's personnel
- Surveys, by phone or in written form, for customers, vendors, and so on to respond to
- Questions within the review work program
- Review of transactions, in which the different types of normal and abnormal transactions are considered
- Review of operations by techniques such as observation, work measurement, time studies, and work performance forms or logs
- Forms analysis
- Analysis of results
- Review and analysis of management information system and related reports
- Compliance reviews, as to compliance with laws, regulations, policies, procedures, goals, objectives, and so on
- Use of computer processing; using computer auditing "through the computer" techniques or review and analysis of computer-produced information

> ### The Best Work Step
> ### for the Situation
> ### Is the One That Works

Reader: Document the work steps—from the preceding list and others—that you would use in the operational review of your organization. Identify each work step as to overall organization and each functional area.

Reader: Review the operational review work program (Exhibit 3.1). Which work steps would you include in the operational review of the purchasing function, or any function, on your organization? Are there other work steps that you would include? What are they?

ENGAGEMENT CONTROL

Before starting the actual operational review, the engagement manager should prepare some form of engagement control tool. Samples of such forms are shown in Exhibits 3.2 through 3.6:

- Gantt Chart (Exhibit 3.2)
- Planning Phase Budget Hours Control, by Personnel and Time Period (Exhibit 3.3)
- Planning Phase Budget Control, by Task and Personnel (Exhibit 3.4)
- Field Work Phase Budget Hours Control, by Personnel and Time Period (Exhibit 3.5)
- Field Work Phase Budget Control, by Task and Personnel (Exhibit 3.6)

Any or all of these forms may be used for control purposes in conducting the operational review, or original forms can be designed.

Reader: Which of the above engagement control forms would you include in your operational review? Are there any others that you would use?

**EXHIBIT 3.1   OPERATIONAL REVIEW WORK PROGRAM:
PURCHASING FUNCTION**

I. COMPANY POLICY AND ORGANIZATION

A. *Organizational Status of Purchasing Department*
  1. Secure or prepare an organization chart of the Purchasing
     Department with descriptions of each work unit's specific func-
     tions. Determine to whom the head of the Purchasing Department
     reports. Perform analytical work to determine whether such report-
     ing is proper or whether it results in operational concerns and
     problems. Analyze each work unit's functions to determine
     whether they are appropriate and proper Purchasing Department
     functions.
  2. Document the duties and responsibilities of each Purchasing
     Department employee. Obtain copies of existing job descriptions,
     and validate through interviewing each employee and related
     supervisor. Observe actual work being performed. Determine
     necessity of all duties and responsibilities.

B. *Responsibility for Purchasing*
  1. Obtain or prepare company policy on purchasing functions and
     activities. Determine that the responsibility of the Purchasing
     Department is clearly defined and understood by Purchasing
     Department personnel and other nonpurchasing employees.
     Ascertain whether the Purchasing Department staff has knowl-
     edge of conflicting purchasing responsibility assumed by other
     departments. Document any principal procurement activities for
     which the Purchasing Department has no responsibility or limited
     responsibility.
  2. Obtain or prepare policy covering other departments' relations
     with vendors as to contacts or discussions with sales personnel or
     correspondence. Analyze such activities within selected operat-
     ing departments to determine the extent of such vendor relations.
     Select a number of heavily used and critical vendors to survey as
     to their relations with the Purchasing Department and other
     departmental personnel. Use both telephone survey and written
     response survey techniques.

C. *Authorization for Purchasing*
  1. Obtain copy or document policies as to:
     • Approval of purchases by departments requiring material

---

EXHIBIT 3.1   CONTINUED

- Approval limits as to types of purchases and amounts
- Capital expenditures
- Budget approval prior to commitment

2. Analyze procedures through the review of selected transactions where the final cost of an order exceeds the amount originally estimated on the purchase order:
   - Where limit of approval of original signer is not exceeded by final cost
   - Where limit of approval of original signer is exceeded
3. Analyze procedures through the review of selected transactions where changes are made in the quantity or specifications of the original purchase requisition.

D. *Decentralized Purchasing*
   1. Determine company policies and procedures on purchases made by decentralized operating units, through petty cash, etc. as to:
      - Limits of authority
      - Reporting responsibility
      - Review or control by central Purchasing Department
   2. Select a number of such decentralized operating units for review. Analyze their operations as to compliance with existing company policies related to decentralized purchasing.

   Note: The purpose of this portion of the review is to learn of the policies and general conditions under which the Purchasing Department operates. The sources of information will usually be the head of the Purchasing Department, other Purchasing Department staff, and company manuals.

   Where policies are lacking or indefinite, there may be weakness in control, duplicating fields of responsibility, or other deficiency that will be evidenced in the course of the review. Also evidenced will be variations between policy and actual operations.

II. PURCHASING DEPARTMENT OPERATIONS

A. *Department Procedures*
   1. Obtain or prepare a copy of the Purchasing Department operating procedures.
   2. Prepare flowcharts of the major purchasing operations, such as the handling of requisitions, processing of purchase orders, control over open purchases, receipt of merchandise, and vendor payment procedures.

EXHIBIT 3.1   CONTINUED

---

3. Review procedures related to bidding by vendors:
   - Dollar amounts of orders on which bidding is required
   - Requests for bids
   - Form of bids (sealed, oral, etc.)
   - Summarization of bids and selection of vendors

B. *Department Forms*
   Obtain a copy of each specialized form used by the Purchasing Department. These should be studied so that the purpose and usage is thoroughly understood. Areas to be considered include:
   - Purchase order form, clear and complete, so that the vendor understands all terms and conditions
   - Protection of blank purchase order forms
   - Routing of copies of purchase order forms
   - Necessity of each copy of the form
   - Forms designed for efficient and simple completion
   - Use of specialized forms to eliminate repetitive processing such as:
     - Traveling requisitions: for repetitive orders of the same item
     - Blanket purchase orders for repetitive purchases from the same vendor

   Note: It is common to find overelaborate routines relating to the preparation of purchasing forms, particularly the purchase order. The result is the unnecessary duplication of files in various departments.

C. *Physical Facilities*
   Prepare a layout flow diagram of the Purchasing Department showing its layout and general facilities, with particular attention to:
   - Work flow efficiencies and inefficiencies
   - Arrangements for reception of and interviews with salespeople
   - Office layout for effective/ineffective operations

D. *Value Analysis Program*
   1. Review the Purchasing Department's value analysis program, including:
      - Determination that price revisions covering changes in materials and methods are negotiated with vendors
      - Review of market trends, particularly on long-term contracts and contracts containing escalation clauses.

EXHIBIT 3.1   CONTINUED

Note: In a value analysis program, the Purchasing Department
works with vendors and with affected company departments (such
as engineering and production) in the analysis of specifications, con-
sumption, and requirements. Through such analysis and cooperative
effort, it is possible to make savings through redesign, change in
specifications, purchase in more economical quantities, or manufacture by the company itself.

E. *Collateral Operations*
  1. Determine and describe all operations performed in the
     Purchasing Department that are not directly concerned with plac-
     ing orders and follow-up for delivery. For example, the Purchasing
     Department may be assigned responsibility for such operations as:
     • Reporting on quantity, quality, and timeliness of received
       materials
     • Authorization of payments to vendors
     • Sale of scrap
     • Purchases for employees
In the review of the collateral operations of the Purchasing
Department, the reviewer will have a twofold concern: first, the
effect that the inclusion of these operations under the responsibility
of the Purchasing Department will have, as far as internal control is
concerned; second, the review of the assigned collateral operations.
     Because of the many variables, it is not possible to specify any
definite program for the review of specific collateral responsibilities
of the Purchasing Department. The reviewer must shape his or her
study to cover each situation, and it may develop that a supplemen-
tary interdepartmental survey of a particular field should be made.

III. REVIEW OF PURCHASE TRANSACTIONS

A. *Selection of Transactions*
  Examine files covering all purchase orders placed over a period of
  XX months. From these, select, for detailed examination, orders that
  include some of each of the following:
     • Purchases made by each buyer
     • Requisitions by each major operating department
     • A number of "Rush" and Confirming Delivery" orders
     • Single orders divided between several suppliers

EXHIBIT 3.1   CONTINUED

- Orders in which purchase is not made from lowest bidder
- Orders in which final specifications or quantities are revised from the original requisition
- Orders in which freight is allowed
- Orders for capital equipment
- Orders in which price is not specified, or that include some variable pricing arrangement
- Orders providing for trade-in allowances
- Orders in which substantial overshipment is made and accepted
- Blanket or continuing orders, in which a number of deliveries are made over a period
- Orders in which specification of item, quantity, or price is not definite
- Orders placed under long-term purchase contracts.

Note: The selection of an adequate sample of orders is of utmost importance. The objective is to set aside for detailed examination a group of purchase orders that will adequately represent both the normal and the abnormal. There must be enough of the normal for the reviewer to verify general policies and procedures and reveal situations that may call for more extensive examination.

B. *Examination of Purchase Transactions Selected*
The examination of each type of purchase transaction selected should be completed in enough detail, through examination of all supporting records, to enable the reviewer to acquire sufficient knowledge as to how each of the operations, from origination and approval of requisition to the completion of the order, was handled. The reviewer must be constantly concerned with what was done and why, and should achieve satisfaction that each order was placed and handled in the best interests of the company.

It is through this examination that the reviewer may become aware of situations, in the Purchasing Department or in other departments of the company, that require further study. The objectives are (1) through verification, to provide the basis for appraisal of current policies and procedures and (2) to give a basis for constructive recommendation. The following list is intended only as a sample of questions that will occupy the reviewer's attention and may be the subject for further inquiry:
- Where an order was divided among several vendors, what was the reason?

EXHIBIT 3.1   CONTINUED

- On Confirming Orders, did some operating department really assume the purchasing function?
- If orders are placed for such items as memberships, just what is gained by clearing these through purchasing routines?
- Are there any indications of favoritism to vendors?
- Where changes are made from original specifications in a requisition or order, are these adequately approved and brought to the attention of those who should be concerned?
- How are allowances and adjustments handled and approved?
- Are transportation allowances verified?
- If price is omitted from an order, why?
- If an order calls for services or materials on a cost-plus or other basis indefinite as to exact amount, how are final charges verified?
- Does the employee approving a requisition appear to have adequate information to enable intelligent approval?
- How are trade-in arrangements determined and approved? (It is often possible to secure more for replaced equipment from outside sale than from trade-in.)
- How completely do possible sources of supply seem to be covered?
- Are FOB points and routings shown and followed?
- Does it appear that effort is made to ship by most economical methods? Is the traffic department consulted regarding routes and methods?
- How were long-term contracts negotiated?
- What consideration is given to the tax status of materials—sales and use taxes, excise taxes, etc.?

IV. RECORDS AND REPORTS

The various records that are used in current operations will have been reviewed and appraised in the study of departmental procedures. This will include such records as those showing sources of supply and numerical listings of purchase orders placed.

Beyond these will be a variety of records and reports that are not required in the normal flow of work but are maintained to provide information considered valuable for administrative response. Examples of this type of record or report are:

- Records of orders placed with each vendor

EXHIBIT 3.1   CONTINUED

- Records of orders placed by each buyer, showing number of orders and total value
- Reports of future commitments
- Reports of departmental operations to management
- Reports of commodity price trends to operating departments
- Reports that have been rendered to management covering special savings or other accomplishments

The examination and appraisal of records and reports has two objectives:

A. First, verification of the accuracy of the records of statements that are maintained or reported. This should be done on a test basis. For example, if a saving was claimed, there should be a test to be sure that the claimed saving was actually realized.

B. After verification of the general accuracy, the second step is appraisal of the value to the department or executive using or receiving the record or report. In this appraisal, the reviewer should ascertain the answers to such questions as:

- Is each record really used?
- Does each report serve a useful purpose?
- Does each report give a complete and accurate picture?
- Are reports incomplete, so that important factors are not brought to management's attention?

The answers to these and other questions that arise will require discussions with those who prepare the records and reports and with those who receive and use them.

EXHIBIT 3.2   GANTT CHART—PLANNING PHASE

Review Work Steps	Budgeted Hours	Personnel Assigned
I. Goals and Objectives		
A. Review legislative/internal materials	6	Mary
B. Planning systems and procedures		
1. Narrative and/or flowchart	12	Bill
2. Determine extent of planning	4	Bill
3. Review present plans	4	Bill
4. Review detail plans	6	Bill
	32	
II. Budgets		
A. Review budget process	3	Bill
B. Review budget justification procedures	2	Bill
C. Analyze budget reporting procedures	6	Bill
	11	
III. Organization Chart and Procedures Manual		
A. Obtain copy or prepare organization chart and analyze	6	Betty
B. Obtain copy of procedures manual and review	8	Betty
	14	
IV. Flowcharts		
A. Familiarize with Purchasing Department and its operations	4	Mike
B. Prepare general systems flowcharts	16	Mike
C. Analyze flowcharts	8	Mike
	28	
V. Reports		
A. Obtain copies of management and operating reports	2	Mary/Cliff
B. Discuss reports and prepare written description	10	Mary/Cliff
C. Review and analyze reports	6	Mary/Cliff
	18	
VI. Personnel		
A. Obtain current job descriptions and review	4	Jane/Roy
B. Review personnel folders	6	Jane/Roy
C. Analyze personnel functions	8	Jane/Roy
D. Prepare summary of positions and compare	6	Jane
E. Observe employees at work	5	Jane/Roy
F. Review employee statistics	4	Jane
	33	
VII. Facilities		
A. Observe and analyze work layout	4	Mike
B. Prepare/analyze layout flow diagram	4	Mike
C. Review use of equipment	2	Mike
D. Analyze general operating procedures	2	Mike
E. Review fixed assets used in operations	4	Jane
	16	
VIII. Review of Planning Phase Results	10	Betty
IX. Preparation of Work Program—By 3-1	24	Betty/Cliff
X. Review Management	40	Betty/Cliff
Total Budgeted Hours	226	

EXHIBIT 3.2   CONTINUED

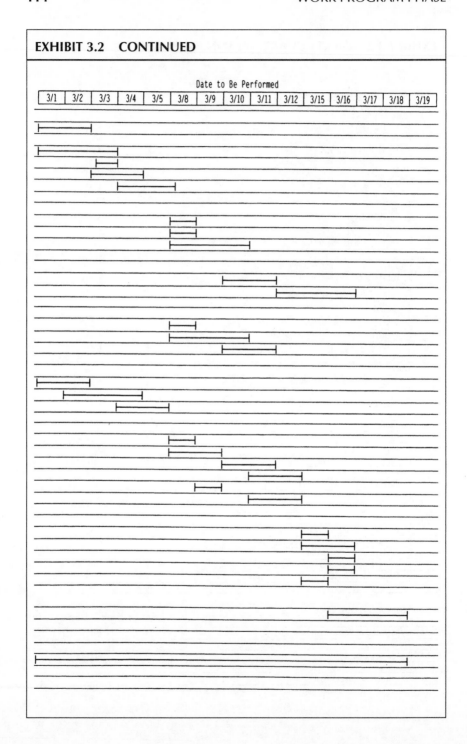

EXHIBIT 3.2 GANTT CHART—FIELD WORK PHASE

Review Work Steps	Budgeted Hours	Personnel Assigned
I. Company Policy and Organization		
A. Organization status of Purchasing Department		
1. Organization chart analysis	20	Bill
2. Employee duties and responsibilities	30	Bill
B. Responsibility for purchasing		
1. Purchase functions/activities	8	Bill
2. Relations with vendors	12	Bill
C. Authorization for purchasing		
1. Approval of purchase	4	Jane
2. Final cost exceeds PO amount	3	Jane
3. Quantity or specification changes	3	Jane
D. Decentralized purchasing		
1. Policies and procedures	6	Joe
2. Review of decentralized units	14	Joe
	100	
II. Purchasing Department Operations		
A. Department procedures		
1. Operating procedures	8	Mike
2. Flowcharts: purchase reqs and orders	32	Mike
3. Bidding by vendors	10	Mike
B. Department forms	20	Mary
C. Physical facilities	12	Roy
D. Value analysis program	8	Cliff
E. Collateral operations	16	Jane
	106	
III. Review of Purchase Transactions		
A. Selection of transactions	20	Joe/Beth
B. Review of transactions	30	Joe/Beth
	50	
IV. Records and Reports		
A. Verification of accuracy	12	Jane
B. Value to the department	22	Jane
	34	
V. Review of Field Work Results	60	Betty/Cliff/Bill
VI. Development of Findings	80	Betty/Bill/Jane
VII. Oral Reporting	20	Mary/Cliff/Roy
VIII. Written Report	40	Betty/Cliff/Bill
Total Review Work Steps	490	
IX. Preparation of Work Program 3-17 to 3-19	40	All
X. Review Management	100	Betty/Cliff
Grand Total Budget	630	

EXHIBIT 3.2   CONTINUED

Week Ending Date of Worksteps to Be Performed

| 3/26 | 4/2 | 4/9 | 4/16 | 4/23 | 4/30 | 5/7 | 5/14 | 5/21 | 5/28 | 6/2 |

EXHIBIT 3.3 PLANNING PHASE BUDGET HOURS CONTROL BY PERSONNEL AND TIME PERIOD

*B = Budget
A = Actual
D = Difference

Reviewer's Name	*	3/1	3/2	3/3	3/4	3/5	3/8	3/9	3/10	3/11	3/12	3/15	3/16	3/17	3/18	3/19	Total Hours
Betty White—Manager	B								3	3	2	3	3	2	4	4	24
	A																
	D																
Bill Brown—Supervisor	B	4	6	8	5	3	6	5									37
	A																
	D																
Jane Plath—Reviewer	B						3	4	4	6	4	4					25
	A																
	D																
Mike Clark—Consultant	B						6	8	8	6	4	6	6				40
	A																
	D																
Cliff Chambers—Purchasing Supervisor	B	1	2	2	2	2											9
	A																
	D																
Roy David—Buyer II	B						3	2	3	4							12
	A																
	D																
Mary George—Standard Specifications Supervisor	B	4	3	2	3	3											15
	A																
	D																
Totals	B	9	11	12	10	8	18	19	18	19	6	13	9	2	4	4	162
	A																
	D																

EXHIBIT 3.4   PLANNING PHASE BUDGET CONTROL BY TASK AND PERSONNEL

Review Work Steps	Budgeted Hours
I. Goals and Objectives	
A. Review legislative/internal materials	6
B. Planning systems and procedures	
1. Narrative and/or flowchart	12
2. Determine extent of planning	4
3. Review present plans	4
4. Review detail plans	6
	32
II. Budgets	
A. Review budget process	3
B. Review budget justification procedures	2
C. Analyze budget reporting procedures	6
	11
III. Organization Chart and Procedures Manual	
A. Organization chart and analysis	6
B. Procedures manual and review	8
	14
IV. Flowcharts	
A. Familiarize: Purchasing Department operations	4
B. Prepare general systems flowcharts	16
C. Analyze flowcharts	8
	28
V. Reports	
A. Management and operating reports	2
B. Discuss reports and prepare written description	10
C. Review and analyze reports	6
	18
VI. Personnel	
A. Job descriptions and review	4
B. Review personnel folders	6
C. Analyze personnel functions	8
D. Prepare summary of positions	6
E. Observe employees at work	5
F. Review employee statistics	4
	33
VII. Facilities	
A. Observe and analyze work layout	4
B. Prepare/analyze layout flow diagram	4
C. Review use of equipment	2
D. Analyze general operating procedures	2
E. Review fixed assets used in operations	4
	16
VIII. Review of Planning Phase and Results	10
IX. Preparation of Work Program	24
X. Review Management	40
Total Budgeted Hours	226
Billing Rates	
Estimated Budget Dollars	$10,770

EXHIBIT 3.4 CONTINUED

Betty White	Bill Brown	Jane Plath	Mike Clark	Cliff Chambers	Roy David	Mary George
						6
	12					
	4					
	4					
	6					
	3					
	2					
	6					
6						
8						
			4			
			16			
			8			
				1		1
				5		5
				3		3
		2			2	
		3			3	
		3			5	
		6				
		3			2	
		4				
			4			
			4			
			2			
			2			
		4				
10						
12				12		
24				16		
60	37	25	40	37	12	15
$80	$60	$30	$75			
$4,800	$2,220	$750	$3,000			

EXHIBIT 3.5 FIELD WORK PHASE BUDGET HOURS CONTROL BY PERSONNEL TIME PERIOD

A = Actual
D = Difference

Reviewer's Name	*	3/26	4/2	4/9	4/16	4/23	4/30	5/7	5/14	5/21	5/28	6/2	Total
Betty White—Manager	B			3			11	16	4	8	6	6	54
	A												
	D												
Bill Brown—Supervisor	B	16	22	12	12	8	8	16	12	6	10	10	132
	A												
	D												
Joe Super—Senior	B	6	14	4	12	4							40
	A												
	D												
Jane Plath—Reviewer	B	10	16			16	18		12	10			82
	A												
	D												
Beth Herman—Reviewer	B			8	18	4							30
	A												
	D												
Mike Clark—Consultant	B		28	22									50
	A												
	D												
Cliff Chambers—Purchasing Supervisor	B	8		3			7	8	6	10	4	4	50
	A												
	D												
Roy David—Buyer II	B		12	4					6				22
	A												
	D												
Mary George—Standard Specifications Supervisor	B		16						6	4			30
	A												
	D												
Totals	B	40	108	56	42	32	44	40	46	42	20	20	490
	A												
	n												

120

EXHIBIT 3.6   FIELD WORK PHASE BUDGET CONTROL BY TASK AND PERSONNEL

Review Work Steps	Budgeted Hours
I. Company Policy and Organization	
A. Organization status of Purchasing Department	
1. Organization chart analysis	20
2. Employee duties and responsibilities	30
B. Responsibility for purchasing	
1. Purchase functions/activities	8
2. Relations with vendors	12
C. Authorization for purchasing	
1. Approval of purchasing	4
2. Final cost exceeds PO amount	3
3. Quantity or specification changes	3
D. Decentralized purchasing	
1. Policies and procedures	6
2. Review of decentralized units	14
	100
II. Purchasing Department Operations	
A. Department procedures	
1. Operating procedures	8
2. Flowcharts: purchase requisitions and orders	32
3. Bidding by vendors	10
B. Department forms	20
C. Physical facilities	12
D. Value analysis program	8
E. Collateral operations	16
	106
III. Review of Purchase Transactions	
A. Selection of transactions	20
B. Review of transactions	30
	50
IV. Records and Reports	
A. Verification of accuracy	12
B. Value to the department	22
	34
V. Review of Field Work Results	60
VI. Development of Findings	80
VII. Oral Reporting	20
VIII. Written Report	40
Total Work Steps	490
IX. Preparation of Work Program	40
X. Review Management	100
Grand Total Budget	630
Billing Rates	
Estimated Budget Dollars	$29,280

EXHIBIT 3.6   CONTINUED

Betty White	Bill Brown	Joe Super	Jane Plath	Beth Herman	Mike Clark	Cliff Chambers	Roy David	Mary George
	20							
	30							
	8							
	12							
			4					
			3					
			3					
		6						
		14						
					8			
					32			
					10			
								20
							12	
						8		
			16					
		8		12				
		12		18				
			12					
			22					
24	24					12		
8	18		22			12	10	10
10						10		
12	20					8		
54	132	40	82	30	50	50	22	30
12	8	4	4	2	2	4	2	2
80						20		
146	140	44	86	32	52	74	24	32
$80	$60	$40	$30	$30	$75			
$11,680	$8,400	$1,760	$2,580	$960	$3,900			

CASE STUDY: JOE SORRY, INC., WORK PROGRAM PHASE

The operational review work program is written for the review of the five selected critical activities as determined in the planning phase, as follows:

1. Review of personnel: manufacturing and quality control
2. Manufacturing systems: review of manufacturing control concepts
3. Manufacturing: facility layout and production procedures
4. Inventory control systems and procedures
5. Four business concepts

The work program becomes the bridge between the planning phase and the field work phase. It is the plan of action for conducting the operational review. The review team considers each significant area previously identified for further review and develops specific work steps that it believe will most clearly demonstrate the extent and cause of the operational deficiency and lead to practical recommendations for positive improvement. The work program is, of course, subject to change based on the actual findings identified during the field wok phase of the review.

All of the members of the review team helped to develop the work program for the review of the selected critical areas of Joe Sorry Company. In the development of the work program, the review team followed four work steps:

1. Identification of control and risk areas for each critical operational area selected for review. These risk areas usually relate to the inability to achieve the operational areas' goals and objectives. For instance, not using manufacturing control concepts available with existing software could result in customer orders not being produced and shipped on time.
2. Development of key questions and work steps to validate and quantify the perceived risk areas. For instance, one might question procedures relative to having materials on hand, determining what job mix to manufacture, how to load work centers, and so on.

3. Identification of the work steps needed to provide answers to the perceived risk areas and key questions. For instance, work steps could include observations, interviews, analysis work, and so on.

4. Development of work plans for each area to be reviewed, including personnel assignments, time schedules, and work program budgets. Personnel should be assigned, based on the skills and abilities needed to perform a specific work step.

The operational review work program developed for the five selected critical areas for review in the planning phase for the Joe Sorry Company is shown in Exhibit 3.7. Note that the sections of the work program and the corresponding areas within each section relate back to these five areas as identified in the planning phase.

EXHIBIT 3.7.   JOE SORRY COMPANY: OPERATIONAL REVIEW WORK PROGRAM

1. *Manufacturing Personnel*
   a. Develop narrative descriptions of each work unit's specific functions for the following areas:
      • Vice President—Production
      • Forepersons
      • Production team leaders
      • Production teams
      • Repairs and maintenance
      • Packers and shippers
      • Receivers
      • Inventory Control manager
      • Quality Control manager
      • Quality Control inspectors
      • Quality Control clerical
   b. Analyze each work unit's functions to determine whether they are accomplishing their purposes efficiently and economically.
   c. Document the duties and responsibilities of each manufacturing department employee.
   d. Interview a selected number of employees from each work unit (including all managers and supervisors) to determine the actual responsibilities and work being done.

EXHIBIT 3.7.   CONTINUED

---

    e. Observe actual work being performed to determine the necessity of all work steps, any areas for improvement, and whether there are better methods for achieving results.

2. *Manufacturing Systems*
    a. Review present MRP II software package JOBEASY to determine system capabilities and whether they can be applied to the Joe Sorry Company.
    b. Determine desired manufacturing procedures for the company by analyzing present methods of operations as to achieving desired results.
    c. Review present operational reporting procedures and document desired reporting features.
    d. Develop proposed operating reporting system together with an implementation plan.
    e. Document necessary changes to JOBEASY software.

3. *Manufacturing Facility and Production Procedures*
    a. Prepare layout flow diagram of the manufacturing facility, noting any areas of inefficiency, bottlenecks, poor working conditions, etc.
    b. Observe production operations, particularly as related to the four product lines—specialty, custom, defense, basic boards.
    c. Develop manufacturing recommendations for each product line as to production procedures, personnel, production scheduling and control, quality control, and so on.
    d. Develop proposed recommendations for plant facility layout incorporating earlier manufacturing recommendations.

4. *Inventory Control Systems and Procedures*
    a. Review and analyze present inventory control procedures, noting any areas of deficiency and proper practices not being followed.
    b. Determine the company's objectives for inventory control and proper levels of expected raw material and finished goods inventory.
    c. Observe physical control and storage procedures as to good practices and control.
    d. Review inventory receipt and issuance procedures.

EXHIBIT 3.7.   CONTINUED

---

    e. Review and analyze present inventory reporting systems and determine adequacy and what is lacking for proper reporting.

5. *Four Business Concepts*
    a. Recast the past three years' income statements by product line: specialty boards, custom boards, defense work, and basic boards.
    b. Analyze customer statistics by these product lines.
    c. Review and analyze present operations as to their impact on the product line concept: production, inventory, quality control, purchasing, sales, engineering, and customer service.
    d. Document recommendations for each of the product lines as profit centers, product lines, and/or separate businesses.

Because the general critical areas to be reviewed have changed from our initial understanding with Joe Sorry as documented in our confirming letter, the review team also needs to update its review budget estimate as to review areas, number of hours, and personnel assigned. Our original estimated budget of 180 hours (200 hours less 20 hours expended on the planning phase) must be reapplied to the developed work program steps. The revised review budget is shown in Exhibit 3.8.

EXHIBIT 3.8   JOE SORRY COMPANY: FIELD WORK AND REPORTING PHASE BUDGET

	HOURS	STAFF
Review Area:		
1. *Manufacturing Personnel*		
a. Narrative descriptions of functions:	12	MM/PH
• Vice President—Production		
• Forepersons		

EXHIBIT 3.8 CONTINUED		
	HOURS	**STAFF**
• Production team leaders		
• Production teams		
• Repairs and maintenance		
• Packers and shippers		
• Receivers		
• Inventory Control manager		
• Quality Control manager		
• Quality Control inspectors		
• Quality Control clerical		
b. Analyze each work unit's functions	8	EH
c. Document duties and responsibilites of each manufacturing department employee	12	SH
d. Interview a selected number of employees from each work unit	12	SH
e. Observe actual work being performed	6	HR
2. *Manufacturing Systems*		
a. Review MRP II package JOBEASY	6	MM
b. Determine desired procedures	4	MM
c. Review operational reporting procedures	6	PH/SH
d. Develop operating reporting system together with an implementation plan	6	MM/PH/SH
e. Document necessary changes to JOBEASY	4	MM
3. *Manufacturing Facility and Production Procedures*		
a. Prepare layout flow diagram	4	HR
b. Observe production operations	6	HR
c. Develop manufacturing recommendations	6	HR
d. Develop recommendations for plan layout	4	HR
4. *Inventory Control Systems and Procedures*		
a. Review and analyze inventory procedures	4	PH
b. Determine objectives for inventory control	2	PH
c. Observe physical control and storage	2	PH
d. Review inventory receipt and issuance	2	PH
e. Review present reporting systems	2	PH

	HOURS	STAFF
EXHIBIT 3.8 CONTINUED		

	HOURS	STAFF
5. *Four Business Concepts*		
a. Recast the past year's income statement by product line	12	PF
b. Analyze customer statistics	6	PF
c. Review and analyze present operations as to impact on the product line concept	14	HR/EH
d. Document recommendations by product line	8	HR/EH
6. *Management Tasks*		
a. Review of field work results	6	HR/EH
b. Development of findings	8	All
c. Oral report	6	All
d. Written report	12	HR/SH/EH
Total Budget	180	

CASE SITUATION: DEFECTIVE MERCHANDISE RETURNS

Reader: Review the following case situation and document your answers to the questions presented. Then review the suggested responses.

A preliminary review of your operational review disclosed the following deficiencies as related to the handling of defective merchandise returns:

Company's Return to Vendors. The company was paying return freight charges on almost 50 percent of defective merchandise returns. This practice was a result of noncompliance with established procedures, whereby return freight charges were not to be paid by the Traffic Department and other operating divisions.

Customer Returns to Company. Some of the company's local customers were returning defective merchandise in company trucks— contrary to company policy.

Cash Discounts Improperly Handled. Cash discounts were being improperly handled when defective merchandise was returned by customers. The amount credited to the customer was the invoice price plus the cash discount. This is in violation of company policy and good business practice.

Questions for Consideration

Document one work step that the reviewer would include in his or her work program for each of the deficiencies noted in the preceding list.

1. *Return Freight Charges*
2. *Returning Merchandise in Company Trucks*
3. *Cash Discounts Improperly Handled*

Suggested Responses

1. *Return Freight Charges*
   a. Analyze sample to determine incidence and amount of return freight charges.
   b. Review procedures in selected operating divisions to determine where practice is being performed.

2. *Returning Merchandise in Company Trucks*
   a. Analyze sample set of returns by local customers to determine extent of use of company trucks for this purpose.
   b. Review procedures in shipping to ascertain whether practices allow for the detection of returned merchandise in company trucks.
   c. Review the present policy of not using company trucks for the return of defective merchandise and ascertain whether the current policy should be changed and whether this would be the most economical method for such returns.
      Note: This may be only indicative of the real problem (a tip of an iceberg situation)—the amount of defective merchandise and the reasons underlying the situation, rather than the method of return.

3. *Cash Discounts Improperly Handled*

 a. Analyze accounting documents and records to determine the amount of cash discounts paid to customers for returned merchandise.

 b. Analyze the system, both manual and computerized operations, to determine whether controls can be established that will prevent this practice from continuing.

 Note that the correction of these operating deficiencies resulted in an annual net savings of more than $140,000, as well as in identifying a significant problem area in the increasing amount of defective items returned by customers. The review scope was therefore expanded to determine the causes for the increase in defective items, and a recommendation was made for major manufacturing and quality control systems and procedures changes.

CASE SITUATION: EQUIPMENT MAINTENANCE REVIEW

As part of the operational review of the production facilities at the Example Company, you identified equipment maintenance as a significant and critical area for review. You found that equipment maintenance costs skyrocketed over the past few years, from $180,000 to $340,000 annually. In addition, the amount of manufacturing equipment downtime increased in like amounts. The objective in reviewing and analyzing this situation is to determine whether operating economies can be achieved while at the same time decreasing the amount of equipment down time.

During the review of this situation, you analyzed the inventory control system and related storage procedures for equipment maintenance items. Based on this analysis, it was found that for more than 70 percent of the 800 items in inventory, on average there were enough equipment maintenance parts and materials for the next 30 months, based on current rates of usage. For the other 30 percent or approximately 240 inventory items, it was found that more than 90 were out of stock, more than 40 were below reorder points, and the other 110 were mainly low usage items.

You believe that such poor inventory control methods and results constitutes a substantial area for which to develop an operational review finding. Not only should improved systems and procedures result in reduced costs, but they should also assist in improving the equipment downtime situation.

Questions for Consideration

The work steps that you might consider for inclusion in your work program are shown in the following chart. Review each of these work steps and then determine which of the five attributes of a finding—condition, criteria, cause, effect, and recommendation—the work step is addressing. Write the attribute next to the work step. Correct responses follow the exercise.

Review Step	Attribute
1. Determine authority as to requisition and purchase items.	
2. Analyze whether anyone exceeded that authority.	
3. Determine what the goals are for Equipment Maintenance (e.g., to keep equipment functioning at the least cost without unnecessary equipment down time).	
4. Determine policy as to how much of each item to maintain in inventory.	
5. Determine how much of each item needs to be in stock and any overages from that quantity.	
6. Calculate cost savings from inventory reductions to more reasonable levels, including any items that need to be increased.	
7. Analyze the inventory control and storeroom operations as to meeting the desired results.	
8. Investigate improvements in inventory control methods and procedures necessary to correct the situation.	

Responses

Review Step	Attribute
1. Determine authority as to requisition and purchase items.	Criteria
2. Analyze whether anyone exceeded that authority.	Condition
3. Determine what the goals are for Equipment Maintenance (e.g., to keep equipment functioning at the least cost without unnecessary equipment down time).	Criteria
4. Determine policy as to how much of each item to maintain in inventory.	Criteria
5. Determine how much of each item needs to be in stock and any overages from that quantity.	Criteria and Condition
6. Calculate cost savings from inventory reductions to more reasonable levels, including any items that need to be increased.	Effect
7. Analyze the inventory control and storeroom operations as to meeting the desired results.	Cause
8. Investigate improvements in inventory control methods and procedures necessary to correct the situation.	Recommendation

REVIEW QUESTIONS

1. What benefits do operational review work programs provide relative to conducting effective and successful operational reviews?

2. In preparing an operational review work program, what are four standards that should be considered?

3. Relative to operational review work programs, mark the following either TRUE or FALSE.

- Serve only as a checklist of work steps to be performed
- Foster individual reviewer initiative, imagination, and resourcefulness

- Are written for the preliminary review of selected activities as determined by the reviewer in charge
- The reviewer carrying out the work step must know why the work step is being done

SUGGESTED RESPONSES

1. What benefits do operational review work programs provide relative to conducting effective and successful operational reviews?

Response

- A systematic plan for work to be performed, that can be communicated to all review team members
- A systematic basis for assigning work to review team staff members
- A means by which review supervisors and other reviewers can compare performance with approved plans, work program standards, and requirements
- Assistance in training inexperienced staff members
- Basis for a summary record of work actually performed on the review
- Aid in familiarizing successive review teams with the nature of work previously carried out

2. In preparing an operational review work program, what are four standards that should be considered?

Response

- Tailor-made to specific assignments.
- Each work step should clearly set forth the work to be done and the reason for performing the work step.
- Flexible and permitting application of initiative in deviating from prescribed procedures.
- Specifically provide for the development of individual findings.

3. Relative to operational review work programs, mark the following either TRUE or FALSE.

Response

- Serve only as a checklist of work steps to be performed? FALSE
    - Used as a guide, but should be flexible permitting changes as the review progresses.
- Foster individual reviewer initiative, imagination, and resourcefulness? TRUE
- Are written for the preliminary review of selected activities as determined by the reviewer in charge? FALSE
    - Activities to review are determined by work performed in the planning phase.
- The reviewer carrying out the work step must know why the work step is being done? TRUE

4

Field Work Phase

This chapter reviews some of the procedures and techniques that can be used by the operational review team in conducting the field work phase.

This chapter will:

- Increase understanding of the purpose of the field work phase in an operational review.
- Present various techniques that can be used in the field work phase.
- Increase knowledge of how to use information gained in the field work phase in the further development of review findings.
- Describe field work phase documentation and operational review work file contents.

Based on the critical areas identified in the planning phase and work steps designed in the work program phase, the following two items are considered in the field work phase:

1. Whether the reviewee's policies, and the related procedures and practices actually followed, are in compliance with basic authorities, statutes, and legislative intent
2. Whether the system of operating procedures and management controls effectively results in activities being carried out as desired by top management in an efficient and economical manner

General tasks that would be performed to assist in reaching the correct conclusions include:

- Fact-finding or verification; for example, are management procedures being followed?
- Evaluation—for example, analyzing deviations from procedures and determining whether the cause is the policy or procedure itself, or other factors.
- Review of findings—for example, meeting occasionally with the review supervisor and other members of the review team to get a better understanding of matters requiring interpretation.
- Recommendations as to the areas having sufficient significance to warrant a more detailed examination directed toward the development of an operational review finding.

Operational review recommendations resulting from effective field work are based on the reviewer's determination as to the adequacy and effectiveness of management and operations.

FIELD WORK TECHNIQUES

Many different field work techniques are used in the field work phase, depending on the particular circumstances of an engagement. However, the best tools are common sense and analytical ability. The reviewer should be able to analyze problems logically, and, in many cases, this is the only tool needed. The review team should also be aware of the various management and operational techniques that have been used effectively in the past or are currently in vogue, such as:

- Total quality management (TQM)
- Participative management
- Benchmarking strategies
- Restructuring, reengineering, and reinventing
- Principle centered leadership
- Learning organizations
- Revision of mental models
- Spirituality in the workplace

- Activity-based costing/management (ABC/ABM)
- Strategic, long-term, short-term, and detail planning
- Flexible budgeting
- Systems theory
- Complexity theory (complex adaptive systems)

Field Work Techniques Are All-Inclusive

Reader: Which of the techniques in the preceding list would you want to use in an operational review of your organization? Which of these techniques do you believe your review team is adequately trained in, and which ones require additional training? Are there other techniques that you would want to use? What are they?

SPECIFIC FIELD WORK TECHNIQUES

Although there are many tools and techniques that can be used in the field work phase, there are a number that are used consistently. The operational reviewer should be most aware of these techniques, which include:

- Interviewing
- Systems flowchart
- Layout flowchart
- Ratio, change, and trend analysis

Following are exercises for you to do with regard to each of these techniques. Respond to the exercise on your own prior to looking at the suggestions.

Sample Interview

1. *Reviewer* (Walks right into Department Manager's office, unannounced): Hi, we're doing an operational review of your area, so I thought you might answer some questions about the inventory system.

2. *Department Manager* (looks up and looks at watch): What! You caught me by surprise. I have a meeting shortly, but I'll see what I can do for you.

3. *Reviewer* (sits down next to Department Manager, picks up pencil from desk): Can you tell me the status of the SRP program?

4. *Department Manager*: Huh?

5. *Reviewer* (louder): SRP program—surplus removal program.

6. *Department Manager*: Oh. We haven't used that in months.

7. *Reviewer*: I know. Can you describe the program?

8. *Department Manager* (obviously disturbed): I told you, it's not currently being used.

9. *Reviewer*: Could you just describe it?

10. *Department Manager* (more annoyed): Okay. The purpose was to transfer surplus inventory to another location where it was needed. We dropped it because we couldn't establish an effective reporting system between locations where we could tell . . . (cut short)

11. *Reviewer*: Uh huh. So, you have to correct your reporting system for SRP to work. What type of inventory records do you keep?

12. *Department Manager*: We use an online computerized record.

13. *Reviewer*: I see. It's my experience that whatever records you use, it's almost impossible to effectively control inventory. In fact, most inventory operations are extremely sloppy. I suppose I'll see for myself how good yours are.

14. *Department Manager* (shocked, sits back in chair): Uh huh.

15. *Reviewer*: What vehicles do you have in your delivery fleet?

16. *Department Manager* (looks confused and disturbed): Two panel trucks, one pick-up, one station wagon.

17. *Reviewer* (writes down answer and asks manager to repeat): Run that by me again.

18. *Department Manager* (in very annoyed tone): Two panel trucks, one pick-up, and one station wagon.

19. *Reviewer*: Is that all?

20. *Department Manager* (extremely annoyed): Yeah, that's all!!!

21. *Reviewer*: Who schedules the deliveries?

22. *Department Manager*: Chief storekeeper schedules deliveries and dispatches drivers.

23. *Reviewer*: Is the schedule formally written?

24. *Department Manager*: No, its not formal! Its just a day-to-day type thing.

25. *Reviewer*: Do you have any delivery records and time spent on them?

26. *Department Manager* (really disturbed): No!

27. *Reviewer*: Have you ever calculated the cost to make a delivery?

28. *Department Manager*: No!

29. *Reviewer*: That's funny; Tony Maroney, the assistant storekeeper told me that they keep detailed records and costs of all deliveries. He thinks we could save a bundle of money if we got out of the delivery business.

30. *Department Manager* (quite disturbed, turns away): You don't say.

31. *Reviewer*: Where do you get your authority over inventories?

32. *Department Manager* (picks up large loose-leaf binder): Look, its right here in the *Company Policies and Procedures Manual* (flips through the book). Here are the sections.

33. *Reviewer*: That's okay. I'll read my copy when I get back to the office. Do you have an organization chart I can have?

34. *Department Manager*: Sure, just a minute. I'll call my assistant. (calls out) Al, get me a copy of our organization chart.

35. *Al* (enters room): I have a chart you can have, but it's about three years old.

36. *Reviewer*: You don't have a current organization chart? How can you run your department without one?

37. *Department Manager* (upset and embarrassed, pauses and stutters): We'll, uh, I'll get you a copy when we update it (nods to Al, who leaves).

38. *Reviewer* (starts to gather up his papers, puts the Department Manager's pencil in his bag): Uh, I've written down the forms I'd like to have copies of (hands piece of handwritten paper to Department Manager).

39. *Department Manager* (looks over paper): Uh huh, Order and Bill, Log of Filled Orders, Manufacturing Order, Inventory Addition

Record, Inventory Status Report, Completed Order, Shipping Documents. Look, I can't get them for you now (looks at watch). I'm already 20 minutes late for my meeting. I'll have to send them to you.

40. *Reviewer:* Okay. I didn't think it was that much trouble (grabs paper back and copies down forms on pad).

41. *Department Manager* (gets up to leave): If you have any more questions, contact my secretary (leaves the office with the reviewer still sitting there).

Reader: For each numbered item in the preceding Sample Interview, document your comments as to what the interviewer did incorrectly based on effective interviewing techniques. Then review the Sample Interview Comments.

Sample Interview Comments

Overall Weak Point: The interview was not planned; it skips from one area to another without any logical sequence. The question of authority over inventory is asked at the end of the interview instead of at the beginning, which would be the most logical place.

1. No appointment was made. The reviewer called on the department manager without making an appointment, establishing a time limit, or reviewing the general agenda. This is a result of lack of proper planning. If the department manager was contacted in advance and given the general agenda or areas to be covered, he or she could have been prepared for the interview. In addition, the department manager might have been able to raise some points the reviewer may not have thought about.

2. The department manager mentions having a meeting shortly but will see what he or she can do. However, the reviewer not only fails to respond to this issue, but offers no apology for just stopping by unannounced, producing an immediate negative image of the reviewer and the review team.

3 to 6. The reviewer jumps right into the interview with no preliminary ice breaking; again putting the department manager ill at ease. In addition, the reviewer starts out with the SRP program—obviously a sore point in the department. This creates a good possibility of putting the department manager immediately on the defensive.

7. The reviewer's question, "Can you describe the program?" is the type of open-ended question to be asked in an operational review interview. However, there is the point of whether this might not be a too-detailed question for a department manager and whether the reviewer could have acquired such detailed information prior to the interview.

8 to 10. The department manager, although obviously disturbed, starts to respond to the question quite adequately, providing good information. However, the reviewer cuts the department manager short and jumps immediately to a conclusion. Had the reviewer allowed the department manager to continue, instead of being presumptuous and dismissing his or her opinions, the reviewer might have gained some valuable information and recommendations.

11. The reviewer, after cutting the department manager short, jumps right into another area (inventory records) without properly concluding the discussion on the SRP Program or introducing the new discussion area.

12 and 13. After the department manager responds that the department uses an online computerized record, the reviewer interjects his or her own poor opinion of any and all inventory operations—again putting the department manager on the defensive. As the interview is unfolding, the department manager will probably hold back and not provide as much and complete information as possible.

14. The department manager, although shocked, allows the interview to continue.

15 to 18. The reviewer does not properly close the discussion on inventory records, but instead jumps right into the delivery fleet. The reviewer writes down what the department manager says about the delivery fleet and then asks him or her to repeat. This can be annoying and distracting, especially to a department manager. Such detailed information should be obtained from someone other than the department manager, and prior to the interview.

19 and 20. The reviewer asks the department manager, "Is that all?" This again implies displeasure and the point that there should be more. The department manager is justifiably "extremely annoyed."

21 and 22. The question, "Who schedules the deliveries?" is again detail data that should have been known prior to the interview. This type of question only puts the person on the spot, implying, You should know the answer, or how can you be running the department?

23 to 28. These questions tend to be of the yes or no type, allowing the department manager to offer no additional information, opinion, or analysis. In addition, the staccato-style questioning suggests a scene in which a bright light might be shone on the department manager as the interrogation gets heavier.

29 and 30. The question, "Have you ever calculated the cost to make a delivery?" is a set-up, and the department manager provides the expected "no" answer. The reviewer, however, rather than pick up on the thread of the discussion and ask for an analysis or opinion of why not, disputes the department manager's information by bringing another employee's (Tony Maroney) input into the discussion. This is not only a breach of confidentiality of the other employee, but it also undermines the confidence of the department manager being interviewed. If the reviewer is that quick to bring someone else's opinion into the discussion, he or she is likely to do the same with the present discussion. In most instances, the other person will be either a supervisor (as in this case) or a supervisee; such a situation creates possible trouble and conflict. This practice also destroys the interviewee's trust in the reviewer and inhibits the openness of the interview.

31 and 32. The reviewer asks, "Where do you get your authority over inventories?" This question should have been asked at the beginning of the interview. In addition, it points to the reviewer's having done insufficient advance preparation. When the department manager offers to show the *Company Policies and Procedures Manual*, the reviewer says, "That's okay, I'll read my copy when I get back to the office." This not only discounts the department manager's offer, but also reemphasizes the lack of preparation.

33 to 37. The reviewer asks for an organization chart, which should have been requested at the time the interview was scheduled or obtained from other sources prior to the interview. What results here is the necessity to engage someone else in the interview (Al, the assistant), ultimately resulting in the reviewer's criticizing the department manager in front of the supervisee. This causes the department manager to become upset and embarrassed, certainly not conducive to a good working relationship, which is necessary for the rest of the operational review.

38. The reviewer begins to end the interview by gathering up papers and keeps the department manager's pencil—rude on both counts. The reviewer then requests certain forms via a handwritten piece of paper. Note that any forms or documents needed should be requested at the time the interview is scheduled. This allows the department manager to have them ready so as to explain their use at the interview. The reviewer should know what to request by proper planning and research in preparation for the interview. Should other items come up in the interview, of which the reviewer was not aware, these could be legitimately asked for.

39. The department manager needs to read the handwritten note to make certain of the request and responds that he or she will have to send such copies to the reviewer, which is quite doubtful based on the content of the interview thus far.

40. The department manager also says, "I'm already 20 minutes late for my meeting." Remember, the department manager had originally stated that he or she had a meeting to go to shortly. However, the reviewer has shown no regard for the department manager's needs during the entire interview.

41. The reviewer's response, "Okay. I didn't think it was that much trouble;" is probably the last straw. Not only has this final comment sent the department out the door, but the reviewer has also not left the door open for the future.

42. The department manager's closing, "If you have any more questions, contact my secretary," while cordial under the circumstances, is more likely a brush-off; and the chance of the department manager's cooperating with the reviewer in the future is remote.

Systems Flowchart

Reader: For each numbered item on the systems flowchart (see Exhibit 4.1), analyze the process step and then document your comments as to what you would question as part of your operational review. Then review the suggested responses.

Suggested Responses

1. a. Procedure and control question as to whether the department heads should be doing the account coding (is this the best use of time?). Normal procedure calls for the requisitioner and/or an account coding clerk to provide such coding. This may also be a tip of the iceberg situation suggesting a larger problem— an organizational pattern of management performing clerical tasks.

EXHIBIT 4.1   SYSTEMS FLOWCHART: PURCHASING—RECEIVING—PAYABLES—DISBURSEMENTS SYSTEM

Purchasing—Receiving—Payables—Disbursements System

Procedure	Personnel	Purchasing	Receiving	Accounts Payable
1. The originating dept. initiates a purchase by preparing a requisition. The requisition is approved by the dept. head who also specifies the account coding. The requisitions are not prenumbered.	Department Head			
2. Upon receipt of requisition, a prenumbered purchase order (approximately 30,000 per year) is prepared in accordance with the company's purchasing manual.	Purchasing Clerk #1			
3. Re-check entries on P.O. and verify math calculations. The prices are compared to current price lists maintained by purchasing.	Purchasing Clerk #2			
4. Review and approve P.O. If new vendor or item is involved, determine that competitive prices are obtained by comparison to industry price lists. P.O.s not approved are returned to originating dept. for correction or clarification.	V.P. Purchasing			
5. Distribute copies of P.O. and requisition as follows: P.O. 1. Vendor 2. Originating Dept. 3. File (numeric) 4. File (vendor) 5. Receiving 6. Accounts Payable Dept. Req. Receiving copy #5 includes quantities and prices.	Purchasing Check Clerk #1			
6. Account for numerical sequence and file.	Secretary to the V.P. of Purchasing			

Flowchart elements (Purchasing column): Originating Department → Department Requisition → Prepare P.O. → Verify P.O. → Approve P.O. → Distribute Documents → P.O. 1, P.O. 2, P.O. 3, P.O. 4, P.O. 5 → Department Requisition → Vendor / Originating Department → Account for Sequence → Alpha File #4, Numerical File #3

Receiving column: Vendor Suspense File — A — To 1-2

Accounts Payable column: Suspense File — B — To 1-3

144

EXHIBIT 4.1 CONTINUED

Purchasing—Receiving—Payables—Disbursements System

Procedure	Personnel	Receiving	Production Control	Accounts Payable
7. When goods are received, count and check for damaged items. (See separate narrative write-up.) Prepare, sign, and date three-part prenumbered receiving report. Attach to bill of lading and P.O.5.	Receiving Clerk #1			
8. Review and compare receiving report, bill of lading and P.O.5 for completeness and any discrepancies. Distribute as follows: P.O. 5. Production Control B of L. Production Control R.R.1. Production Control 2. Accounts Payable 3. Head of receiving dept. Note: the two receiving clerks may rotate steps 7 & 8 as both are involved.	Receiving Clerk #2			
9. Check numerical sequence of receiving report. Prepare daily listing of receiving reports and forward to accounts payable.	Head of Receiving Dept.			
10. Update inventory records. (See separate flowchart on inventory system for detailed discussion.)	Inventory Control Clerk #1			

145

EXHIBIT 4.1 CONTINUED

Purchasing—Receiving—Payables—Disbursements System

Procedure	Personnel	Accounts Payable	Orig. Dept.

11. Match all related documents and hold in suspense file pending receipt of vendor invoice.

  Accounts Payable Clerk #1

12. Vendor invoices are forwarded from the mail room daily. Duplicate invoices are stamped as such. Match vendor invoices with other documentation.

  Accounts Payable Clerk #1

13. Review file of unmatched invoices and receiving reports daily. Notify V.P. Purchasing of unmatched items over 10 days old for his follow-up.

  Head of Accounts Payable dept.

14. Approve invoice for payment when all documents have been received and matched. Exceptions are brought to the attention of the head of Accounts Payable dept., who is responsible for corrective action. Upon resolution, the documents are returned to the head of the originating department for approval.

  Head of originating dept.

EXHIBIT 4.1 CONTINUED

Purchasing—Receiving—Payables—Disbursements System

Procedure	Personnel	Accounts Payable	Cash Disbursements
15. Match invoice and supporting documentation to related entry on daily listing of goods received and indicate that items have been matched by initialing the list. Check all documentation, verify math computations, agree quantities, check for proper discount, verify account distribution, check for approval, and indicate work by initials. At end of month, prepare accrual on the basis of open items on daily receipts list.	Accounts Payable Clerk #2		
16. Prepare prenumbered voucher (approximately 35,000 per year). Includes all information necessary for posting to accounting records and preparation of check by E.D.P. Accumulate net amount of vouchers on adding machine tape as a control total for each day's transactions. A supply of prenumbered checks is given to computer operator.	Cash Disbursement Clerk #2		

147

EXHIBIT 4.1 CONTINUED

Purchasing—Receiving—Payables—Disbursements System

Procedure	Personnel	EDP
E.D.P. documentation consists of the source programs, operator instructions and record layouts.		
17. The vouchers are entered via data terminal in E.D.P. An interactive edit routine is performed as data are entered.	Data Terminal Operator	
18. Computer operator processes data file through an edit program. The edit program checks that all numeric fields are numeric and checks for missing voucher numbers. The conversion process is verified by the use of record counts. Any vouchers that are detected as errors are returned to cash disbursements clerk #1. The voucher is corrected within two days and sent back to E.D.P. for reprocessing.	Computer Operator (all operators are capable of running this series of programs)	
19. The daily transaction data file is used to prepare the checks and the check register. In addition, a month-to-date transaction file of checks issued is maintained to accumulate and prepare the monthly posting to the general ledger by account. The data file has internal header and trailer labels that are tested by the program. The daily transaction data file and the month-to-date file are maintained for one week. The final MTD file is kept for 13 months.	Computer Operator	
20. End of the month procedure: The end of month file is processed to prepare a summary of the checks issued, which serves as the source document to post the journal entry in the general ledger.	Computer Operator	

EXHIBIT 4.1   CONTINUED

Purchasing—Receiving—Payables—Disbursements System

Procedure	Personnel
21. The daily adding machine tape control total of vouchers is compared and reconciled to the check register. The check sequence is accounted for.	Cash Disbursement Clerk #1
22. At end of month journal entry is prepared based on summary report prepared by E.D.P. J.E. is not approved.	Cash Disbursement Clerk #2
23. Invoices and supporting documentation are collected with the voucher and checks.	Cash Disbursement Clerk #1
24. Sign checks using facsimile plate. Checks over $10,000 require manual signatures of two executives (Chairman, President, V.P. Finance, V.P. Operations).	Secretary to V.P. Finance
25. Review checks and supporting documentation, noting payee amount, approvals, and manual signatures as required.	Accounting Supervisor
26. Checks and supporting documents filed as follows: Voucher • Vendor File	Cash Disbursement Clerk #2

Check   1 Mail Room
        2 * Vendor file
        3 File alpha
        4 File numeric
Inv.   1 * Vendor file
        1 Mail Room
R.R. 1 *Vendor file
R.R. 2   · · · ·
B of L   · · · ·
P.O. 5   · · · ·
P.O. 6   · · · ·
Dept. Req
*Cancel and file by vendor

149

   b. Purchase requisitions are not prenumbered. Numerical control over purchase requisitions ensures that all purchases are processed by the Purchasing Department, and no requisitions are processed more than once. Normally, such control is exercised by the requisitioning department and, accordingly, must be performed uniformly throughout the organization.

2. Approximately 30,000 purchase orders are prepared annually by one Purchasing Clerk. This appears to be a large number for one person to handle. The reviewer would want to analyze the procedures for preparing purchase orders to clarify this situation.

3. a. Another Purchasing Clerk rechecks entries on the purchase order and verifies math calculations. The preparation of purchase orders (particularly for 30,000 per year) is usually done on a computerized basis with today's technology. If so, this step could be eliminated. This may also suggest a larger problem, in which computer equipment and resources are available, but not properly utilized.

   b. The prices are compared with current price lists maintained by the Purchasing Department. The operational reviewer should note this as an area for further analysis to determine accuracy and up-to-dateness of the price list.

4. a. The VP of Purchasing reviews and approves all purchase orders, which again is not the best use of management time.

   b. If a new vendor or item is involved, the VP determines that competitive prices are obtained by comparison with industry price lists. This is another area for further analysis.

   c. Purchase orders not approved are returned to the originating department for correction or clarification. The operational reviewer should determine what reasons constitute disapproval. There is also no mention of whether a check is made against the approved plan/budget prior to the preparation of the purchase order. Other than this, there would not appear to be any other reason to return purchases to the issuing department, particularly after the purchase order is prepared.

5. Distribute copies of purchase order and requisition.

   a. The purchase requisition should be returned to the issuer as proof of processing (or some other method of notification), and not to accounts payable.

b. The originating department needs to receive notification of its open purchases, but not necessarily a copy of the purchase order. With a computerized system this could take the form of a data file or open purchase listing. These data are then used to control the processing of open purchase requisitions and subsequent open purchase orders.

c. Two copies of the purchase order (one maintained in numeric sequence and one in alphabetic sequence) are kept in the Purchasing Department. Again, with a computer system, only one copy (filed numerically) is needed, as the computer system can enable the user to go from numeric to alphabetic and back.

d. The receiving department normally receives a copy of the purchase order as its authorization to receive the goods. However, it has no reason to have prices on its copy. Quantities usually are on the receiving copy, so that the receivers know what is authorized for receipt and proper control is maintained over partial receipts. Another method is not to provide quantities, thereby forcing receivers to count everything. However, this method does not provide an open item quantity with which to reconcile to the actual receipt. The operational reviewer should determine which method works best in a specific situation.

6. The secretary to the VP of Purchasing accounts for numerical sequence of the purchase orders and files both the numerical and alphabetical copies. The computer system should maintain strict numerical sequence and eliminate the sorting and filing of alphabetical copies. In addition, at the present time, this does not appear to be a function that needs to be done by the secretary to the VP of Purchasing.

7. a. Damaged items procedure. This is an area for additional analysis to determine whether proper control and handling is exercised for damaged items upon receipt.

b. Prepare a three-part receiving report. Good business practice is never to re-record information that already exists in the system. In this instance, receiving data are already shown on the purchase order copy. Therefore, this document should be used as the receiving report without any unnecessary rerecording. At all times, the open purchases awaiting receipt should equal the open purchases maintained in the Purchasing Department. For partial receipts (where the full quantity of an item or all the items on the PO are not received at the same time), a copy is made of the purchase order to be used as the receiving copy, the partial shipment data is noted on the original copy of the receiving PO, and the original PO is refiled as a purchase awaiting receipt for the remaining open items.

8. Review and compare the receiving report and the PO copy. With the use of the PO itself, there is, of course, no need to compare with receiving reports.

9. Check numerical sequence of receiving reports and prepare daily listing of receiving reports by the head of the Receiving Department. This step would also be eliminated by the use of PO receiving copies, greatly reducing the amount of paper within the system.

10. Update inventory records. At present this is done on a manual basis independent of other updating. This inventory updating should be integrated and simultaneously processed within a computer system.

11. Match all related documents and hold them in a suspense file pending receipt of vendor invoice. This step is necessary; but notice the number of documents already accumulated in the process.

12. Vendor invoices are forwarded from the mail room. The reviewer may want to review mailroom procedures to determine whether this is the most efficient manner of receiving and processing vendor invoices. An effective alternative might be to receive vendor invoices directly by the Accounts Payable Department or via a lock box system.

13. Review unmatched invoices and receiving reports. Analyze the current situation and determine whether unmatched items are proper. Note that unmatched invoices more than 10 days old may indicate the nonreceipt of receiving reports from the receiving department (inefficiency in the receiving department); and unmatched receiving reports may indicate the nonreceipt of vendor invoices from the mail room (inefficiency in the mail room). In addition, this is not a function that the head of accounts payable, nor the VP of Purchasing, needs to be involved with.

14. a. Approve invoice for payment. This is a necessary step; however, note the number of documents which need to be reviewed and filed.

    b. Exceptions brought to the attention of the head of accounts payable for corrective action. Analyze what types of exceptions are being experienced and how they are being corrected.

    c. Upon resolution, the documents are returned to the head of the originating department for approval. This step is unnecessary, and the documents should not leave the accounts payable department.

15. a. Matching invoice and support documentation and verifying math, discount, account distribution, and so on. This procedure should be tested on a sample basis to determine the accuracy of such operations. Consider reduction and elimination of these procedures by changes in receiving procedures and computerization.

    b. End of month accrual based on open items on daily receipts list. Computer system should provide this automatically.

16. a. Prepare prenumbered voucher (approximately 35,000 annually). As the purpose of the voucher is to provide the necessary data in an orderly manner for subsequent data entry, alternative procedures might be considered for this purpose, such as circling the original document and recording data onto a rubber stamp impression directly on the document.

    b. Data entry control procedures should be reviewed to ensure that the present process of controlling by the total net amount of the vouchers is the most efficient and best.

    Reference to EDP (computer systems) documentation:

    This is the first indication in the system that data processing procedures are in existence. The operational reviewer should determine the extent of computer processing used, the overall capability of present computer resources, the effectiveness of use, and the efficient use for present systems concerns. In this situation, the operational reviewer might recommend the increased use of computer procedures for the present system under review to provide for the economies, efficiencies, and effectiveness previously discussed. In the development of his or her recommendations for the increased use of computer procedures, the operational reviewer should consider the providing of a computer systems design for the implementation of recommended computer procedures. The systems design document should include items such as input formats, offline and online controls, data record layouts, processing procedures, and information and report layouts.

With regard to the present procedures being reviewed on the systems flowchart, the operational reviewer should:

17. Review data terminal operations to determine that proper computer controls exist to ensure that only authorized transactions are processed and no others, that error identification and correction procedures are adequate, and that edit routines contain all necessary checks and validations.

18. a. Review edit routines embedded in the computer edit program to ensure that all edit checking is proper and that there are not other edits that should be included in the program. The edit program should also be tested (possibly through the computer) to determine that it is working as documented.

   b. Review all internal processing controls, such as the use of record counts in the conversion process, to ensure that no data records are lost, added, or suppressed during processing.

   c. Review error detection and correction procedures to ensure that all error conditions are properly identified, controlled, and resubmitted back into computer processing correctly. This is an extremely critical area, as it is subject to abuse and laxity if not properly controlled.

19. The present systems flow within computer processing should be reviewed as to efficiency and the production of necessary operating and management information. The various data files used in computer processing and their physical and processing controls and purposes should also be reviewed. As part of this review, computer processing procedures relative to system run-to-run controls should be determined as to their operating properly. In addition, offline control total procedures should be reviewed to ensure that the computer system is being properly controlled by the users.

20. The end-of-month procedure consists of computer processing preparing a monthly check summary listing. This listing then serves as the source document for re-inputting the same data for computer posting to the general ledger. This is an indication of the improper use of computers; as the principle to be applied is to use the same data sources for all integrated purposes. In this case, computer processing should automatically post to the general ledger without such re-inputting.

21. Offline daily control procedures to reconcile the results of computer processing should be reviewed to determine that controls over the results of computer processing are adequate.

22. An end-of-month journal entry is prepared, based on the summary report prepared by computer processing. This processing should be done automatically by the computer system with integrated processing procedures.

23. Invoices and supporting documentation are collected with the voucher and checks. This is another point at which the reviewer should look at the accumulation of documents and determine what can be eliminated.

24. a. Sign checks, using a facsimile plate. The controls and safeguards for the use of this plate should be reviewed. In addition, review the check signing procedure and determine whether the Secretary to VP of Finance needs to be involved.

    b. Checks for more than $10,000 require manual signatures of two executives. Determine whether this is a proper limit and whether procedure is working.

25. Review of checks and supporting documents by Accounting Supervisor. Determine whether this step is necessary and, if so, whether the Accounting Supervisor needs to be involved.

26. Checks and supporting documents filed. As can be seen, the present systems and procedures have created an enormous amount of paperwork necessary for the purchasing, receiving, payables, and vendor payment functions. Each document that can be eliminated results in the reduction of forms cost, preparation costs, handling time, filing time, and file costs. In looking at the documents to be disposed of, the following could be considered for elimination:

    a. Voucher

    b. Check copies

    c. Receiving report

    d. Department requisition

Layout Flowchart

Reader: For each numbered block (or blocks) on the layout flowchart (see Exhibit 4.2), analyze the possible function or activity, and then document your comments as to what you would question as part of your operational review. Then review the suggested responses.

Suggested Responses

Note: The following responses correspond to the numbers shown on the layout flowchart for each person/job function.

1 to 4. These employees all appear to be performing the same function, with No. 2 most likely being the titular supervisor or head worker. This function should be reviewed as to efficiency. In addition, reporting relationships should be analyzed, including their reporting to No. 26, who appears to be acting as a controller.

5 to 12. These employees appear to be performing an offline or staff function in an isolate capacity to the remainder of the work group. Their only reporting, which is indirect (as shown by the dotted lines), appears to be with No. 13, who appears to be performing the role of dispatcher.

13. This employee is performing the role of dispatcher—on an indirect basis. He or she is interfacing in this capacity with No. 5 through 12, No. 14, and No. 21. The detailed tasks of this function should be looked at as far as necessity.

14. This employee is performing the role of controller. He or she is controlling materials from No. 22 and No. 16 on an indirect basis, and from Nos. 26 and 18 on a direct basis, and is then routing to No. 13 on an indirect basis. The operational reviewer should determine whether there is any value added effort being made or whether this is strictly controlling.

15. This employee appears to be an isolate with only an indirect interest in materials coming from the outside and from No. 13, and then routing them on to No. 21.

16 to 18. There appears to be an inverse pyramid with materials coming from No. 14 and then distributed downwards from No. 18 to No. 16. The function being performed should be reviewed as to

EXHIBIT 4.2   EXAMPLE OF LAYOUT FLOWCHART

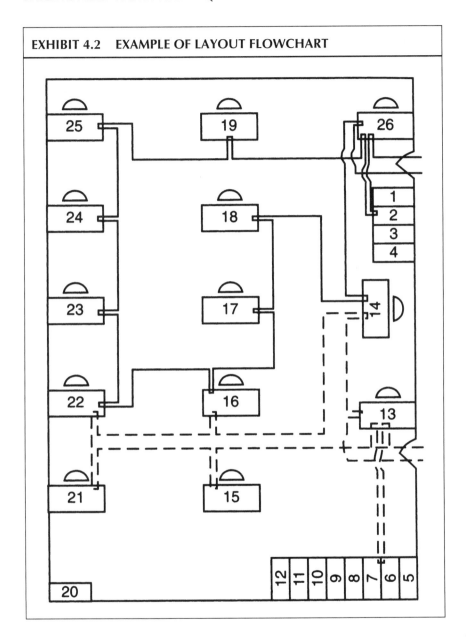

necessity of all three employees. No. 16 at the bottom of the pyramid, relates to No. 22 on a direct basis, and to No. 22 and No. 14 on an indirect basis.

19. This employee is performing the role of controller between No. 26 and No. 25. This is a typical role for a manager over two supervisors. That is, there is a review of one area's output prior to routing it to another area. This is often an expensive and unnecessary function.

20. This employee is an absolute isolate, bearing no direct or indirect relation to any- one else in the work area. This could be a staff resource person who is sometimes necessary and sometimes just a nice luxury.

21. This employee appears to be an isolate with only indirect relation to No. 22 and No. 15. Ask, again, is this a necessary function?

22 to 25. This is another inverse pyramid similar to Nos. 16 through 18. Work is routed by Nos. 19 to 25, who then appears to distribute the work downward through Nos. 24, 23, and 22. No. 22 relates directly to No. 16 (the reviewer should find out what is happening here) and indirectly with No. 21.

26. This employee performs the role of controller, receiving work from No. 2 and from the outside and routing it back to the group of employees Nos. 1 through 4 and, when satisfactory, routing the work to either No. 14 or No. 19.

Ratio, Change, and Trend Analysis: Petty Cash Fund Review

Situation: A work unit in the Example Company that should be processing its purchases through the Purchasing Department was found to have a petty cash fund of $3,000. In the preceding year, fund reimbursements totaled $102,000.

An analysis of a sample of 200 petty cash vouchers disclosed that 150 of them were for amounts between $40 and $50; and that 130 of the 150 vouchers were for books. Of the other 50 vouchers, 30 were found to be from repetitive vendors who, as a practice, submitted their charges on a vendor's invoice for subsequent payment. These 30 vouchers averaged more than $32. The remaining 20 vouchers were for cash payments, with an average amount of $8.46.

The total number of petty cash payment vouchers was 3,200. Analysis of Purchasing Department policies revealed the policy that "all purchases over $50 must be processed by the central Purchasing Department via a purchase requisition procedure."

Reader: Document which ratios you might use to arrive at a conclusion as to a possible findings as part of the operational review. Then review the following suggested responses.

Suggested Responses

Ratios

Petty Cash Turnover

$102,000 total / $3,000 petty cash fund = 34 times per year.

Note: A petty cash fund is normally set up for low-amount and/or cash emergency purchases. Within this framework, it is normally expected that the fund will be replenished about once a month. In this situation, it is being replenishing about every week and a half, which is far too often.

Average Amount of Petty Cash Payment Voucher

$102,000 / 3,200 vouchers = $31.88

As mentioned, the petty cash fund should be for low-amount purchases. The present average amount of $31.88 appears to be too large for normal petty cash purposes.

Petty Cash Vouchers between $40 and $50

Sample: 150 / 200 = 75%
Extrapolation: $102,000 × 75% = $76,500 estimate of vouchers between $40 and $50
Books: 130 / 150 × $76,500 = $66,303 for books between $40 and $50
Other Vouchers: $102,000 − $76,500 = $25,500 less than $40
Vendor Invoice Type: 30 = 60% × $25,500 = $15,300
Remainder: Cash Type: $25,500 − $15,300 = $10,200

Estimated Monthly Reimbursement: 320 vouchers (10% of 3,200) @ $8.46 = $2,707 estimated annual reimbursements

$2,707 / 12 = $225 petty cash fund based on monthly reimbursement

Conclusion: Petty cash fund could be lowered to $225 on a monthly reimbursement basis if vouchers that appear to be central purchasing items were processed correctly through the central Purchasing Department. This would allow the company to invest less of their funds in petty cash (this practice may also exist in other work units) and achieve the economies of central purchasing. The reviewer might also want to analyze whether the policy of all purchases over $50 going through central purchasing is appropriate.

Ratio, Change, and Trend Analysis: Inventory Usage Review

Situation: The Example Company raw materials inventory approximated 6,000 items valued at about $350,000 at the end of last year. An operational review test, based on accepted statistical sampling procedures, of 113 listed raw material inventory items disclosed the following:

1. Total value of tested items: $15,000
2. Total zero usage items: 20
3. Total value of zero usage items: $4,000
4. Total number of items whose usage was greater than 1 1/2 times their prior year's usage: 45
5. Total value of items in No. 4: $6,200

Reader: Document which ratios you might use to arrive at a conclusion as to a possible findings as part of the operational review. Then review the following suggested responses.

Suggested Responses

Zero Usage Items

Number of Items: 20 / 113 = 18% × 6,000 items = 1,080 items

Dollar Value: $ 4,000 / $15,000 = 27% × $350,000 = $94,500

Conclusion: Eighteen percent of 6,000 inventory items, estimated at 1,080 items, had no usage during the year. Twenty-seven percent of inventory value, estimated at $94,500, had no usage for the year. These data could be used to determine the cost of carrying inventory and the company's return on investment to determine the cost of carrying such a relatively high percentage of inventory having no usage.

Analysis could also be made as to why so many items with no usage were allowed to build up in inventory during the past year. These items should also be reviewed as to disposition: used in the future, sold, returned to vendor, or scrapped.

Usage Greater Than 1 1/2 Times Prior Year

Number Of Items: 45 / 113 = 40% × 6,000 items = 2,400 items
Dollar Value: $ 6,200 / $15,000 = 41% × $350,000 = $143,500

Conclusion: Approximately 40 percent of inventory items, estimated at 2,400 items and a dollar value of $143,500, had more than 1 1/2 times usage over the prior year. These facts, coupled with the high increase in zero usage items, could indicate a change in product lines manufactured, without corresponding changes in raw material forecasting and ordering.

Therefore, further analysis could be made to determine whether reorder points and reorder quantities have been changed to reflect accurately the recent increase in usage. Analysis could also be made to determine the number of resultant stock-outs and the related cost to the company.

WORK PAPERS

The following are the sections that should be included in the current operational review work paper files:

- Work paper index
- Work program
- Review checklist
- Time control

- Engagement status reports
- Supervision notes
- Correspondence (both in and out)
- Minutes of meetings
- Planning papers
- Fact finding: statement of condition
- Fact finding: establishment of criteria
- Analysis and conclusions
- Development of recommendations: alternatives
- Development of recommendations: final
- Presentation outline: oral reporting
- Written report: draft
- Written report: final copy
- Bulk material

Reader: Using the preceding list, document for your review team the contents of your operational review work paper file.

CASE STUDY: JOE SORRY, INC., FIELD WORK PHASE

The review team's work performed in the planning phase for the Joe Sorry Company indicated five priority management and operational areas for positive improvement:

1. Review of personnel
2. Manufacturing systems
3. Manufacturing facilities and production procedures
4. Inventory control systems and procedures
5. Four business concepts

The review team then developed its work program, which is the plan for conducting the work steps in the field work phase, to determine that there definitely are such weaknesses and whether to expend additional time and effort on an in-depth analysis and review. Based on the work steps performed in the field work phase, particular areas are identified in which to develop specific findings to present to Joe and Flo.

For those areas in which the review team decides to proceed with an in-depth development of a review finding, the information gathered and the analysis work performed in the field work phase provide a basis from which to proceed. The work steps performed in the field work phase not only provide an understanding of the specific areas for improvement, but also help the review team to understand the organization, department, and function. In the field work phase, the work steps are performed as defined in the work program phase, as is any additional analytical work necessary to develop the finding. In addition, additional critical areas discovered during the field work phase are considered for further analysis. For our case study purposes, we will develop one work step as it would be performed in the field work phase for each of the major critical areas.

Manufacturing Personnel

Based on our work program work steps, we reviewed and analyzed each manufacturing related function by:

- Developing narrative descriptions
- Analyzing each work unit's functions
- Documenting the duties and responsibilities (Note that the Job Responsibilities Questionnaire previously completed by all employees saved us considerable time.)
- Interviewing a selected number of employees from each work unit (including all managers and supervisors)
- Observing actual work being performed

Results of Work Steps

As a result of performing these work steps, we found the following conditions to exist:

Vice President—Production. This position is really one of plant manager or overseer of production operations. Joe has orally delegated authority to Ed Harrison to run manufacturing. However, Joe has not effectively released Ed to do this and created the autonomy Ed needs to be successful. In effect, Joe continues to control production by dictating to Ed what needs to be done and establishing his own priorities and creating crises.

Ed appears to be competent for the job, both from a background and credential basis and in his knowledge and abilities. The plant is still being controlled on a manual reporting basis, even though a fully integrated MRP II (Manufacturing Resource Planning) computer system with both software and hardware exists. Ed stated that he wants to get the system up and running, as he is used to working that way. In addition, he has a number of good ideas (e.g., production team focus) that we agree would improve operations, productivity, and profits.

Under present conditions, Ed is being highly paid (at $74,000 per year) and ineffectively used. In effect, at present, he is somewhat superfluous, as Joe effectively controls operations. Many of the production employees see Ed as a joke and as Joe's shadow. Often, when an answer is needed, they will bypass Ed and go directly to Joe. Ed stated he would consider leaving the company, but with present conditions he has no place to go. Nevertheless, Joe seems to like the idea of having someone of Ed's caliber on staff and having a Vice President of Production. Although the company's production operations could probably continue as is without Ed's presence, we would recommend that Ed should get the MRP II system operational and improve manufacturing operations as identified by our review.

Forepersons. There are six forepersons, whose responsibilities are to ensure that the production teams assigned to them are functioning effectively as to:

- Having necessary materials
- Being properly trained
- Receiving proper online supervision by a production team leader
- Working productively
- Completing jobs on time

We interviewed all six forepersons, and not one of them was quite sure what he or she was supposed to be doing. They were supposed to be on the production floor to oversee their production team leaders and their production teams. However, there was no place for them on the floor and they only succeeded in getting in the way. The production teams did not see the need for both a foreperson and a production team leader and tended to ignore the foreperson. This left the job of the foreperson as one of gofer or hustler, at the whims of Joe, Ed, production team leaders, or production team members. At present, these positions could be eliminated with minimal impact to operations. However, as these personnel are quite knowledgeable of the company's operations, they could be used effectively to assist in implementing the MRP II system and then become database operators and analyzers (at least three of the six). Four of the six are former production team members, who could possibly be used in production.

Production Team Leaders. These are really chief workers for each of the six production teams (specialty, custom, (two) defense, and (two) basic). Their major responsibility is to ensure that production is done on time based on Joe's priorities. As all are former production team members, they tend to be cohesive with the production team in their animosity toward the forepersons, Ed, and Joe. They are better production workers than they are team leaders. In fact, we observed many times that they would perform specific production tasks themselves rather than the production employee, just to get the job done. This concept seems to be creating a supervisory duplication of effort and a loss of qualified production assistance. It appears that the company is emphasizing control over production employees rather than releasing them to do their jobs. What is really needed here is a number of roving trainers, coaches, and facilitators (probably three).

Production Team Members. The 36 production employees are divided into six production teams of six members each, as follows:

- Specialty boards: one team
- Custom boards: one team
- Defense (government) contracts: two teams
- Basic boards: two teams

Our observations of each of these work teams disclosed that they predominantly did what they were told. These employees all seem to be knowledgeable and know their jobs. However, very little is asked of them, so that knowledge and ability are wasted. We observed, a number of times, these employees shaking their heads as they were instructed what to do by Joe, Ed, or a foreperson (primarily). When we asked them why they did not say anything or why they just did as they were told, they said "What's the use? They're not going to listen to us anyway."

We found that we could not separate the job functions from the production systems in this instance. Although each production team member has an assigned job function within the team, we needed to determine the purpose for the number of teams, the reason for six members in each team, and the respective differences of each team by product. Our review disclosed the following four factors:

1. The team concept originated with Joe's former employer, ACE Electronics. However, at ACE these teams were more autonomous. Joe merely carried over the concept, but maintained the control.

2. When Joe started his business, he was manufacturing specialty boards only. This type of manufacturing required six work steps or operations—initial set-up, component placement, wiring, soldering, completion, and final testing—hence, six work positions. When Joe started taking custom orders, he kept the same manufacturing procedures.

3. As sales of specialty and custom boards started to peak and level off because of slackening demand and competition, Joe took on defense work (which now designates all government contracts) to take up the production slack. This type of work tended to be different, as it could be one-time production, prototype development, outside purchase with inside inspection, subject to main contractor or government inspection, and so forth. In other words, each job needed to be set up individually, not as a standard job with six work stations. This created the need for two production teams, which has resulted in more idleness and downtime. Joe Sorry, Inc., should consider whether it is worth staying in this defense business, and if so, how to do it.

4. The basic board business was another venture Joe got into to use production capacity and increase the sales numbers. Basically, the company buys these boards from outside (mainly from Asian countries), provides some add-on capability or just Joe Sorry, Inc. identifier materials to justify their being assembled in the United States, and then resells them. This is Joe's only repetitive

type business, but it is more highly competitive. It requires the company to maintain higher levels of inventory and to sell the product at lower per unit prices, thus requiring greater sales efforts to achieve an acceptable profit margin. The six-member team concept was again applied to this product line, where most often no more than two employees are required. Joe also established two teams for this product so that more than one type of board could be worked on at the same time.

We believe that the company needs to consider the manner in which it manufactures. Although the six-member production team works in a number of instances, for specialty and custom boards, it is a costly process. We observed a number (more than 20) of these jobs, and found each time that production was less efficient and more costly than performing the job with the right number of personnel.

For defense and basic boards, the six-member team does not fit at all. These are both different types of manufacturing and should be considered separately. It appears that the company is giving more emphasis to these two products, which make up the smallest and least profitable of the four products, while the specialty and custom board businesses suffer. With efficient adjustments, the company should be able to increase productivity with fewer employees and less cost, reduce backlogs, better control inventories, conserve production capacity, and increase profits.

Repairs and Maintenance. The repairs and maintenance crew consists of five employees whose primary function is to keep all of the equipment in good working order and to maintain the facilities in a clean and orderly fashion. Most of the pieces of equipment used in manufacturing are hand tools (wiring grips, solder irons, pinchers, etc.) that require minimal repair on-site that can be done by the workers themselves. Other, more major repairs are sent outside, or a piece is just replaced when replacement is less costly than repair. Rather than disturb the work teams by having them do maintenance work, Joe believes that these individuals are worthwhile in that they free up the production teams.

During the day, two of these employees are assigned to the repair bin, where they are supposed to be sharpening and fixing the production tools. However, our observation found them mainly engrossed in conversation with each other and various production personnel.

Our work sampling over a five-day period disclosed that there is no more than a half a day's work to be done by one individual each day. Most of this work probably does not need to be done by these individuals.

The other three crew members are assigned to facility maintenance during the day, which consists of keeping the work areas clean so that the production teams can work unencumbered. Although this provides a clean-looking work area, it is an expensive method of accomplishing this result. It appears that the production teams themselves could be responsible for keeping their areas clean as they go. As it is, the company is encouraging the production teams to be sloppier than necessary, as they rely on the maintenance crew to clean up for them.

The repairs and maintenance crew typically works a standard eight-hour shift, with two members coming in early before production starts to make sure the work areas are clean and ready, and three members leaving later to clean up at the end of the day. This has been the work pattern since the inception of this unit. However, with the current amount of backlog and overtime, the later crew is leaving before the end of the production day. This means that the later crew has little to do at the end of their day, whereas the early crew must do all of the clean up at the beginning of the day. Based on our observations and analysis, we believe that this entire crew could be disbanded, with the possible exception of one individual to be available for regular tool maintenance, emergency repairs, and auxiliary facility maintenance duties.

The bulk of tool repairs should be sent outside, or the company should merely replace nonfunctioning tools. Ongoing maintenance of the work areas should be the responsibility of the work crews, as it is more efficient for them to keep the areas clean as they go than to clean up the mess after the fact. Morning and evening facility maintenance should be jobbed to the outside at reduced cost with better results. The company is presently using an outside maintenance group for the office, which could possibly handle the plant facility as well at minimal additional cost.

Packers and Shippers. The packing and shipping crew includes four individuals who are responsible for packing the products and shipping them to the customers. They have a separate work area for these functions. However, at present it is being physically merged with the receiving area due to the volume of materials coming in and going out.

Our observations of these procedures disclosed that because production is by customer, there is a bottleneck of customer orders waiting to be packed and shipped. As items are completed by the production teams, they are thrown into large bins, which in turn are brought to the packing area. Because the packers are backed up at present, most of these bins are waiting and clogging up the packing work area.

In addition, some customer orders cannot be shipped until the full acceptable quantity is available. These bins are normally shoved to the side to await the additional quantities. Based on our review, they will stay that way until a customer crisis arises. Some of these orders in the wait state have been packed; others have not. This is an alarming situation, in that Joe's policy is to overproduce so as to satisfy present and future customer demands. We believe the amount of rejected items is much greater than the amount being reported—possibly a real customer problem. In addition, a number of times, we witnessed production employees "borrowing" items from the bins in waiting, causing additional problems when the previously expected shortage is produced and matched to the quantity still in the bins, resulting in another shortage. Some of these orders were found to be more than six months old.

We believe that the company should consider online packing procedures—that is, move the packing operation to the back end of the production line. In this way, the goods are counted and packed as they are produced (after final testing) and ready for shipment.

For customers that require an exact quantity or more (usually one should allow up to 10 percent), for which production is short, there should be an integration with inventory and other customer orders to ascertain whether this quantity of this item is in-house or must be produced. Typically, only a small quantity is needed, which could be effectively produced by a small (two individuals) work crew. This would be more effective and efficient than holding the order in a wait state and causing inventory concerns.

Receivers. There are three receivers who are responsible for receiving all materials from vendors and returns from customers. The production system was set up so that materials would be received to coordinate with a customer order-oriented production schedule. As this system has become unworkable, materials are being received with no real place to go. The inventory storeroom was not set up for the amount of materials coming in, and these materials are therefore sitting in the receiving area, production areas, or anywhere else the receivers can find a place. We found a number of instances in which materials were on hand but could not be found when needed for production, and so were reordered.

As mentioned earlier, due to these problems in the packing and shipping and receiving areas, the two areas have become merged. Because of this, we observed some instances in which finished goods were sent to production and raw materials were wrapped for shipping. The company has to clean up both of these areas, as they are starting to cost the company sales and customers. Receiving must be recoordinated with the production system.

On a daily basis, the quantity of materials being received is less than can be controlled by one individual, but because of the previously discussed conditions, two receivers were recently hired. This treats the symptoms but does not eliminate the cause. We recommend that these two individuals be used to clean up both the systemic and the physical problems and then implement adequate systems to keep the receiving area working. Once the cause of the problem (lack of integration with production) has been eliminated, there should no longer be any use for these two additional individuals in receiving.

Inventory Control Manager. Production systems were originally set up to minimize raw material and finished goods inventory levels. Raw materials were to be ordered and scheduled for receipt as the customer order was to go into production. The production schedule started to slip almost immediately, and Joe gave up on the computerized MRP II systems and went back to his manual methods of scheduling—basically by customer crisis. Such crisis methodology resulted in backing up scheduled production, so the corresponding materials backed up also, with no place to put them.

As Joe got more and more concerned and crises became the daily norm, work-in-process and finished goods in partial quantities started stacking up in the production area. Consequently, production employees neglected to record these items in the inventory system, making the computerized system almost totally unreliable. This has resulted in the inventory control manager becoming more of an inventory chaser than a controller.

Quality Control. This department consists of a quality control (QC) manager, Bill O'Halaran, six QC inspectors, and two clerical staff. As previously mentioned, this department is located in the office area, although most of its work is done in the production area. The QC unit is responsible for establishing production QC standards; inspecting and testing raw materials and components, work in process at established stages of production, and finished goods prior to packing and shipping; and dealing with customers as to quality problems and returns.

Their inspection work stations, which are located at various points throughout the plant facility, consist of various pieces of test equipment. The locations were set up to minimize the movement of materials to be inspected. However, often the QC inspectors are not at the stations when goods arrive to be tested (repairs and maintenance personnel are being used to move the materials back and forth), as they are back in the office area. This results in a production holdup while the materials wait for an inspector. Quality Control uses random sampling testing procedures (e.g., 8 items randomly selected out of a production run of 86). However, the entire production run is brought to the QC station, where the inspector then selects the sample. We would recommend doing such QC work-in-process testing on an inline basis; that is, select the items randomly and perform the testing right at the production line. This would mean moving the inspectors into the production area, where they should be anyway to achieve the greatest efficiency and increase productivity and timeliness.

Finished goods inspection could be performed in the same manner, with the goods being packed as they are approved—again resulting in maximum efficiency and timely customer deliveries. Raw material inspection for boards and electrical components purchased from outside vendors should be set up close to the receiving area. In this manner, only acceptable raw materials will be moved into production or temporary storage. Those items identified as defective can be controlled and returned as soon as possible, either to be replaced by their vendor or reordered from another vendor. At present, such incoming inspection is performed at the time the materials are placed into production, causing not only production problems but also material return and replacement problems. Either way, the customer order is delayed.

Each of the six QC inspectors is presently assigned to a production team: one for specialty, one for custom, two for defense, and two for basic. This has resulted in an uneven distribution of work, as the production teams do not produce their output on the same basis. For instance, basic boards primarily require incoming inspection and very little work-in-process inspection, whereas specialty and custom boards require a larger amount of work-in-process inspection, and defense work requires more finished goods inspection owing to government requirements. Because of the nature of the various products and their QC requirements, we have observed individual inspectors being overwhelmed while other inspectors sit idly by or in their office. We believe the use of inline inspection methods and the reassignment of QC inspectors based on work requirements would reduce the required number of inspectors to no more than four.

The QC manager is responsible for managing all QC operations. However, presently each QC inspector is managing his or her own area. This leaves very little for the QC manager to do except meet with Joe and/or Ed or the inspectors, write reports and memos (mainly unnecessary), or talk on the telephone. Bill O'Hallaran appears to be quite knowledgeable and capable, but his talents are being wasted. He was hired to work with the MRP II system, which, of course, is not operable. At this time, his job, as described, is unnecessary. This function of overseeing the QC inspectors could be handled by a plant manager. In the meantime, Bill could work with Ed Harrison in implementing the MRP II system and getting it operable.

The two clerical staff assigned to the quality control unit have little to do. Most of the QC reports are prepared manually, for internal use only, resulting in filing requirements only. Those QC reports that go to the outside (i.e., government) are low volume, requiring minimal typing. Although the QC manager produces some clerical requirements (word processing on a PC), again this is minimal. The positions for two clerical staff were based on the data entry, update, and inquiry requirements of the fully implemented MRP II system. Although this never came about, the two clerical staff remain. This appears to be a tip-of-the-iceberg situation, where clerical staff are assigned to each operating department; this situation should be further reviewed as to need. QC clerical requirements could be handled at present by a clerical pool–type operation, with the QC inspectors being responsible for filing their own reports.

Manufacturing Systems

Following our work program work steps, we performed five field work tasks:

1. Reviewed and analyzed MRP II software package JOBEASY as to systems features and applicability to Joe Sorry, Inc.
2. Analyzed present manufacturing methods
3. Reviewed present operational reporting procedures and documented desired reporting features
4. Developed proposed operating reporting system
5. Documented necessary changes to JOBEASY software

Results of Work Steps
Through the performance of these work steps, we found the following conditions:

Review of JOBEASY Software. We reviewed the systems documentation and performed an online walk-through of the JOBEASY MRP II based software package. The package is really a set of integrated subsystems, as follows:

Sales Forecasting

Order Entry and Invoicing

Master Production Schedule

Bill of Material Processing

Material Requirements Planning

Capacity Planning

Shop Floor (Routing) Control

Inventory Control

Production and Cost Control

Purchasing

The JOBEASY package is primarily designed for repetitive type manufacture—that is, one that manufactures and sells the same products over and over again (such as an appliance manufacturer)—which requires a somewhat detailed bill of material with multiple levels and a number of work centers. The package is fairly complete for what it is intended to do.

The Joe Sorry Company, however, is primarily a custom job shop (i.e., specialty and custom boards) manufacturing to customer specifications with a limited bill of material (more of a parts list) and basically one work center per order. Although a particular customer may reorder the same product, another customer normally would not, so repetitiveness is minimal. Although the basic board business has a strong element of repetitive sales of the same product, minimal manufacturing is really involved.

This is a typical situation in which the customer buys the software and then tries to make it fit the situation. The Joe Sorry company has to define its systems specifications as to what elements are needed in a manufacturing control system and then locate the software package that best fits its needs. We believe that the JOBEASY software cannot be effectively applied to the Joe Sorry Company, as it is designed for a different type of manufacturer. The major elements that should be provided by a manufacturing software package for the company include:

Production and delivery schedule based on sales forecasting. Most of the company's sales are ordered by customers and known to the company long before it gets into production. In fact, it is always working with future production. Similar customer orders also need to be combined for production purposes so that they can be manufactured more efficiently than on a strict customer order basis.

Production scheduling based on customer production and delivery requirements. There is a need here to maximize use of plant capacity and satisfy all customer needs at the same time. The company has to know of under- and overcapacity conditions and the level of productivity throughput that is needed at any time.

Material requirements controls. As most of the products start with a limited number of standard boards and most of the components are interchangeable between products, the company must work better with their vendors, and effectively negotiate through purchasing, so that it can minimize raw material inventory.

Finished goods coordination with customer delivery schedules. That is, as the goods are finished in manufacturing, they are packed and shipped directly to the customer. With proper production scheduling and shop floor control, this should become a reality, resulting in minimal finished goods inventory.

Work-in-process controls, so that each job in the mix is being worked on and completed on schedule. The present system of crisis job shuffling must be discontinued and strict shop floor controls implemented. These procedures should keep work-in-process moving and include reports to management as to what action has to be taken to keep to the schedule.

Inventory control, which is simplified as raw materials and finished goods inventory are minimized. The job of inventory control becomes one of using up existing inventory rather than continual reordering—in other words, always pushing toward zero inventory. The object is to get out of the inventory business, not to have large amounts of inventory to store and control.

Cost control. This must be considered so that the company knows what its costs are and where it needs to push costs down (i.e., material, labor, indirect, customer, and function), as well as determining its lowest possible costs and related selling prices. Such cost control, based on activity-based costing/management should be a natural product of manufacturing and operational data collection; for example, material costs are derived directly from the purchasing system multiplied by quantity, and labor costs are derived directly from work center reporting as time multiplied by labor cost. We suggest that the company use cost-price-volume analysis as a way of determining recovery of all costs—material, labor, and indirect—rather than using individual job overhead allocations. These tend to become confusing for effective decision making, and no matter what basis is used (e.g., labor hours × rate), the results always contain some inaccuracies.

Integration with other systems, such as purchasing, accounts payable, billing, accounts receivable, labor distribution and payroll, cost accounting, sales statistics, and customer statistics.

We do not believe that the JOBEASY software can be effectively modified to meet the needs of the Joe Sorry Company. A more effective approach is to develop the necessary systems specifications to solve the company's situation and then find the software package that most closely fits its needs with any necessary systems modifications. This project should be initiated as soon as possible, as present procedures are crippling the company.

Manufacturing Methods. We observed and analyzed present manufacturing methods and noted the following factors:

Production is being scheduled based on Joe's decision as to which customer orders are priorities. Each customer order then becomes a unique manufacturing order. This means that materials are ordered specifically for each job, it is entered into production as a unique production job, its finished items are identified for the particular customer, and it is not shipped until the entire order is complete.

There are six work centers (one specialty, one custom, two defense, and two basic), each with a team of six members. Regardless of the type of product, it is produced by a six-member team. Although some of the jobs (approximately 20 percent) could fit into this six-workstation pattern, most of the jobs could be produced more efficiently with fewer work stations (e.g., number of workstations for basic boards reduced from two to one).

The present six work steps or operations—initial setup, component placement, wiring, soldering, completion, and final testing—can be simplified and modified by product being produced, resulting in increased efficiency and productivity. For instance, initial setup and component placement could be done by the foreperson or coach/facilitator, and final testing should be done by quality control on a test basis.

Quality control procedures (initial, midpoint, and final) are being done on an offline basis. That is, the QC inspector moves the items from the work center to a central inspection station. It would be more efficient to move QC to an online position at the workstation. Furthermore, most of the jobs do not require three inspections; a final testing would be sufficient. In addition, initial inspection could be better accomplished by vendor reliability (eliminating receiving inspection at the site) or at receiving for boards and components as necessary to identify defects and return the defective items to vendors. Midpoint inspections can be made the responsibility of the workers, eliminating the need for QC inspections. Final inspections can then be made by QC personnel on an exception basis.

Finished goods (completed customer order items) are brought to shipping, where they are held unless production has completed the correct quantity. The order waits until such missing quantities are subsequently produced. This is a very costly procedure and has resulted in many partial completions sitting for long periods of time. We recommend bringing packing and shipping directly to the work center and better controlling quantities so that these functions can be done as the items are completed and then shipped and billed.

The company has basically four product lines—specialty boards, custom boards, defense (government) business, and basic boards—

all of which it is treating in the same manners. The specialty and custom board businesses are somewhat similar, as they produce to customer specifications. Although there is reordering of a product by some customers and some ordering of the same product from different customers, these businesses are primarily custom job shops (which is the strength of the company). Defense and other government contracts are singular in nature, mainly acquired on a bid basis, with minimal likelihood as to reorders because they call for mostly prototype work. The basic board business is really a purchase for resale business, with the main add-on being the company's identifier.

We believe that the company should concentrate on its main product strengths: specialty and custom boards. Manufacturing systems and controls should be based on these products. Customer order requirements as to materials, production processes, and flexibility should be combined with those of other products and customer orders for economy and efficiency. The company should move its emphasis from the inviolate customer order in manufacturing to a consideration of the overall needs for all customers. In addition, sales and engineering efforts should be geared more to standardizing among various customer needs and requirements, as opposed to the present procedure of making each specialty and custom product ultimately unique.

The defense business, which takes up two six-member workstations, is the smallest part of the total business. Based on present cost systems, it would be difficult to determine whether this part of the company is even making any money. The company should determine whether it should remain in this business, particularly in light of the present cut backs in government spending. It is taking up an unequal amount of production space and time as compared with its contribution. The company is in a critical position, in which more profitable business (i.e., specialty and custom) is waiting as backlog while defense work uses one-third of plant capacity.

The basic board business is really that of a distributorship: the company buys the product, puts on its own identifiers (which takes up two work stations in manufacturing), and then resells the product. It should be buying product ready for resale and bypassing the manufacturing process. It would then become a business of customer sales and deliveries (if possible, avoiding inventory).

Operational Reporting. We reviewed operational reporting procedures to determine the level and effectiveness of present practices as well as desirable reporting elements for a proposed reporting system. Our review disclosed the following:

As mentioned previously, the JOBEASY manufacturing control system software contains all of the standard production scheduling, production control, work-in-process, shop floor control, inventory control reports, and so forth. However, such reporting is not being used, as the computer system is not being updated to make it effective. Its main present use is to track customer jobs on the floor, as to where they are in the process, and to accumulate job costs (although inaccurate).

As discussed earlier, the JOBEASY software is not easily adaptable to the reporting needs of the Joe Sorry Company. We will have to analyze operational reporting requirements as part of our systems specifications to determine what is needed to manage and control the company's manufacturing operations. Such reporting should be incorporated into the purchased software package, provided through system modifications, or internally provided through a system-provided report generator module.

The main operational reports being used at present are manually prepared by the forepersons for their jobs, as follows:

- Job status report, showing each job being worked on, the last work step completed, the remaining scheduled work steps, and scheduled completion/shipment date
- Daily time report and labor distribution, showing for each production worker the jobs he or she worked on, amount of time charged to the job, number of units completed, number of units still to be completed, and amount of nonjob time

A proposed operational reporting system needs to consider the following elements:

- Integration of system's modules, such as sales forecasting, order entry, master production scheduling, material requirements planning, capacity planning, shop floor control, inventory control, cost control, and purchasing
- Integration with other support-type systems (either part of the software package or separately purchased modules) such as accounts payable, billing, accounts receivable and collections, labor distribution and payroll, cost accounting, sales statistics, general ledger, operating reports, and key operating indicators

Key operating indicators and other key reporting elements that should be included in the proposed reporting system include the following:

- *Customer orders*: forecasted, in-house, scheduled for production, work-in-process control, on-time deliveries, price/cost/ profit or loss summary
- *Production*: job control, work center reporting, standard versus actual (material, quantity, labor, rejects), over/under capacity planning, production scheduling
- *Inventory*: material requirements planning, on-hand control (zero inventory concepts), reorder control (using up on-hand first), finished goods control
- *Quality control*: number of rejects (receiving, work-in-process, completed items), returned goods, rework (quantity and cost), and causes of rejects/returns/rework
- *Cost control*: standard versus actual (materials, labor, quantities, loss in production), cost versus pricing, productivity, overtime, and so on

A proposed implementation plan would be as follows:

- Production scheduling and control (including QC)
- Inventory control
- Cost control
- Sales forecasting, customer orders, and sales statistics

Manufacturing Facility and Production Procedures

Based on our work program work steps, we performed four field work tasks:

1. Prepared layout flow diagram of present manufacturing facility
2. Observed production operations for four product lines
3. Developed proposed manufacturing flow for each product line
4. Prepared proposed layout flow diagram based on recommendations

Results of Work Steps

Present Layout Flow Diagram. The layout flow diagram of the present manufacturing facility is shown in Exhibit 4.3. Areas of inefficiency,

EXHIBIT 4.3   PRESENT LAYOUT FLOW DIAGRAM

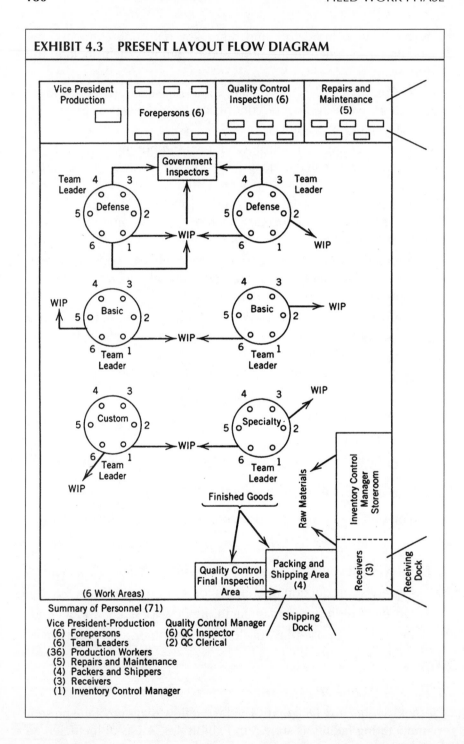

bottlenecks, poor working conditions, and so on, were found to be as follows:

- Six work centers—one for specialty, one for custom, two for defense, and two for basic boards—causing uneven distribution of work load and nonprioritized allocation of space.
- Six-member work teams not always necessary. All customer orders for any one of the product lines are set up in this manner. However, in most instances less personnel and fewer work steps are necessary (e.g., two work steps for basic boards).
- Packing/shipping and receiving are merging into each other's work areas.
- Inventory: raw materials, work-in-process, and finished goods are stored about the production floor.
- Quality control is performing offline inspections, which delays the production process for each customer order. In addition, QC is housed away from the production area in the office area.
- The presence of six forepersons and six team leaders results in these individuals getting into each other's way rather than enhancing productivity.
- The amount of unnecessary inventory, coupled with the lack of sufficient inventory storage space, has resulted in physical inventory getting in the way of production, inability to find specific items, and lack of overall inventory control.

Observation of Production Operations. The company recently (less than six months ago) moved into a new production facility in a brand new industrial park. However, it has not taken advantage of the increased space. Already, production facilities are cramped, with the six work centers encroaching on one another. Moreover, with the increase in inventory, many parts are spread around the production facility, not only overcrowding needed production facilities but also making it difficult to control physical inventory.

Quality control, which should be an integral part of production, had to be housed in the office area. This makes it difficult to find QC personnel at times when they are needed. In addition, they have been forced to conduct their testing on an offline basis in a separate room at the far end of the manufacturing facility. It appears that it would be more economical and efficient to conduct the testing online directly in the work centers. However, the present overcrowding prevents this.

The receiving and packing/shipping areas, which were intended to be separate, have been forced together, creating enormous confusion as to what is coming in and what is going out. Employees in these areas are presently working right on top of each other.

Inventory was intended to be minimal, to be ordered "just in time" for a customer order going into production. This is not working, as raw materials (mainly standard boards for the various types of products) are stacked everywhere. The inventory control manager does not appear to be sure what he has on-hand and is probably ordering additional quantities of existing inventory. The bulk of the finished goods inventory for specialty, custom, and defense-type products is supposed to be shipped out by customer order. However, again there is an enormous amount of such finished goods in inventory, when quite possibly the same items are being manufactured for specific customers. In addition, these items should be addressed for salability; if they are salable, a concentrated effort should be launched to get them out of inventory.

Production operations are set up in six work centers by product line, as follows:

- Specialty: one center
- Custom: one center
- Defense: two centers
- Basic: two centers

Each such work center consists of six workstations for standard operations, as follows:

- Initial setup
- Component placement
- Wiring
- Soldering
- Completion
- Final testing

We observed that for most specialty and custom board customer orders, these six steps were unnecessary. Generally, initial setup and component placement can be combined, wiring and soldering can be done by the same worker, completion can remain the same, and final testing should be done by QC inspectors on a test basis only. As previously mentioned, the company should get out of the defense business, which does not lend itself to the six-step approach at all, and eliminate (or greatly reduce) the manufacturing requirement for basic boards (mainly purchase and resale).

Proposed Product Line Manufacturing Recommendations. The main production facility should be devoted to specialty and custom board manufacturing. Production jobs should be based on realistic sales forecasts and/or real customer orders; using the "greater than" theory (i.e., when real customer orders exceed the sales forecast, use the amount of real orders and vice versa). Through coordination of the engineering and sales departments, standardization of products should be maximized. This will allow scheduling more jobs by product than by customer, providing efficiencies of material ordering, inventory control, production scheduling and control, shop floor control, and the ability to deliver on time. The manufacturing process should also be analyzed for each specialty and custom product so that the most efficient methods and the smallest number of work steps can be used. The production layout can then be set up on a flexible basis, considering the various possibilities (e.g., two work steps or four work steps) and mix of products at any one time.

Through the elimination of the defense business, the present space being allocated is freed up for increased specialty and custom board production—a much more efficient use of this space. In addition, the conversion of the basic board business to a sales distribution-type business frees up additional production space. To the extent the company can have vendors ship directly to the basic board customers, additional space will be made available. At the minimum, some space will have to be allocated to receiving, repacking, and shipping of basic boards.

Proposed Plant Layout Flow Diagram. Our proposed layout flow diagram of the plant facility, which incorporates the preceding comments and recommendations, is shown in Exhibit 4.4.

Among the features and basic assumptions of the proposed plant layout intended to make it most effective are:

- The capability to schedule production, to the extent possible, by product or finished good part number through standardization and

EXHIBIT 4.4   PROPOSED PLANT LAYOUT FLOW DIAGRAM

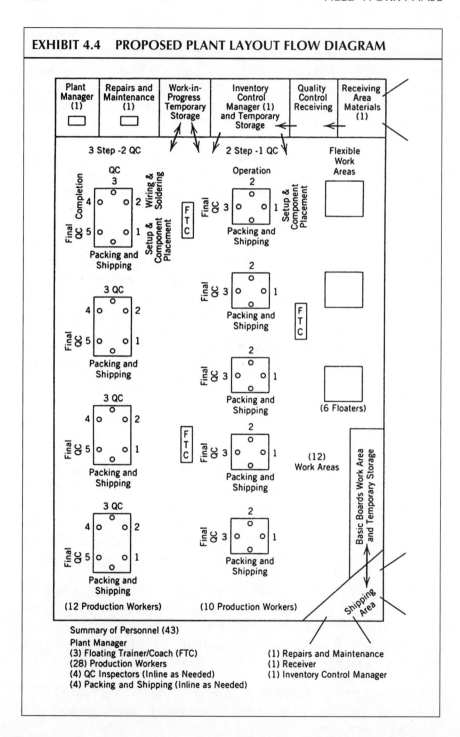

the ability to separate out add-on options. The proposed computer system specifications should allow for this capability.

- Flexibility in production as to type of processes and number of work steps. The proposed layout is set up for a three-step and a two-step process. However, any combination of work steps and quality control inspections can be set up based on the needs of the product to be produced.

- Use of production personnel based on job to be manufactured. To be most effective, each worker should be flexible as to what tasks he or she can perform—cross-training should be established.

- Effective use of three floating trainer/coaches who would be responsible for helping and facilitating each worker's doing what he or she does best even better, helping workers learn from each other, and improving areas where specific workers may need additional help.

- Use of a plant manager to ensure that everything is done correctly and on-time—from a helping and problem-solving standpoint rather than that of a disciplinarian.

Fix the Problem,
Not the Blame

- Quality control inspectors to be part of the production schedule and the production process, with the ability to move from job to job as needed without delaying the production process.

  Packers and shippers to work together online with the production teams so that as parts are finished, they are packed and routed to shipping for immediate customer delivery.

- A production schedule to take into account periods of under- and overcapacity conditions, with the company able to make effective decisions as to what to do. We recommend that when additional production facility is needed (more jobs than can be handled or overcapacity), the company network with other small electronics manufacturers to pick up the slack at previously agreed-upon costs, develop a network of ex-employees and others to come in part time, use flexible scheduling to increase production at no additional cost, and do anything that avoids additional employees, overtime costs, and so on. For undercapacity conditions (not enough work to fill plant capacity), we suggest that the company consider having the six floaters as part time or contractors, negotiate arrangements to perform work for others, attempt to bring projected sales in earlier, and the like.

- Eliminating the defense business and developing the basic board business as a sales distribution business, with a large amount of such basic board sales being shipped directly by the vendor to the customer.

- Coordinating customer sales with basic boards ordered from vendors, deliveries from vendors, and customer delivery schedules. In other words, having the vendor hold the company's inventory and either ship directly to the customer or deliver to the company based on the customer's delivery schedule. This will allow the company to get out of the basic board inventory business and only have to allow for a temporary storage area.

- Effectively controlling work-in-process so that no production jobs sit in production for any length of time (i.e., no more than one day of planned production queue time) and customer delivery schedules are met. This will then require only a minimum work-in-process temporary storage area, which can be better controlled and managed.

- Maintaining only one repair and maintenance employee to handle necessary and emergency tool repairs and maintenance needs. Other tool repairs should be sent to outside facilities, or the tools replaced. Ongoing maintenance, as previously recommended, should be contracted to the outside. Note that with each production crew responsible for cleaning up as they go, such maintenance should be kept to a minimum.

- Stressing specialty and custom boards as the company's main business, coupled with greater standardization, should allow it to better negotiate with its vendors as to parts needed, at what time (their delivery schedule coordinates with the company's production), and at what level of quality (e.g., 98 percent). In effect, the company is making its vendors the keepers of its raw materials inventory until needed for production. These factors (the pluses and the minuses) will have to be considered in negotiations with vendors. Should it be successful in this area, the company should be able to get by with one receiver, a relatively small temporary storage area for materials, and a clean job for the inventory control manager.

- The company may want to consider becoming a distributor for one or more of its major vendors. Typically, this approach allows the company to purchase product at a lesser cost, sometimes on consignment (not paying until used or resold), and to have materials on hand when needed. This approach will, of course, require more storage space, but it might be offset by savings and other benefits.

- Through the implementation of the proposed plant layout and its underlying features and assumptions, the company should also be able to increase productivity (we estimate by at least 25 percent), work more efficiently, reduce inventory levels, increase customer on-time deliveries and satisfaction, improve cash flow, and increase employee morale.

Inventory Control Systems and Procedures

The following five work steps were performed in the field work phase in accordance with our review work program:

1. Reviewed and analyzed present inventory control procedures
2. Determined the company's objectives for inventory control
3. Observed physical control and storage procedures
4. Reviewed inventory receipt and issuance procedures
5. Reviewed present inventory reporting system

Results of Work Steps

Present Inventory Control Procedures. The company presently has an inventory control manager, Jim Phillips, who is responsible for maintaining the computerized JOBEASY computer system and keeping raw material and finished goods inventories to a minimum. As a result of our review, we found that the computerized system is presently not being kept up-to-date because of the volume of inventory receipt and issue transactions. In addition, with present levels of raw material and components, and finished goods inventories far exceeding the capacity of storeroom facilities, these inventories are being stored all over the production facility. In effect, such physical inventory is getting in the way of production, is creating difficulties in locating inventory items, and is eroding effective inventory control, resulting in Jim chasing rather than controlling inventory. The end result at present is that there are no effective systems—computerized or manual—to control raw materials and components and finished goods inventories.

Objectives For Inventory Control. The company is presently operating on a crisis-oriented production system. That is, the order for the customer that screams or has a scheduled (sometimes promised) delivery coming up is pushed through production. This is a primary cause of the loss of control over these inventories. The company's objectives for inventory control, and proper levels of expected raw materials and components and finished goods inventories, should be as follows:

Raw materials and components. The production schedule is to be based on sales forecast and/or real customer orders so that the company can negotiate with its vendors as to price, delivery schedule (to coordinate with the production schedule), and level of quality (98 percent). With such vendor negotiations and performance in place, the company will effectively make these vendors its inventory storeroom until such materials are needed in production. These procedures will simplify inventory control systems, reduce in-house storage needs to a small temporary storage area, establish standard material costs, and eliminate the storage of materials throughout the production area.

Finished goods. Implementing a production schedule and control techniques based on real customer orders and related delivery schedules places the emphasis on production to meet all such delivery dates (98 percent on time deliveries). This ensures having all customer orders completed on-time for packing and shipping directly to the customer. Dependent on the degree of success, this effectively eliminates in-house finished goods inventory. With a 98 percent on-time delivery target, this should be accomplished, particularly by having packing/shipping working together online with the production teams.

Observation of Physical Control and Storage Procedures. As previously stated, present storeroom facilities are overextended, with raw material and components and finished goods inventories stored all over the production areas. At present, there are no adequate storeroom control practices. Present procedures are search and find on a crisis basis.

Inventory Receipt and Issuance Procedures. There are three receivers in the receiving area who are responsible for receiving all raw materials and components. At present, such items are ordered per customer order, and when received are to be taken to production. However, because production is never ready for the materials when received, and because the materials cannot be placed in the already overcrowded storeroom, the receivers must find a place for these materials somewhere in the production area. When the materials are ultimately needed for the customer order by production, it becomes a search and find mission to locate the appropriate materials. We observed a number of times when such materials could not be found and an emergency purchase order had to be placed, the materials were found but the quantity was short, or other different materials had been added. In effect, raw material and component issuance procedures are working in an uncontrolled environment.

Inventory Reporting Systems. Although the computerized inventory control system provides for effective inventory control reporting, it is not being used. Proper inventory control reporting encompasses:

Inventory level control via part categorization, such as:

- MRP II flexible (i.e., only order when needed for production schedule and planned customer delivery).
- MRP II fixed (standard lot size to be ordered based on ongoing repetitive type production).
- Reorder point/reorder quantity based. When the on-hand inventory level hits the reorder point, reorder the reorder quantity. Such a statistical inventory method could be used for spare parts, low-ticket/high-ticket sale items, and parts to be used universally.
- Min/Max levels for parts necessary to be on hand, but desirous to be kept to a minimum.
- Critical items necessary to be on-hand when needed. This category is normally for high-ticket or long-delivery-time items that

would cause production stoppages or difficulties if not available when needed.

Note that the inventory system should be flexible so as to allow for the identification and control of each material and component in inventory into one of these categories (or others) as defined by the user of the system.

- Inventory usage statistics as to items being used regularly and items sitting in inventory (becoming obsolete).
- Inventory cost control to prevent ongoing fluctuations in material costs. Proper vendor negotiations, as discussed, should prevent this from happening.
- Part similarity and replacement capability, by identifying for each item the finished product it goes into and what other material(s) could be used as substitutes.
- Quantity control, including on-hand, on order, and when due, reserved for specific production job(s), available balance, and over/under conditions.
- Integration with production schedule as to quantities needed and at what time, with flexibility to change as production schedule changes.
- Material requirements planning, which provides the ability to foresee all material requirements for the period in which customer orders are entered into the system.
- Inventory exception reporting, such as out-of-stock conditions, excess quantities, short conditions, no usage (possible obsolete), obsolete items, price variances, unusual usage (wide swings up or down), variance of physical count to system quantity, and inaccurate use in finished part.
- Cyclic counting procedures whereby the physical quantity on hand can be reconciled to the quantity shown on the record, with proper variance reporting so that differences can be investigated and properly corrected.

Note that all of these reporting features (and any others) should be incorporated into the company's proposed computer system specifications.

Four Business Concepts

Based on our work program, we performed the following four work steps as related to analysis of the company's four product lines—specialty boards, custom boards, defense business, and basic boards—and the determination of the course for each as a separate business entity:

1. Recast the past three years' income statements by these product lines or businesses.
2. Analyze customer statistics by product line.
3. Review present operations as to their impact on the product line or separate business concept.
4. Document recommendations for each of the product lines.

Results of Work Steps

The performance of these work steps provided us with the following information:

Recast of Income Statement. We reviewed the previous year's income statement and performed the necessary analysis to develop individual income statements for each of the four product lines. In the development of such income statements, we divided the line items for each of the product lines on the following bases:

Net sales. Analyzed actual invoices for the year and distributed sales amounts to the respective product lines

Cost of goods sold. Material, labor, and manufacturing expenses allocated to product lines based on totals derived from actual manufacturing orders and production data

Operating expenses. As actual costs related to product lines would be difficult to determine, we prorated these expenses based on the percentage of sales to total sales

The recast income statement is shown in Exhibit 4.5, together with some significant operating ratios (Exhibit 4.6). In addition, as we analyzed invoices and sales data, we also developed customer statistics (for major customers equal to approximately 80 percent of the total and all other customers) by product line (Exhibit 4.7).

EXHIBIT 4.5   COMPARATIVE INCOME STATEMENTS BY PRODUCT LINE

	Total Sales			Specialty			Custom Boards			Defense			Basic Boards		
	20X1	20X2	20X3	20X1	20X2	20X3	20X1	20X2	20X3	20X1	20X2	20X3	20X1	20X2	20X3
Net Sales:	3240	4680	6250	2400	2720	2950	840	1060	1350	—	300	800	—	600	1150
% of Total				74	58	47	26	23	22	—	6	13	—	13	18
Cost of Goods Sold:															
Material:	480	860	1130	330	360	380	150	170	180	—	100	190	—	230	380
Labor:	970	1170	1630	680	710	800	290	320	390	—	80	260	—	60	180
Mfg. Expense:	640	860	1040	450	500	520	190	180	200	—	70	160	—	110	160
Total Cost of Goods Sold:	2090	2890	3800	1460	1570	1700	630	670	770	—	250	610	—	400	720

Mfg. Profit:
1150 1790 2450 940 1150 1250 210 390 580 — 50 190 — 200 430

Gross Profit Margin %:
35.5 38.2 39.2 39.2 42.3 42.4 25.0 36.8 43.0 — 16.7 23.8 — 33.0 37.3

Operating Expenses:
530 940 1300 390 545 582 140 215 250 — 56 166 — 124 302

Operating Profit:
620 850 1150 550 605 668 70 175 330 — (6) 24 — 76 128

Operating Profit Margin %:
19.2 18.1 18.4 22.9 22.2 22.6 8.3 16.5 24.4 — (2.0) 3.0 — 12.7 11.1

EXHIBIT 4.6   SELECTED OPERATING DATA AND RATIOS

	Specialty			Custom Boards			Defense			Basic Boards		
	20X1	20X2	20X3	20X1	20X2	20X3	20X1	20X2	20X3	20X1	20X2	20X3
1. Analysis by Product Line												
Total Sales	2400	2720	2950	840	1060	1350	—	300	800	—	600	1150
Units Sold (in 1000s)	20.0	24.8	31.0	6.0	8.5	11.7	—	5.0	16.0	—	15.0	32.8
Average Unit Price	$120	$110	$95	$140	$125	$115	—	$60	$50	—	40	$35
2. Backlog Statistics												
Backlog	$272	$490	$990	$96	$195	$420	—	$50	$260	—	$112	$530
% of Sales	11.3	18.0	33.6	11.4	18.4	31.1	—	16.7	32.5	—	18.7	46.1
3. Accounts Receivable												
Total Amount	$450	$640	$840	$150	$250	$380	—	$70	$240	—	$120	$400
Turnover	5.3X	5.0X	4.0X	5.6X	5.3X	4.3X	—	4.3X	4.9X	—	5.0X	4.4X
Days Collect	68.5	85.9	104	43.5	86.2	103	—	85.2	110	—	73.2	127
4. Inventory												
Total Amount	$590	$700	1200	$210	$275	$540	—	$80	$340	—	$145	$600
Turnover	4.1X	4.2X	3.1X	4.0X	3.9X	3.3X	—	3.8X	3.8X	—	4.1X	3.1X
Average Age	89.0	86.9	118	91.3	94.8	111	—	96.1	96.1	—	89.0	118

EXHIBIT 4.7.	CUSTOMER STATISTICS BY PRODUCT LINE					
	20X1		**20X2**		**20X3**	
Customer Name	**Sales**	**%**	**Sales**	**%**	**Sales**	**%**
Specialty Boards						
Apex Electronics	$320	13.3%	$440	16.2%	$380	12.9%
Consolidated Electronics	160	6.7	180	6.6	140	4.7
Delta, Inc.	250	10.4	220	8.1	180	6.1
Kontrol Electronics	240	10.0	340	12.5	380	12.9
Peterboro, Inc.	460	19.2	440	16.2	460	15.6
Samson Electric	280	11.7	250	9.2	330	11.2
Textron, Inc.	180	7.5	210	7.7	230	7.8
Total Major Customers	$1890	78.8%	$2080	76.5%	$2100	71.2%
All Other Customers	510	21.2	640	23.5	850	28.8
Total Sales	$2400	100%	$2720	100$	$2950	100%
Custom Boards						
Delta, Inc.	$140	16.7%	$160	15.1%	$210	15.5%
Kontrol Electronics	—	—	110	10.4	140	10.4
Peterboro, Inc.	220	26.2	180	17.0	240	17.8
Roadway Spas	130	15.5	160	15.1	220	16.3
Samson Electric	160	19.0	180	17.0	210	15.5
Total Major Customers	$650	77.4%	$790	74.5%	$1020	75.6%
All Other Customers	190	22.6	270	25.5	330	24.4
Total Sales	$840	100%	$1060	100%	$1350	100%
Defense/Government						
Dept. of Defense	$—	—	$300	100%	$540	67.5%
EPA	—	—	—	—	80	10.0
Northrup—Subcontractor	—	—	—	—	180	22.5
Total Sales	$—	—	$300	100%	$800	100%
Basic Boards						
Ace Appliances	$—	—	$140	23.3%	$180	15.6%
Broadway Electric	—	—	—	—	120	10.4
Eager Specialties	—	—	120	20.0	150	13.1
Katchup Novelties	—	—	180	30.0	240	20.9
Seize the Day, Inc.	—	—	—	—	160	132.9
Total Major Customers	$—	—	$440	73.3%	$850	73.9%
All Other Customers	$—	—	160	26.7	300	26.1
Total Sales	$—	—	$600	100%	$1150	100%

CASE SITUATION: CLERICAL PROCEDURES

During the planning phase of the operational review, the reviewer observed that the office area of the Purchasing Department appeared to be grossly overstaffed. Accordingly, the review team wanted to perform operational review procedures during the field work phase and included such techniques in their work program. Although the office manager agreed that there might be a little overstaffing, she pointed out that a recent company report showed their office expense per purchase order processed was no higher than that of other similar companies, including those operating in lower-cost areas.

Reader: What work steps would you perform in the field work phase to substantiate your preliminary finding of overstaffing in the office area? Document your work steps here and then review the suggested work steps.

Suggested Work Steps

Work steps that could be performed include:

- Expanded review of office payroll to verify total office payroll costs being reported, and to make sure all costs are being included (e.g., the office manager being charged to the executive payroll)
- Interviews with each of the employees to determine exactly what tasks they perform and to what extent
- Layout/flow diagram of the office area and major operations to determine smoothness of operational flow
- System flowcharts for each operating procedure to determine whether procedures could be simplified, steps eliminated, and duties realigned
- System flowcharts and layout/flow diagrams of proposed systems for increased efficiency with reduced staff

Note: As a result of these review work steps being performed, it was determined that office costs were understated by $84,000 and that in actuality overall costs were greater than those of similar companies. You should be aware that such comparisons are only to be used as yardsticks and do not actually measure the economy, efficiency, and effectiveness of the entity being reviewed.

The performance of these work steps provided the following results:

- Purchase order processing simplified
- Manual procedures eliminated that were the same as computerized
- Number of reports eliminated where information was duplicated
- Personnel duties realigned, resulting in increased efficiency
- Overall staff to be reduced by six positions

    (Note that it is not the operational reviewer's responsibility to identify specific personnel to be dismissed, but only to document job positions or functions that can be eliminated. It is management's responsibility to decide what to do at that point—that is, reassign personnel, change responsibilities, dismiss employees, and so forth. The dismissal of good employees is to be discouraged.)

The total net annual savings resulting from these operational review findings and conclusions amounted to more than $250,000.

REVIEW QUESTIONS

1. Planning phase work identifies possible management weaknesses or operational areas for improvement. During the field work phase, additional information is gathered to determine whether an in-depth examination should be performed. What are the two major considerations in performing the field work phase?

2. What are some of the more common field work techniques that the operational review team can use during the field work phase?

3. An evaluation of systems flowcharts can provide information relative to the operations and activities in a process. What can the operational reviewer learn from these flowcharts?

4. Work papers serve as the connecting link between the operational review work program, the work done, and the review report. What are some of the uses that workpapers serve?

SUGGESTED RESPONSES

1. Planning phase work identifies possible management weaknesses or operational areas for improvement. During the field work

phase, additional information is gathered to determine whether an in-depth examination should be performed. What are the two major considerations in performing the field work phase?

Response

- Whether policies and related procedures and practices are in compliance with laws, regulations, policies, and procedures
- Whether operations are being carried out in an efficient and economical manner

2. What are some of the more common field work techniques that the operational review team can use during the field work phase?

Response

- Interviewing—responsible officials and direct operating and support personnel.
- Flowcharting—systems and layout flowcharts
- Ratio, change, and trend analysis
- Surveys and questionnaires
- Analytical procedures

3. An evaluation of systems flowcharts can provide information relative to the operations and activities in a process. What can the operational reviewer learn from these flowcharts?

Response

- How the operations are actually carried out
- The necessity or usefulness of the various steps in the processing of transactions
- The effectiveness of the controls provided
- Inefficiencies in the system, such as:
  - Unnecessary handling
  - Inefficient routing
  - Unused information
  - Inadequate planning or delegation of work

- Inadequate instruction to employees
- Insufficient or excessive equipment
- Poor utilization of computer processing capabilities
- Bad work scheduling
- Inappropriate work backlogs

4. Work papers serve as the connecting link between the operational review work program, the work done, and the review report. What are some of the uses that work papers serve?

Response

- Repository of information obtained.
- Identify and support problems, events, or actions occurring during the engagement.
- Support discussions with operating personnel.
- Provide support for report.
- Line of defense when facts, conclusions, or recommendations are challenged.
- Basis for supervisory review—work performed per the work program.
- Basis for appraising the individual reviewer's technical ability, skill, and working habits.
- Background and reference for subsequent reviews.

5

Development of Review Findings

This chapter reviews the attributes of a well-developed, convincing operational review finding and how the operational review team can put the relevant principles into practice.

This chapter will:

- Increase understanding of the importance of the proper development of an operational review finding.
- Familiarize the reviewer with the five operational review attributes—statement of condition, criteria, cause, effect, and recommendation—and their significance in the development of review findings.
- Increase knowledge as to how to use proper review finding presentation as an effective reporting tool.
- Provide hands-on experience in the development of operational review findings.

The most important single element of the operational review is the development of specific findings—this is the heart of the operational review. Furthermore, the acceptance and implementation of these findings by management is the yardstick for operational review success. A good rule of thumb is that if the review team can persuade management to accept at least 50 percent of its findings and recommendations, the team has been successful.

```
┌─────────────────────────────────────────────┐
│              All Review Findings              │
│             Have Common Structure             │
└─────────────────────────────────────────────┘
```

OPERATIONAL REVIEW FINDING ATTRIBUTES

To develop a specific operational review finding, the reviewer should be aware of, and use effectively, the following attributes or building blocks:

- Statement of Condition
- Criteria
- Cause
- Effect
- Recommendations

These attributes are summarized below:

Statement of Condition
- What did you find?
- What did you observe?
- What is defective, deficient, or in error?
- *This is the what-when-where-how step.*

Criteria
- What should they be?
- What do you measure against?
- What is the standard procedure or practice?
- *This is the comparing what is with what should be step.*

Cause
- Why did it happen?
- What is the underlying cause of the deficiency?
- Why have operations become inefficient or uneconomical?
- *This is the identification of the cause and not the symptom step.*

Effect

- So what?
- What is the effect of the finding?
- What is the end result of the condition?
- *This is the present or potential impact on the operations step.*

Recommendations

- What is recommended to correct the condition?
- What recommendation is practical and reasonable for acceptance?
- Who should implement the recommendation?
- *This is the what needs to be done to correct the situation step.*

OPERATIONAL REVIEW CRITERIA STANDARDS

Operational review criteria standards include:

Internal to the Organization

- Organizational policy statements
- Legislation, laws, and regulations
- Contractual arrangements
- Funding arrangements
- Organizational and departmental plans: goals and objectives
- Budgets, schedules, and detail plans

Developed by the Operational Reviewer

- Performance of similar individuals or functions (internal bench-marking)
- Performance of similar organizations (competitive benchmarking)
- Industry or functionally related statistics (industry benchmarking)
- Performance of functions outside the company (best-in-class bench-marking)
- Past and present performance of the organization
- Engineered standards

- Special analysis or studies
- Reviewer's judgment
- Sound business practices
- Good common business sense

Example

Objective: To provide meaningful, accurate, and timely financial information

Criteria

- Information provided is relevant to management's needs
- Information supplied is accurate
- Information is received in sufficient time after the reporting period to be useful for its intended purpose
- Information is easily understood

Reader: Check off those criteria in the preceding list that pertain to your organization. Are there other criteria used in your organization? What are they? Are these criteria effective in appraising and evaluating your organization's operating results?

SOME POSSIBLE TYPES OF CAUSES

Possible types of causes include:

- Ineffective or lack of adequate planning systems and procedures
- Confusing, ineffective, or faulty organizational structure
- Superfluous or unwieldy organizational hierarchy
- Lack of effective delegation of authority, commensurate with related responsibilities
- Inability or unwillingness to change, as exemplified by resistant attitudes: "We've always done it that way"; "It's industry practice"
- Lack of effective or sufficient management or supervision
- Inadequate, misleading, or obsolete policies, procedures, directives, or standards

- Lack of effective personnel procedures relative to hiring, orientation, training, evaluation, promotion, and firing
- Ineffective use of computerization
- Inadequate management and/or operational reporting systems
- Lack of effective communication
- Personal inadequacies such as negligence, carelessness, unfamiliarity with expected requirements, failure to use good sense or judgment, dishonesty, and lack of effort or interest
- Inadequate resources, including people, equipment, materials and supplies, and facilities
- Ineffective operating systems and procedures
- Deviation from expected standards or criteria
- Lack of knowledge that a problem or condition exists

Reader: Which of the preceding causes exist in your organization? How do they create operational problems? Are there other causes in your organization? What are they?

EFFECTS OF OPERATIONAL REVIEW FINDINGS: POSSIBLE INDICATORS

Possible indicators of the effects of operational review findings include:

Management and Organization

- Poor planning and decision making
- Too broad span of control and/or poor channels of communication
- Badly designed systems and procedures
- Excessive crisis management
- Excessive organizational changes and/or inadequate delegation of authority

Personnel Relations

- Inadequate hiring, orientation, training, evaluation, and promotion procedures

- Lack of clearly communicated job expectations
- Idle, excessive, or not enough personnel
- Poor employee morale
- Excessive overtime and/or absenteeism
- Unclear responsibility/authority relationships

Manufacturing and Operations

- Poor manufacturing methods (e.g., excessive rework, scrap, or salvage)
- Inefficient plant layout and/or poor housekeeping
- Idle equipment and/or operations personnel
- Insufficient or excessive equipment
- Excessive production or operating costs
- Lack of effective production scheduling procedures

Purchasing

- Not achieving best prices, timeliness, and quality
- Favoritism to certain vendors
- Lack of effective competitive bidding procedures
- Not using most effective systems such as blanket purchase orders, traveling requisitions, and electronic and telephone ordering
- Excessive emergency purchases
- Purchase of unnecessary expensive items
- Unmet delivery schedules
- Excessive returns to vendors

Financial Indicators

- Poor profit/loss ratios
- Poor return on investment
- Unfavorable cost ratios
- Unfavorable or unexpected cost/budget variances

Complaints

- Customers: bad products or poor service
- Employees: grievances, gripes, or exit interview comments
- Vendors: poor quality or untimely deliveries
- Production: schedules not met, material not available, deliveries not on time, quality poor, and so on

Reader: Which of the effects in the preceding lists exist in your organization? Check them off. What other effects can you identify in your organization? What are they?

REVIEW FINDINGS DEVELOPMENT CHECKLIST

Are any of the finding attributes—statement of condition, criteria, cause, effect, recommendation—missing? Why? What can or should we do about it?

- Is it a presentation defect or a symptom of an incomplete review?

Are attributes mixed up with one another in a way that impedes clarity?

- Are facts distinguishable from opinions?

Is the condition statement valid?

- Have we indicated that it is a fact or that it was told to us?

Are the *criteria* unclear or unconvincing?

- Are they weak or unsound from a professional standpoint?
- Do they contain subjective bias?

Have we explained the *cause*? Have we given the real cause, or is it a symptom?

- Is the information on the cause incomplete? Superficial?
- Does it get to the heart of the matter?

Has *effect* been understated? Exaggerated? Quantified when possible?

Is the *recommendation* unnecessarily vague? Too rigid?

- Does it take care of the past but not the future?
- Is it punitive rather than constructive? Is it out of harmony with cause?

Reader: Evaluate the preceding review finding development checklist. Is it sufficiently complete to ensure the correct inclusion of all attributes? Are there other items or questions that should be added to the checklist? What are they?

CASE STUDY: JOE SORRY INC., DEVELOPMENT OF FINDINGS

The review team, in the field work phase for the Joe Sorry Company, identified areas for the development of findings in the following functional activities:

- Manufacturing personnel
- Manufacturing systems
- Manufacturing facility
- Inventory control
- Product line operations
- Four business concepts

Manufacturing Personnel

Based on the completion of the review team's work steps in the field work phase relative to manufacturing personnel, the review team identified the following areas for the development of findings and recommendations:

- The present Vice President of Production position is unnecessary. As plant operations are presently controlled by Joe, based on his priorities, using a manual system, all that is needed is a plant manager or overseer. Ed Harrison, the Vice President of Production, should be used to get the MRP II system operational and improve operations per our review.
- The six foreperson positions are superfluous at present. All of these positions could be eliminated with minimal impact on plant operations. These personnel could be used to assist in implementing the MRP II system, and then at least three retained to function as database operators and analysts.

- The production team leaders (six) are really functioning as chief workers. Their emphasis is on controlling production and workers rather than being helpers. With increased backlog and the need to increase productivity and satisfy customer demands, these personnel (probably three) could be better used as roving trainers, coaches, and work facilitators. The other three could be better used as production workers to improve productivity and meet production and delivery schedules.

- The production teams (six teams of six members each) are currently divided by product type (one specialty, one custom, two defense, and two basic teams). This team concept needs to be reevaluated, as the present methods of production are contrary to this concept. By developing more efficient production methods that are flexible and relate better to the product being produced, the company should be able to increase productivity with fewer employees and less cost, reduce backlogs, better control inventories, conserve production capacity, and increase profits.

- The entire five-employee repairs and maintenance unit could be disbanded, with the possible exception of one person for regular tool maintenance and emergency repairs and auxiliary facility maintenance duties. Other tool repairs should be done on an outside vendor basis, or the faulty tool should be replaced. Ongoing maintenance of the work areas should be the responsibility of the work crews, with morning and evening maintenance jobbed to the outside.

- The packing operation should be moved online with production, so that goods are counted and packed as they are produced and ready for shipment.

- The packing/shipping and receiving areas need to be unclogged and cleaned up so that materials and finished goods can be separated cleanly and the two operations can function properly.

- Consideration should be given to controlling production by product rather than by customer order. This should work cleanly for basic boards and, to some extent, specialty boards. For custom boards, where there is a greater likelihood that another order for exactly the same product is not in the system, production by customer order may have to continue. The defense (government) business needs to be reevaluated as to whether the company should remain in this business.

- For those customers requiring an exact quantity or more, there should be an integration with inventory and other customer orders to determine whether this quantity is in-house or needs to be produced. If it needs to be produced, a small work crew of two individuals should be set up, which would be more effective than holding the order in a wait state.

- Receiving needs to be recoordinated with the production system. Once this is done and conditions have been cleaned up, there is no need for more than one of the three receivers.

- Inventory control has become uncontrollable, with the inventory control manager becoming a chaser rather than a controller. The inventory control portion of the MRP II system has to be reimplemented to minimize the amount of raw materials and finished goods on hand. The present chaotic condition of these inventories must be cleaned up and the system put back in place and kept that way.

- Quality Control work stations should be brought inline with production by moving the six QC inspectors into the production area. This would create the maximum efficiency for work in process and finished goods inspections. Quality control personnel should be used based on work requirements per job rather than the present assignment by production team. Work-in-process inspections should eventually become the responsibility of each worker.

  Raw material inspections should be set up close to the receiving area so that only acceptable raw materials are moved into production or temporary storage. Defective materials can be controlled and returned as soon as possible. Such receiving inspections should be looked at for elimination as vendor reliability increases.

  The results of these two findings should enable the company to reduce the number of QC inspectors from six to no more than four immediately, with ultimate reduction to two—for only necessary work-in-process and finished goods inspections.

- The QC manager's job at present is unnecessary. Each QC inspector is managing his or her own area, and the MRP II system for QC is inoperable, leaving very little for the QC manager to do. This function could be handled by the recommended plant manager.

- The two clerical staff assigned to QC have very little to do. They were hired for data entry, update, and inquiry of the MRP II system, which is not implemented. Present QC clerical requirements could be handled by a clerical pool operation. This whole area of clerical personnel assigned to all operating areas should be reviewed, as this appears to be a companywide, costly problem.

Development of Review Finding

Condition. Our review of manufacturing personnel levels and use disclosed the following:

- Vice President of Production is unnecessary at present.
- Foreperson positions (six) are superfluous at present.
- Production team leaders (six) are functioning as chief workers.
- Production teams (six teams of six members each) divided by product type are ineffective as to productivity.
- Repairs and maintenance unit (five employees) could be disbanded.
- Receiving can be accomplished by one employee rather than three, as at present.
- Quality control inspectors can be reduced from six to four, ultimately to two.
- The QC manager's job could be eliminated and handled by a plant manager.
- Quality control clerical staff of two can be eliminated.

Criteria. An efficient business operates with the fewest possible number of employees. Additional employees are not hired unless they are absolutely necessary.

Cause. The present levels of manufacturing personnel were established based on Joe Sorry's criteria to emulate his former employer, to control operations based on levels of management/supervision, and the requirements of an implemented MRP II system. These levels of personnel have never been reviewed as to their necessity, and have built up as the business has been monetarily successful.

Effect. The overuse of personnel in manufacturing operations has resulted in less efficiency and causing a number of functions and personnel to get in each other's way. In addition, the excess number of personnel is costing the company more than $500,000, as follows:

Vice President of Operations	$ 74,000
Forepersons (six @ $24,000)	144,000
Repairs and maintenance (four @ $24,000)	96,000
Receivers (two @ $10,000)	20,000
Quality control inspectors (two @ $22,000)	44,000
Quality control manager	26,000
Quality control clerical (two @ $16,000)	32,000
Total Cost of Personnel	$436,000
Less Cost of Plant Manager	36,000
Net Cost of Personnel	$400,000
Plus: Fringe Benefits @ 32%	128,000
Net Savings	$528,000

Recommendations. Eight recommendations were made in regard to manufacturing personnel:

1. Eliminate Vice President of Production and six foreperson positions immediately, or use these personnel to assist in implementing the MRP II system and procedures. You could also consider retaining at least three of the forepersons as data base operators and analysts, or hire less expensive personnel once the MRP II system is operational. Hire a plant manager or use the present forepersons in this capacity.

2. Use present production team leaders (probably three) as roving trainers, coaches, and work facilitators. Use the other three as production workers to improve productivity, reduce the use of overtime, and meet production and delivery schedules.

3. Reevaluate the production team concept of assigning a six-member work team by product type. Consider a more flexible method based on the product being produced.

4. Eliminate the repair and maintenance unit by using outside vendors for tool repairs or replacing tools, and using an outside vendor for morning and evening maintenance. One individual might be considered for retention for regular tool maintenance, emergency repairs, and auxiliary maintenance.

5. Recoordinate receiving with the production system and clean up present conditions, necessitating only one receiver.

6. Bring QC work stations inline with production, and use QC inspectors based on work requirements; set up raw material inspections close to the receiving area. This will enable the company to reduce present staff form six to four. By developing programs for vendor reliability (reducing incoming inspections) and placing in-process QC responsibility directly on the workers, QC staff can be reduced to two.

7. Eliminate the QC manager's position and have this function handled by the plant manager.

8. Eliminate the two QC clerical positions by using a clerical pool concept for this and other areas.

Manufacturing Systems

Based on the review team's completion of work steps in the field work phase relative to manufacturing systems, the review team identified the following areas for the development of a review finding:

JOBEASY MRP II software package is not presently being used. However, although this package is relatively complete for what it is intended to do, it is not compatible with this company's needs.

- The company must define its systems specifications for what it requires in a manufacturing control system, and then locate the software package that best fits its needs.
- The major elements to be considered in such a package include:
  - Sales forecasting
  - Production scheduling and control
  - Material requirements planning
  - Capacity requirements planning
  - Inventory control
  - Cost control
  - Integration with other systems modules (e.g., billing)
  - Operating reporting
- Manufacturing systems and procedures need to be modified to fit the various product lines: specialty, custom, defense, and basic. Consideration should be given to customer order control, work center by product line, QC procedures, packing and shipping concepts, use of

personnel (forepersons, production team leaders, six member production teams), and inventory storage and control.

- There should be concentration on main product strengths— specialty and custom boards—with manufacturing systems based on these product lines. Sales and engineering efforts should be directed toward more standardization among various customer needs, increasing the ability to more accurately forecast these sales.

- It should be determined whether the company should remain in the defense (government) business. It takes up an unequal amount of production space for its limited contribution to profits (if any).

- The basic board business, which is really that of a distributor, should become a business of buying and reselling (bypassing inventory and manufacturing processes).

- Production capacity is being overextended while customer order backlogs are increasing. Manufacturing systems and methods need to be streamlined so that productivity can be increased. Emphasis on specialty and custom boards, standardization, and manufacturing processes geared to individual products needs to be addressed.

Development of Review Finding

Condition. The defense (government) business is presently the smallest part of the Joe Sorry Company. In the current year, this segment of the business contributed $800,000 in sales and $24,000 in net income (estimated), out of a total of $6,250,000 (or about 13 percent) in total sales and $1,150,000 in net income (3 percent). However, this segment takes up about one-third of the total plant capacity (two work centers out of six)—an unequal distribution of production as compared with its monetary contribution.

Criteria. Production space should be allocated to the product lines that maximize the contribution to company income. Profit center segments should be analyzed periodically to determine their contribution relative to resource allocation, and then a determination made as to the course of action to be taken.

Cause. Joe Sorry decided to get into the defense/government business in the preceding year to help the company boost its total sales to meet his desire to achieve more than $500,000 in sales per month. Although this segment contributed $300,000 and $800,000 in sales for the last two years, it is not contributing its share of net income. The government is cutting back spending on contracts of this type, and those it does allow are expected to be performed at less cost than in the past. This segment has not been analyzed by the company and should be reconsidered.

Effect. The defense business is taking up one-third of the company's production capacity, while contributing minimally to company sales and net income. In addition, more profitable business segments (specialty, custom, and basic boards) are building up customer orders in backlog.

Based on disbanding the defense business, converting the basic board business to a sales distribution business, adapting our other manufacturing recommendations, and concentrating on the two core businesses of specialty and custom boards, we estimate the company can:

- Increase production by over 50 percent (at less cost).
- Eliminate present specialty and custom backlog ($1,320,000).
- Increase sales of specialty and custom products by at least 20 percent or $860,000 (20 percent of $4,300,000).
- Increase overall annual sales by more than $2,500,000.
- Provide additional net income of at least $625,000 (estimated at 25 percent of $2,500,000).

These figures do not include additional sales and net income to be generated by converting the basic board business into a sales distribution business.

Recommendation. The company should determine whether it should remain in the defense and government contract business. We believe the company would become more efficient and increase overall productivity and resultant net income by disbanding this segment of the business and allocating the resulting plant capacity to the other more profitable segments of the business.

Manufacturing Facility

As a result of the review of manufacturing facilities including present plant layout, production operations and procedures, product line concerns, and proposed plant layout concepts, the review team identified the following for the development of a review finding:

- Present plant layout and work flow based on six work centers by product line (one for specialty, one for custom, two for defense, two for basic boards) is causing uneven distribution of work and misuse of available space.
- Six-member work teams are an inefficient allocation of personnel and a negative factor in productivity. For almost all jobs, fewer personnel are required, normally two or three.
- The present plant layout and manufacturing methods have created the following adverse conditions:
  - Packing/shipping and receiving are becoming merged.
  - Inventory: raw materials, work-in-process, and finished goods are stored all over the production area, resulting in a lack of overall inventory control.
  - Quality Control performs offline inspection procedures, resulting in production delays.
  - Concept of six forepersons and six team leaders, one each for each work team, is counterproductive.
- Quality Control is housed in the office area and not readily available to production. Testing is done offline in a separate room at the back of production.
- The main production facility should be devoted to specialty and custom board manufacturing. Production should be based on realistic sales forecasts and/or real customer orders. Standardization of parts and products should be maximized by the engineering and sales departments working together.
- Manufacturing processes should be analyzed so that each specialty and custom product uses the most efficient methods of production.
- Production layout and procedures should be set up on a flexible basis, considering the number of work steps and mix of products at any one time.
- Strong consideration should be given to getting out of the defense (government contracting) business.
- The basic board business should become a sales distribution business, with vendors storing and shipping as much of the product as possible.

Development of Review Finding

Condition. The company recently (lees than six months ago) moved into a new production facility in a brand-new industrial park. However, it has not taken advantage of the increased space. Already, production facilities are cramped, with the six work centers encroaching on one another and inventory (raw materials, work-in-process, and finished goods) spread all over the production facility. Production space is so overcrowded and working conditions so cramped that Joe Sorry is already looking for additional plant facility space.

Criteria. It is management's responsibility to maximize the efficiency and effectiveness of limited resources such as finite plant capacity—maximizing productivity, minimizing inventory levels, and producing the best quality product at the least possible cost, resulting in customers satisfied as to product quality, cost, and on-time deliveries.

Cause. Production processes were established based on a standard work center of six work stations for the production of specialty products. This concept was implemented by Joe Sorry based on the methods used by his previous employer. The same manufacturing procedures were also employed with the other product lines—custom boards, defense business, and basic boards—as the company started production into these areas. However, for most of these products, including specialty boards, such a six-step process is unnecessary.

Effect. As a result of inefficient manufacturing procedures, the company has diminished its potential productivity, has inventory out of control, has production employees getting in each other's way, has increased the amount of rejected items and rework, is experiencing more than 20 percent overtime for production workers, and has a delivery on-time record of less than 40 percent. In addition, present manufacturing procedures are resulting in excess personnel and inefficient methods, which is costing the company more than $1 million annually in unnecessary costs. We estimate that the company can conservatively save more than $900,000 in annual personnel costs alone as shown in Exhibit 5.1 by implementing our proposed plant layout and related operating procedures.

These estimated savings do not include the additional amount of productivity to be accomplished through these recommendations,

EXHIBIT 5.1   SCHEDULE OF PRESENT AND PROPOSED PERSONNEL COSTS

	Present Condition			Proposed Condition			Savings	
#	Position	Dollars	#	Position	Dollars	#	Dollars
1	VP-Production	$74,000	1	Plant Manager	$36,000	—	$38,000
6	Forepersons	144,000	—	—	—	6	144,000
6	Team Leaders	132,000	3	Trainer/Coach	66,000	3	66,000
36	Production	576,000	28	Production	448,000	8	128,000
5	Repair/Maint	120,000	1	Repair/Maint	24,000	4	96,000
4	Packer/Shipper	52,000	4	Packer/Shipper	52,000	—	—
3	Receivers	30,000	1	Receiver	10,000	2	20,000
1	Inv. Cont. Mgr.	18,000	1	Inv. Cont. Mgr.	18,000	—	—
1	QC Manager	26,000	—	—	—	1	26,000
6	QC Inspectors	132,000	4	QC Inspectors	88,000	2	44,000
2	QC Clerical	32,000	—	—	—	2	32,000
71		$1,336,000	43		$742,000	28	$594,000
	Overtime 20% (Team Leaders & Production)	141,600			—		141,600
		$1,477,600			$742,000		$735,600
	Fringe Benefits @ 32%	472,832			237,440		235,392
	Totals	$1,950,432			$979,440		$970,992

estimated to be at least 25 percent of present specialty and custom board production levels.

Recommendations. Implement our proposed plant layout and manufacturing procedural change recommendations, as presented to company management together with specific recommendations, features, and basic assumptions at our final progress meeting.

Paramount to achieving the economies, efficiencies, and effectiveness of these recommendations are the implementation of the following 14 specific recommendations:

1. Disband the defense/government contracting business.
2. Develop the basic board business into a sales distribution–type business.
3. Stress specialty and custom boards as your main business.
4. Do production scheduling by product or finished goods part number.
5. Coordinate with materials vendors so that delivery schedules coordinate with your production schedule.
6. Standardize specialty and custom parts, with the ability to separate out add-on options.
7. Maintain flexibility in production as to the type of processes and the number of work steps.
8. Promote flexibility and interchangeability of production workers.
9. Effectively use floating trainer/coaches.
10. Integrate QC inspection and packing/shipping into the online production process.
11. Build effectiveness in responding to periods of under- or overcapacity plant conditions and the ability to make effective decisions.
12. Institute effective control over work-in-process directed toward meeting customer delivery schedules.
13. Institute effective inventory control procedures, resulting in lowering levels for raw materials, components, work-in-process, and finished goods inventories.
14. Change manufacturing attitude to one of increased productivity, working together and helping each other, fixing the problem and not the blame, and customer rather than crisis orientation.

Inventory Control

The review team's analysis of present and proposed inventory control procedures identified the following items for the development of review findings:

- The present JOBEASY computer system is not being properly maintained and kept up-to-date because of the volume of receipt and issue transactions.

- Raw materials and components and finished goods inventories are not being kept to a minimum; the present storeroom is filled beyond capacity, and materials are stored all over production.

- The inventory control manager cannot effectively do his job, resulting in his chasing rather than controlling inventory.

- Raw materials and components are being ordered based on customer order crises, rather than integrated with a controlled production schedule.

- Finished goods inventory is not being shipped out as completed in production based on customer delivery schedules, owing to short quantities, inability to ship, crises taking priority, and so on. This has resulted in finished goods being stored all over the plant facility.

- There are at present no adequate storeroom control procedures in place, with the storeroom capacity overextended, materials sitting all over the production area, and items located strictly on a search-and-find basis.

- Inventory receiving procedures are chaotic because materials received for a customer order cannot be placed into production or the overcrowded storeroom, but must be placed somewhere in the production area.

- When materials are needed to be issued into production, it becomes a search and find mission to locate the correct materials. Often the materials cannot be found, the quantity is short, or other different materials have been added.

- Although the computerized JOBEASY inventory control system provides for effective inventory control reporting, it is not being used. Accordingly, there are no proper inventory control reporting procedures, which has resulted in an uncontrolled inventory control environment. All of the desired inventory control reporting features should be incorporated into the proposed computer system specifications.

Development of Review Finding

Condition. Total inventory levels and corresponding inventory turnover and average age of inventory have worsened during the three years the company has been in existence, as follows:

Year Ending	Dollar Value	Inventory Turnover	Average Age of Inventory
20X1	$ 800,000	4.1 times	89.0 days
20X2	$1,200,000	4.2 times	77.7 days
20X3	$2,680,000	3.2 times	114.1 days

Inventory levels have also grown over the three years for each of the four product lines, as follows:

Year Ending	Specialty Boards	Custom Boards	Defense Business	Basic Boards
20X1	$ 590,000	$210,000	$ —	$ —
20X2	$ 700,000	$275,000	$ 80,000	$145,000
20X3	$1,200,000	$540,000	$340,000	$600,000

Criteria. Inventory levels and related investment in inventory should be kept to the absolute minimum as dictated by the demands of the specific type of business. Material inventory ideally should not be brought on-site until it is needed for production, but should be available at the appropriate vendor site. Finished goods inventory should be completed for customer orders and shipped and billed immediately, to the extent possible. Inventory should be controlled so as to meet these objectives, pushing toward zero inventory levels.

Cause. The present JOBEASY computerized inventory control system is not being maintained or kept up-to-date. In addition, the present storeroom is filled above capacity, with additional inventories stored all over the production area. There are no effective systems at present—computerized or manual—to control inventories.

The company is presently operating on a crisis-oriented production system—the order for the customer in need gets pushed through production. This is a primary cause of the loss of control over these inventories, as materials received cannot get into production and must be stored in the production area, and completed jobs are not being shipped on a timely basis and must also be stored in the production area.

Effect. The result of inadequate inventory control procedures is that raw materials and components and finished goods are stored all over the plant facility. Frequently, when materials are needed in production, the materials cannot be found (and may result in emergency reorders), quantities are short, additional different materials have been mixed in, and multiple quantities are found. This process of search and seek as materials are needed is also costly in terms of the time required to locate items, as well as inefficient production with these materials (and finished goods) in the way.

The related costs of having finished goods sitting in storage and not being shipped include the lost cost of shipping and collecting from the customer, the cost of carrying this inventory, the cost of not locating the order in whole or in part and having to redo production, the lost value of the money tied up in inventory, the cost to the company's cash position, the cost of customer dissatisfaction and the loss of customers. Although we cannot quantify many of these costs, such as for the process of locating inventory items or the cost of customer dissatisfaction and lost sales, and the cost imposed by the uncontrolled inventory control environment, we can estimate the cost of carrying inventory, based on the electronics industry standard of 20 percent of inventory value, to be approximately $536,000 (20 percent of present inventory of $2,680,000).

The present inventory condition will have to be cleaned up, with inventory maintained in a controllable environment, as it affects all aspects of manufacturing and is costly in dollars as well as manageable operations.

Recommendations. In the area of inventory control, the following seven recommendations were made:

1. Develop desired systems specifications for a proposed computerized inventory control system to include all necessary features to effectively control raw materials and components and finished goods inventories.
2. Through the disbanding of the defense business, turn the present inventory of $340,000 into cash by using in specialty or custom

board production, returning it to vendors, selling it to other customers, selling it to other manufacturers, and selling it for scrap. Finished goods inventory should be delivered and billed.

3. The basic board inventory of $600,000, which is mostly finished goods, should be reduced by turning it into sales and then concentrating on making this a sales distribution business, as previously discussed.

4. Raw materials and components inventories for specialty and custom boards must be controlled as to what exactly is on-hand and which parts can still be used in production. This should be coordinated with customer orders in-hand and in backlog so as to use these materials in production as soon as possible and not reorder them.

5. Raw materials and components that cannot be used (obsolete) or will not be used in production in the near term (within six months) should be disposed of (converted to cash) by returns to vendors, sales to others, modifications so that it can be used in production, sold as scrap, and so forth.

6. The remaining raw materials and components inventory (hoped to be minimum) has to be physically controlled and integrated with an adequate record keeping system.

7. Finished goods inventory of specialty and custom boards must be analyzed as to what orders are readily shippable, what orders need to be cleaned up or require additional production before they can be shipped, and what items are excess inventory. Action should be taken to convert excess inventory items to cash through special sales efforts to present customers. However, before this is done, management should determine the impact these sales will have on other present and future sales.

Product Line Analysis: Four Business Concepts

The review team analyzed present manufacturing operations as to their impact on the various product lines and identified their findings as follows:

Specialty and Custom Boards

Presently, these products are controlled by customer order. The main difference internally between a specialty and a custom order is that a custom order is normally to solve a specific problem (and the product does not exist), which requires more customer definition, more internal engineering, and a much longer lead time in development and manufacturing. A specialty board is also built for a special purpose, but it is a recurring or repetitive purpose rather than a new product design.

Typically, the company waits for the customer to order, then logs in the order on the production schedule as backlog awaiting availability. Scheduling of a specific order into production is done by Joe, based on his relationship with the customer or an impending customer crisis. There is no consideration as to maximizing production job mix or completion of orders by expected customer delivery date. We analyzed current customer order backlog and found almost 20 percent of the total backlog to be three months old or older. We were unable to determine how many orders customers canceled prior to getting into production, owing to the lack of adequate record keeping. We observed three different customer orders being canceled, in the total amount of $420,000.

The sales manager and the two sales staff assigned to specialty products are primarily responsible for order taking and customer contact (usually initiated by the customer). We observed minimum sales staff initiated contact with customers. Each order is treated individually, and unless it is a reorder of a product previously manufactured, the order write-up is routed to engineering for product design. Engineering looks at each such order separately, with little if any coordination between previous orders or other customer's orders.

Once the customer order is set for production, materials are ordered through purchasing, based on the engineering specifications. Purchasing is mainly processing purchase orders, with no coordination between customer orders or overall material needs. The company is paying higher prices for this type of ordering. Although this was not within the scope of our review, we analyzed four such transactions in which the materials were exactly the same and found that if the company had combined its requirements, it would have saved more than $4,000 based on the vendor's quantity discount policy. Purchasing is responsible for ordering materials for delivery at the time of the planned production start. However, other than setting up the scheduled delivery date, we found no evidence that purchasing controls such deliveries or that delivery dates are changed to correspond with changed production start dates. This has resulted in materials coming in and sitting in inventory all around the plant facility.

Once these specialty or custom orders are ready for manufacture, they follow basically the same path—the six step production process; offline initial, mid, and final QC inspections; and offline packing and shipping. As the company controls by customer order, we found many partial orders sitting around the manufacturing floor, some more than two months old (one order more than six months) from the date of production completion. This situation is extremely costly and has gotten out of control.

The customer service unit was established to deal with customer problems after the sale, delivery, and installation of the product. There are so many of these types of postinstallation problems that the present three-person unit is backed up more than a month. In fact, it has the two clerical staff dealing with these customer concerns as well. In addition, the numerous calls from customers (as to where their orders are, are they in production, when will they be shipped?) are being handled by this unit as well.

Defense Business

The defense/government business is primarily a contract bid business. The company presently has contracts with the U.S. Department of Defense, the Environmental Protection Agency, and a subcontract (also Defense Department work) with Northrup Company totaling $800,000.

Although the company has been able to increase its business in this area from last year (the first year of government business) from $300,000 to the present $800,000, this is basically a decreasing market owing to government cutbacks. In addition, bid prices are typically lower than can be achieved for commercial products, and internal costs for such things as bid proposing, negotiating, engineering, production specifications, QC testing, and special packing and shipping are much higher. This segment of the business is operating at marginal profit (estimated at 3 percent for 20X3) with many of its inherent costs not being accounted for.

The company presently allocates two each of six-member work stations, QC inspectors, sales staff, and engineers to this segment. This is not a growth area, and this allocation of plant facility and personnel can be better used in the main specialty and custom board businesses. The company should push to complete its current contracts and not pursue any additional business in this area. The sooner it can get out of this business, the more quickly it can start achieving the manufacturing efficiencies previously proposed with our plant facility recommendations.

Basic Boards

This segment of the business was started last year and has grown from $600,000 in sales and $76,000 in net income to $1,150,000 in sales and $128,000 in net income this year. The business is basically a purchase and resale of lower priced boards ($30 to $50 range) to repetitive customers. The company presently is bringing the completed boards in-house, using two six-member work stations to put the company identifier data (company name, logo, etc.) on the product and then repacking and shipping. As mentioned elsewhere, the company should pursue making this a total sales distribution business, with vendors shipping directly to the customers. Again, the two workstations can be better used by the specialty and custom board products.

This is a definite growth area, which should require minimal space and personnel allocation. Although profit margins are less than those for specialty and custom boards (11 percent as compared with 22 to 24 percent), we believe that this is additional revenue accruing to the company for each additional dollar in sales. Moreover, with the elimination of any in-house manufacturing (product identification), overall costs should be reduced significantly, even with additional vendor costs and possibly increased inventory investment and storage.

The company should stress sales efforts to increase sales to the many potential customers that are presently out of the company's customer base. Presently, five major customers make up close to 75 percent of total sales. As the sales staff is primarily on commission for sales shipped and collected, this should require minimal up-front, out-of-pocket costs. The commission (8 percent) is already calculated into the selling prices. This appears to be an untapped and profitable marketplace for the company. In addition, there is the residual effect of this part of the business bringing in additional customers for the specialty and custom product lines and vice versa.

General Findings

The product line analysis yielded five general findings:

1. Sales prices have come down each of the three years the company has been in business. This is a result of more competition, the customer's push to lower their costs and prices, and an overall down economy. The company can probably expect further erosion of sales prices for its products. While there is still good potential for increased unit sales, this never makes up for loss of

selling price. The company needs to become more competitive in engineering, manufacturing, and cost containment.

2. The total customer order backlog is currently more than 35 percent of last year's sales ($2,200 of $6,250); 33.6 percent for specialty, 31.1 percent for custom, and 46.1 percent for basic boards. This is entirely too high, particularly in light of the company's current shaky cash position. This backlog must be converted into sales and collections before it disappears to the competition.

3. Accounts receivable is at an uncontrollable level; the collection period has gone over 100 days. The situation is mainly due to Joe's push to get sales, create production crises, and relax credit terms, and to customer complaints and held back payments for less than quality merchandise.

4. Inventory levels have risen to uncontrollable proportions, with turnover ratios of about three times per year and the average age of inventory more than 100 days. This situation is not only contributing to the poor cash position, but is also clogging the plant facility.

5. The company is dependent on a limited number of customers in each of its primary businesses (specialty, custom, and basic boards). Although this is advantageous in working with these customers as to assisting them to define their needs, forecast their purchases, and more effectively service them, it leaves the company open to possible quick losses of revenue and income should any one of these customers pull its orders and start to use one of the competition. This is particularly critical with the company's current large backlog, inability to meet delivery dates, large amount of customer complaints, the amount of returned and defective merchandise, and so on. The company needs to better service these customers as well as look for an additional customer base.

Product Line Recommendations

Three recommendations were made in regard to product line:

1. *Specialty and Custom Boards.* Main business: Expand customer base; standardize materials and products to the extent possible; maximize manufacturing throughput to meet customer delivery schedules.

2. *Defenses Business.* Disband: Finish present contracts and get out of the business; reallocate space to specialty and custom products.

3. *Basic Boards.* Expand: Move toward a sales distribution business with vendors shipping directly to customers; minimize inventories.

Development of Review Finding

Condition. The company's backlog of customer orders has grown in each of the three years it has been in business, indicating an inability to service customers' needs adequately, as follows:

Year Ending	Total Sales	Backlog in Dollars	Backlog % of Sales
20X1	$3,240	$ 368	11.4%
20X2	$4,680	$ 847	18.1%
20X3	$6,250	$2,200	35.2%

The backlog has also grown over the three years for the three main product lines—specialty, custom, and basic boards—as follows:

	Year Ending	Total Sales	Backlog in Dollars	Backlog % of Sales
Specialty Boards	20X1	$2,400	$ 272	11.3%
Custom Boards		840	96	11.4
Basic Boards		—	—	—
Specialty Boards	20X2	$2,720	$ 490	18.0
Custom Boards		1,060	195	18.4
Basic Boards		600	112	18.7
Specialty Boards	20X3	$2,950	$ 990	33.6
Custom Boards		1,350	420	31.1
Basic Boards		1,150	530	46.1

Criteria. Customer orders should be put into production, manufactured, shipped, billed, and collected in the shortest time possible. In effect, the company is not in the customer order backlog business. Customer order backlog should be kept to a minimum—ideally at zero—so as to provide adequate customer service and not take the chance of losing the customer order.

Cause. The present policy of putting customer orders into production, based on Joe's relationship with the customer or a specific customer crisis, has resulted in many other customer orders not being placed into production and remaining as backlog. In addition, the inefficient use of plant facilities (such as two work stations for both the defense business and basic boards) has resulted in specialty and custom customer orders remaining in backlog. The use of inefficient production methods (such as forepersons, production team leaders, six-member production teams, and offline quality control and shipping/packing) has created less production throughput than possible, which has also had an impact on the amount of customer backlog.

Effect. The result of this buildup of customer backlog has resulted in reduced and canceled sales from some of the company's major customers. For instance, Apex Electronics accounted for $440,000 in specialty board sales in 20X2, but only $380,000 in 20X3. Discussions with this customer's representatives attributed the drop in business to Joe Sorry Company's inability to produce and deliver on time—otherwise, it would have increased its business. Other major customers related the same story.

The total of $2.2 million in present customer backlog could be converted to sales, producing an operating profit of approximately $400,000 (18 percent operating profit margin plus efficiencies).

Recommendations. Adopt the proposed plant layout and related features and production method changes, as recommended previously, so as to increase throughput and productivity of specialty and custom board orders, and at the same time phase out the defense business and move toward making the basic board business a sales distribution business.

CASE STUDY: FINISHED GOODS SHIPMENTS

You are the supervisor of finished goods warehouse operations for an electrical component manufacturer. At the end of each day, shipments are set up for effective loading onto company and private carrier trucks the following morning. Each planned shipment is palletized and waiting in the correct truck loading dock or position. As the trucks arrive as scheduled, the corresponding pallets are at the front of the line for efficient loading via mechanized fork lift equipment. This system has been in effect for more than a year and has worked quite effectively. As long as planned shipments are prepared the night before and the trucks arrive according to schedule, the system will continue to function properly.

This morning when you arrived, you found that the proper shipments were all in the correct loading position. It was less than 15 minutes before the arrival of the first trucks, and the forklifts should have been moving the items from the warehouse onto the loading docks. You were greatly concerned, as there was no forklift available for any of the 16 loading docks. If the materials were not ready, private carriers would not wait and would most likely charge the company for the time anyway. Your own company trucks could wait; however, it would cost the company to pay its drivers for waiting. In addition, the entire day's schedule would be out of whack, and items out of place or not picked up would have to be juggled around in the warehouse— and some customer orders would not be delivered.

You immediately went back to the forklift area and found all 16 pieces of equipment with dead batteries. A new policy had recently been installed to economize on the use of electricity, whereby all forklift equipment was to be recharged overnight, with the corresponding circuit breaker thrown by Hank, the forklift supervisor, prior to his leaving each night. However, last night Hank had to leave early, and no one else was directed to throw the circuit breaker.

Reader: Listed in Exhibit 5.2 are some thoughts you might have related to this situation. Place an X in the column of the attribute (if it is an attribute) that corresponds to each of your thoughts. The completed chart is shown in Exhibit 5.3.

OPERATIONAL REVIEW FINDINGS EXERCISE: IDENTIFICATION OF ATTRIBUTES

Reader: Each of the following statements has been excerpted from an actual operational review finding. Record to the left of each statement the attribute or attributes of a finding that would be associated with it:

   A = Condition, B = Criteria, C = Cause, D = Effect,
   E = Recommendation

The correct answers follow the exercise.

EXHIBIT 5.2   RELATING THOUGHTS TO ATTRIBUTES

	Condition	Criteria	Cause	Effect	Recommendation	None
1. This makes me angry.						
2. Let's borrow the three batteries from the raw materials storeroom forklifts.						
3. The forklifts won't start.						
4. We'll mess up the schedule.						
5. There should be system backups.						
6. It's too early in the morning.						
7. The circuit breaker wasn't thrown.						
8. Hank never told anyone what to do.						
9. I knew not to trust this system.						
10. The first trucks are due.						
11. Customers won't get their orders.						
12. Let's use the four new batteries in the storeroom.						
13. My boss will be angry.						
14. Critical items should have sufficient spares available.						
15. The batteries are dead.						

EXHIBIT 5.3 RELATING THOUGHTS TO ATTRIBUTES—SUGGESTED RESPONSES

	Condition	Criteria	Cause	Effect	Recommendation	None
1. This makes me angry.				X		
2. Let's borrow the three batteries from the raw materials storeroom forklifts.					X	
3. The forklifts won't start.	X					
4. We'll mess up the schedule.				X		
5. There should be system backups.		X				
6. It's too early in the morning.						X
7. The circuit breaker wasn't thrown.			X			
8. Hank never told anyone what to do.			X			
9. I knew not to trust this system.						X
10. The first trucks are due.				X		
11. Customers won't get their orders.						X
12. Let's use the four new batteries in the storeroom.					X	
13. My boss will be angry.				X		
14. Critical items should have sufficient spares available.		X				
15. The batteries are dead.	X					

Note that these excerpts are being used only for identification purposes and are not to be construed as good or excellent examples.

1. In fact, the total project cost was $16,685 on May 30, 20XX, with the institution sharing $2,302 of the total cost, which was more than the required 10 percent of the total project cost.

2. The above conditions existed because the property custodian did not have adequate control over the receipt of equipment.

3. Furthermore, procedures were not established to make a review of the activities of these employees.

4. The necessary ledger accounts should be established and maintained on a current basis to provide control over funds.

5. We believe that these procedures also result in wasted effort and unnecessary costs in maintaining duplicate records.

6. The Internal Revenue Service, Circular E, Employer's Tax Guide, states that students working for a school, college, or university are taxable for federal income tax withholding.

7. We were told that there were only oral contracts between the department manager and the individual performing the service.

8. In our opinion, timely and accurate final expenditure reports from local offices are essential to proper management and control of funds.

9. As a result, we estimate that the administrative costs of the department were overstated by $287,584.

10. The approval of project proposals is one of the Director's most important responsibilities, and we believe that management should take whatever action is necessary to improve review procedures.

Suggested Response

A = Condition, B = Criteria, C = Cause, D = Effect,
E = Recommendation

A
&
B
   1. In fact, the total project cost was $16,685 on May 30, 20XX, with the institution sharing $2,302 of the total cost, which was more than the required 10 percent of the total project cost.

C   2. The above conditions existed because the property custodian did not have adequate control over the receipt of equipment.

C   3. Furthermore, procedures were not established to make a review of the activities of these employees.

E   4. The necessary ledger accounts should be established and maintained on a current basis to provide control over funds.

D   5. We believe that these procedures also result in wasted effort and unnecessary costs in maintaining duplicate records.

B   6. The Internal Revenue Service, Circular E, Employer's Tax Guide, states that students working for a school, college, or university are taxable for federal income tax withholding.

A   7. We were told that there were only oral contracts between the department manager and the individual performing the service.

B   8. In our opinion, timely and accurate final expenditure reports from local offices are essential to proper management and control of funds.

D   9. As a result, we estimate that the administrative costs of the department were overstated by $287,584.

B   10. The approval of project proposals is one of the Director's
&   most important responsibilities, and we believe that manage-
E   ment should take whatever action is necessary to improve
           review procedures.

DEVELOPMENT OF REVIEW FINDING: EMPLOYEE LEASED AUTOMOBILES

As part of the operational review of the Purchasing Department, procedures were reviewed as performed by the Buyer II responsible for administering automobile leasing arrangements and the use of the cars by assigned staff personnel for the fiscal year 20XX. Analysis of these 87 leased cars disclosed that 24 cars were being used consistently for only short distances each day. In addition, 37 employees' personal cars, although not driven on company business every day, were still driven sufficiently on company business each month to justify using a leased car as opposed to reimbursing such employees at the rate of

30 cents per mile. Analysis of the entire situation, along with recommendations as to the reassignment of leased cars, demonstrated that the Example Company could realize a savings of more than $44,000 per year.

Reader: Develop an operational review finding for this situation using the five-attribute format of a finding. The suggested response follows the exercise.

1. *Statement of Condition*
2. *Criteria*
3. *Cause*
4. *Effect*
5. *Recommendation*

Suggested Response

The operational review finding in response to this situation was as follows:

1. *Statement of Condition.* Our analysis of the use of leased cars by your assigned personnel for the fiscal year 20XX disclosed the following:

   a. Of 87 leased cars, we found that 24 of these were not being used sufficiently to justify the lease payment. It would be more economical to the company to allow these employees to use their own personal cars and reimburse them at the current rate of 30 cents per mile.

   b. For 37 employees who presently use their personal cars and are reimbursed at 30 cents per mile, the total reimbursement for the fiscal year exceeds the cost of leasing an automobile.

2. *Criteria.* It is normal business practice to lease automobiles for employees in situations where the cost of the lease is expected to be less than the reimbursement for the use of their own cars.

3. *Cause.* We found that a procedure does not presently exist whereby the use of leased cars and personal automobiles on a reimbursement basis is analyzed periodically. Accordingly, the present situation has evolved over a number of years.

4. *Effect.* The present situation has resulted in the company's paying excess costs of more than $44,000 per year.

5. *Recommendation.* We recommend that a procedure be implemented to analyze the use of leased and personal automobiles on an ongoing basis. To correct the present situation, we recommend the reassignment of leased cars which will result in a present savings to the company of over $44,000 per year.

DEVELOPMENT OF REVIEW FINDING: LOW-DOLLAR AND LOCAL PURCHASES

As a result of an operational review of the purchasing function at the ABC Pipe Supply subsidiary, the following findings were uncovered:

Twenty percent of all purchase orders issued were for a value of less than $25.

Thirty-two percent of all purchase orders were for a value between $25 and $50.

Sixty-six percent of all purchase orders were issued to local vendors.

The cost to process a purchase order in the central Purchasing Department has been calculated at $51. Present Example Company policy states that all outside purchases (including those from subsidiaries) of more than $50 should be processed through the central Purchasing Department. Although the Purchasing Department has the authority to alter this policy, this has not been done for ABC Pipe Supply.

Reader: Develop an operational review finding for this situation using the five-attribute format of a finding. The suggested response follows the exercise.

1. *Statement of Condition* (What did you find?)
2. *Criteria* (What should it be?)
3. *Cause* (Why did it happen?)
4. *Effect* (So what? What is the effect of the finding?)
5. *Recommendations* (What is recommended to correct the situation?)

Suggested Response

The suggested finding is as follows:

1. *Statement of Condition* (What did you find?)
   a. Twenty percent of all purchase orders were for less than $25.
   b. Thirty-two percent of all purchase orders were for $25 to $50.
   c. Sixty-six percent of all purchases were issued to local vendors; should be part of another finding.

2. *Criteria* (What should it be?). In our opinion, purchase orders should not be issued for purchases under $50 by ABC Pipe Supply, as it costs $51 to process a purchase order in the Example Company central Purchasing Department.

3. *Cause* (Why did it happen?). The discussed conditions exist because present company policy states that all outside purchases over $50 must be processed through the Example Company Purchasing Department. The Purchasing Department, however, has the authority to allow operating departments and subsidiaries to purchase directly for amounts under a certain limit (i.e., $50). Such delegation of authority has never been made. Accordingly, the ABC Pipe Supply purchasing function presently processes all purchases as purchase orders, regardless of the amount.

4. *Effect* (So what? What is the effect of the finding?). The processing of purchase orders by ABC Pipe Supply for under $50 results in unnecessary purchasing, overstaffing in the purchasing function, excessive paperwork, and wasted time in the purchasing/receiving cycle. As a result, we estimate a realizable savings of approximately $87,000 (less the costs of alternative procedures) of purchasing function costs by eliminating the need for purchase orders for purchases under $50. (The reviewer provides the data to show the actual savings and what can realistically be reduced or eliminated, as well as the cost of recommended alternative procedures.)

5. *Recommendations* (What is recommended to correct the situation?) We believe that such a high proportion of small value purchase orders (52 percent under $50) warrants consideration of a more economical ordering system. We recommend that you consider the use of a telephone ordering system for purchases under $50. This system does not require the processing of a purchase order, but rather, the order is placed directly over the tele-

phone from a copy of the purchase requisition. We estimate that this system will reduce the cost of processing a purchase order by at least 60 percent of present costs, resulting in an annual savings of $52,200.

CASE SITUATION: SHIPPING AND RECEIVING PROCEDURES

During the course of an operational review at a plant location, the reviewers reviewed the shipping and receiving functions. As part of this review, they observed that freight cars at the plant location siding in shipping and receiving were loaded and unloaded by eight employees (two four-person teams).

Shipping Procedures

The reviewers observed that products to be shipped were all similarly boxed and stored on pallets in the storeroom. A forklift operator would pick up the loaded pallets and bring them to the appropriate shipping area. The eight-employee crew would then unload the pallet and stack the boxes in the freight cars, returning the pallets for reuse. This was in accordance with company policy, not to use pallets in shipping, as there had been past incidences of many lost pallets.

Upon checking with the client's 12 major customers (accounting for over 80 percent of total sales), the reviewers found that 10 of these customers were reversing the client's procedure (unloading the rail car onto pallets) and would be willing to provide the client with pallets so they could use palletized shipments.

Receiving Operations

The review of receiving operations disclosed that the bulk of freight car receipts were for commodities in 50-pound bags, 55-gallon drums, standard-size boxes, and so on. All of these were shipped in full railcars and stacked one on top of another. The eight-person crew would unload the rail car by stacking the items onto pallets. The forklift operator would then pick up the loaded pallets and take them to the appropriate storage area. The reviewers checked with the four major suppliers (more than 80 percent of material purchases) and found that each of them transported the product from storeroom to railcar on pallets and then had the product taken from the pallets and placed on the railcar—similar to what the client's plant location was doing with shipments as described previously.

Reader: What would you recommend to correct these operating deficiencies? The suggested responses follow the exercise.

Shipping Procedures

Receiving Procedures

Suggested Responses

The operational review recommendations are as follows:

Shipping Procedures

1. Palletize shipments for the 10 major customers who are willing to provide pallets, and who wish to have palletized shipments.
2. Conduct further review and study as to palletizing shipments for other customers who order in sufficient quantities and where palletizing would be appropriate.

Receiving Procedures

1. Provide the four major material suppliers with sufficient pallets to cover those that would be in transit, so that they can ship product to the client on pallets.
2. Initiate a policy to analyze all other receiving (and shipping) situations for the possibility of using palletized shipments whenever possible and appropriate.

The net cost savings of these recommendations for the initial year were estimated at $80,000 annually.

CASE SITUATION: ACCOUNTS RECEIVABLE AND COLLECTIONS

The review team performing an operational review of the accounts receivable and collection functions at a bank credit card operation, found that the policy for sending out delinquent payment notices was as follows:

- First notice: 10 days after payment due date
- Second notice: 10 days after first notice
- Third through eighth notices: every 5 business days
- After 60 days: to credit department for further action

Each overdue payment notice was prepared automatically by the computer system as long as the customer had any amount overdue. The last 60-day notice, prior to credit department intervention and credit card cancellation, was hand signed by the Accounts Receivable manager and sent "Certified Mail, Return Receipt" at a cost of $2 each.

The reviewers' analysis disclosed that many overdue accounts, approximately 28 percent, were of that status as the customer was questioning an item(s) on the bill and Customer Service was investigating. The client's policy was that the customer did not have to pay for an item under investigation. However, there was no mechanism to code the customer's account on the computer system. Generally, customers would phone Customer Service when they received the overdue letters, and Customer Service would tell them to ignore the letters until the situation was cleared up.

As part of the review, it was also discovered that another 24 percent of these delinquent payment accounts were for account balances of less than $20. The primary reason for most of these (more than 90 percent) was the questioning by the customer of improper computer recording of finance charges while an account was being investigated by Customer Service. Bank policy prohibited the waiver of any finance charge without proper approval by Accounts Receivable management.

Reader: What would you recommend to correct these operating deficiencies? The suggested responses follow.

Suggested Responses

The operational review recommendations are as follows:

1. Reappraise the philosophy of credit card operations being in the short-term loan business, thus increased emphasis on customers' paying down bills plus finance charges rather than on nonpayment of bills. The credit card operation makes more money on finance charges than on retailers' fees for using the charge card service (which does not usually cover operating costs). This is an area for further analysis.

2. Eliminate the practice of sending out delinquent notices for amounts of less than $20 (calculated as the approximate cost to process and follow-up a delinquent notice).

3. Revise the delinquent payment notice schedule to allow customers sufficient time to remit payments. For example: first notice 30 days after delinquency, second notice after 60 days, third notice after 90 days, fourth notice—termination.

4. Make the necessary changes to computer processing so that accounts under investigation by Customer Service can be properly identified, so as to eliminate the preparation of delinquent notices and the calculation of finance charges for these items.

5. Change the existing policy requiring Accounts Receivable management to approve the waiver of all finance charges. Allow for the delegation of these finance charge waivers to appropriate Accounts Receivable and Customer Service staff for amounts under a certain limit (e.g., $20).

The net cost savings of these recommendations were estimated at $140,000 per year.

REVIEW QUESTIONS

1. The most important single element of the operational review is the development of specific review findings. What are the two major steps involved in the development of a review finding?

2. What are the five attributes of operational review findings? Discuss each one briefly.

3. What are the six steps mentioned in this chapter in the basic approach to developing an operational review finding?

SUGGESTED RESPONSES

1. The most important single element of the operational review is the development of specific review findings. What are the two major steps involved in the development of a review finding?

Response

- Data collection, relative to obtaining as much pertinent, significant information about each finding as is realistic
- Evaluating the finding, in terms of cause, effect, and possible courses of corrective action

   2. What are the five attributes of operational review findings? Discuss each one briefly.

Response

- Statement of Condition:
    - What did you find? What did you observe? What, when, where, how step.
- Criteria:
    - What should it be? What do you measure against?
    - What is the standard procedure or practice?
    - Note: In the absence of standards, use alternative approaches:
      —Comparative analysis
      —The borrowed standard
      —The test of reasonableness
- Effect:
    - So what? What is the effect of your finding?
- Cause:
    - Why did it happen?
- Recommendation:
    - What can correct the situation?

   3. What are the six steps mentioned in this chapter in the basic approach to developing an operational review finding?

Response

- Review and analyze operating policies, systems, and procedures and the practices actually being followed to determine whether they will produce the desired results, if performed correctly and adequately.

- Accumulate valid evidence related to the operational area under review and its corresponding transactions.

- Compare operational transactions with systems and procedures to determine whether procedures are being followed correctly and desired results are being achieved.

- Quantify the effect in dollars lost, ineffectiveness, and so on resulting in the failure to achieve desired results.

- Determine the cause why desired results are not being achieved, together with appropriate and sufficient evidence.

- Develop recommendations as to how to improve the situation as to economy, efficiency, and/or effectiveness.

6

Reporting Phase

This chapter reviews the principles of good operational review reporting that should ensure the review team greater success in getting operations management and staff to implement recommended operational improvements. Remember, to be successful, the review team does not have to persuade management to follow all recommendations; action on more than 50 percent of the significant findings is usually adequate.

This chapter will:

- Increase understanding as to the purpose of good operational review reporting
- Increase knowledge of the types of operational review reporting— oral and written, informal and formal
- Increase understanding of the basic characteristics of good operational review reporting
- Increase ability to decide the significance of findings—what to include in the formal report and what to report informally
- Increase understanding of the types of information to be included in the operational review report
- Increase understanding of the relationship of developed operational review findings to the reporting phase
- Increase knowledge of positive factors related to more effective written communications

• Increase understanding of the format of a completed operational review report by presenting a sample letter and regular report

---

> ### To Be Successful, the Report
> ### Must Persuade Management to
> ### Follow Its Recommendations

CHARACTERISTICS OF GOOD REPORTING

There are many characteristics of good reporting. Among the most basic:

• Significance
• Usefulness and timeliness
• Accuracy and adequacy of support
• Convincingness
• Objectivity and perspective
• Clarity and simplicity
• Conciseness
• Constructiveness of tone
• Organization and positivity

> ### Good Reporting Equals
> ### Good Results

Reader: Discuss the value of each of the listed characteristics of good reporting with regard to their importance in convincing and persuading management to take the appropriate action.

EXAMPLES OF REPORTING OPERATIONAL REVIEW RESULTS

Each of the following three examples relates to the reporting of an operational review result. An example of unclear writing is shown for each one. Remember, reporting needs to be objective, clear, concise, and understandable. The reader needs to know what is actually being reported—for example, what is wrong and what needs to be done.

Reader: Rewrite each of the three examples in a clearer, more easily understood language so that the reader understands what is wrong and what needs to be done.

Example 1: Inadequate Facts

The Purchasing Department, many times could not process purchase requisitions due to inadequate controls and procedures relative to the proper recording of account charges by the various operating departments.

Rewrite:

Example 2: Use of Internal or Technical Jargon

Inventory requirements in the ASP are determined by the use of RP and EOQ formulas. IC is responsible for updating these formulas, together with related min and max levels.

Rewrite:

Example 3: Unclear Conclusion or Recommendation

The existence of an in-house equipment and maintenance unit cannot be justified as related to the economies of using an outside service organization.

Rewrite:

Suggested Rewrites

Example 1: Inadequate Facts

The Purchasing Department many times could not process purchase requisitions due to inadequate controls and procedures relative to the proper recording of account charges by the various operating departments.

Rewrite:

The Purchasing Department is delegated authority to process all departmental purchase requisitions for purchases over $50. However, each operating department is responsible for proper coding of account charges per the company's approved chart of accounts. Purchasing Department personnel do not have the authority to change any incorrect account charges recorded at the departmental level, but are required to review them for completeness and accuracy and return any improper purchase requisitions to the originating department for correction. We analyzed 364 purchase requisitions submitted by various operating departments and found 146 to have incorrect account coding.

Example 2: Use of Internal or Technical Jargon

Inventory requirements in the ASP are determined by the use of RP and EOQ formulas. IC is responsible for updating these formulas, together with related min and max levels.

Rewrite:

Inventory requirements for items included in the Accelerated Surplus Program are determined by the use of reorder point and economic order quantity formulas. The Inventory Control Unit is responsible for updating these formulas, together with the establishment of quantity on hand minimum and maximum levels.

Example 3: Unclear Conclusion or Recommendation

The existence of an in-house equipment and maintenance unit cannot be justified as related to the economies of using an outside service organization.

Rewrite:

The present in-house equipment maintenance unit is costing the company more than $280,000 per year. Based on our analysis of completed equipment maintenance work orders for last year, we found the work load of the equipment maintenance unit to be less than 40 percent of total available work hours. This has resulted in many of the eight employees assigned to the equipment maintenance unit being idle a good part of their working hours. In addition, our analysis of completed work orders disclosed an average overage of 160 percent of standard. By contracting with an outside service firm at an annual cost of $60,000 to handle the present equipment maintenance work load, the company can obtain a net savings of $220,000 per year. The present eight-person equipment maintenance unit should be reassigned to production units where needed, such as production scheduling, inventory control, subassembly, and assembly operations.

ABCS OF EFFECTIVE REPORT WRITING

For the review team to produce more effective reports, it sometimes helps to think in terms of the ABCs of effective report writing, as follows:

Accuracy. The reviewers should be accurate in presenting facts, spelling, punctuation, grammar, and usage. Accurate description of problems, conditions, and situations is an absolute necessity. If management is to rely on the information given by the review team, it must be accurate in all respects. The reviewers cannot shade the facts or manipulate them to their unfair advantage. If they do, they shake management's faith in their reporting.

Brevity. The reviewers should strive for brevity, using the short, concrete word and the short, simple sentence. Their report should be exactly the right length—long enough to cover the subject, short enough to be interesting. Lengthy narratives and long paragraphs are to be avoided; listings and tabulations should be used instead.

Confidence. The reviewers should be confident that they have something of value to say. If they are—and this is basic to an effective report—then they must say it confidently, positively, and sincerely, as well as simply and directly.

Defense. As the saying goes, there are two sides to every story, so the reviewers should be sure to present management's defense and reaction to their findings and recommendations. Failure to present management reactions detracts from the value of the report to management and wastes time. Management may agree with the review teams' findings and conclusions in whole or in part, or may totally disagree.

Explain. The reviewers must explain, interpret, and describe, since many times facts have to be interpreted for management. Tabulations, charts, and graphs may present the overall picture, but the reviewers have to tell management what the facts mean.

Format. In presenting the review report, there is the conflict between formatting it in free style, based on the creativity of the reviewers, or using a strict formula in which the reviewers fill in the spaces. A recommended middle ground is to define some basic directions, but to avoid strict standardization.

> ### Remember Your ABCs
> ### of Effective Reporting

CASE STUDY: JOE SORRY, INC., REPORTING PHASE

In the reporting phase of the operational review, the review team communicates the results of its review and analysis of operations. As demonstrated in the results of our field work steps, significant findings were identified and developed for the Joe Sorry Company. These findings were presented to company and operational management during the course of the field work phase, in both oral presentation and written formats, for management's response.

In fact, management and operations personnel have already begun to implement the steps necessary to correct the identified deficiencies. For instance, the following review findings and related recommendations were being addressed and corrective action implemented as we concluded the operational review:

- Phasing out of the defense business
- Taking steps to become a sales distributor of basic boards, and negotiating with vendors to ship directly to customers
- Engineering review of product specifications of specialty and custom boards for standardization of parts and manufacturing processes, combining of finished goods products, product development procedures, and coordination with sales and customers

- Revamping of manufacturing procedures for specialty and custom boards, including the plant manager concept, elimination of foreperson position, use of three team leaders as trainer/coaches, establishment of manufacturing processes or work steps based on simplest requirements, use of online QC and packing/shipping
- Proactive sales efforts to work with major customers and others to help them forecast their needs, develop meaningful production and delivery schedules, and provide improved customer service
- Initiating a project, with our assistance, to develop computer systems specifications as to operating, reporting, and control requirements

In this situation with the Joe Sorry Company, because it had already begun to implement many of our major review findings, our report became more a summary of the operational review performed, which documented:

- What we had accomplished as a result of the review
- What we found during the course of the review
- The effect or extent of the operational deficiencies disclosed
- The steps that have been taken by company personnel thus far to correct these situations

The review report (both oral and written) is also the review team's opportunity to get the undivided attention of management and operations personnel. It also provides the opportunity to display the benefits of the operational review process and what the operational review team has to offer. The goal of operational review reporting is to provide useful and timely information on significant operational areas in need of positive improvement and to recommend specific improvements in the conduct of these operations.

Operational review reporting, therefore, has two major functions, which are to communicate the results of the review and to persuade management to take the appropriate action. Remember, to be successful, the review team does not have to persuade management to follow all of its recommendations—action on more than 50 percent of the significant findings is usually adequate.

We closed out the operational review of the Joe Sorry Company with an oral presentation highlighting the results of the review, as well as a written report summarizing what we had accomplished as shown in Exhibit 6.1.

EXHIBIT 6.1   JOE SORRY, INC.: OPERATIONAL REVIEW REPORT

Mr. Joseph Sorry, President
Joe Sorry, Inc.
#8 Lucky Chance Industrial Park
Broadacres, XX XXXXX

Dear Mr. Sorry:

Reider Associates is pleased to submit this report to the Joe Sorry
Company relative to our findings and conclusions as a result of our
review and analysis of your manufacturing-related activities. During the
course of this operational review, we reviewed and analyzed the
following areas:

1. Manufacturing personnel, including assigned responsibilities,
   number of personnel, use of personnel, and work accomplished
2. Manufacturing systems, including present and proposed computer
   systems, manufacturing procedures and operations, and operating
   reporting requirements
3. Manufacturing facility and production procedures, including
   present and proposed plant layout, and production operations as
   related to specialty boards, custom boards, defense business, and
   basic boards
4. Inventory control systems and procedures, including present
   procedures, objectives for inventory control, physical control and
   storage procedures, inventory receipt and issuance procedures, and
   inventory reporting systems
5. Four business concepts, including recast of income statements by
   product line, customer statistics by product line, present operations
   by product line, and related recommendations

BACKGROUND

Joe Sorry Company senior management has been aware of the need for a
comprehensive operational review and analysis of manufacturing
procedures. Although the company has had good success in the areas of
sales and net income in the three years it has been in business, customer
order backlog and inventory levels have greatly increased. In addition,
manufacturing operations have not been able to keep up with demand,
and too many customer delivery dates have been missed and the number

EXHIBIT 6.1   CONTINUED

of rejected and returned items has increased. Accounts receivable have also gotten large and out of control. As a result of all of these factors, the company is presently experiencing a cash liquidity problem.

Although the scope of manufacturing activities has greatly expanded in response to these changing internal and external requirements, basic production related procedures have remained relatively stable since the start of the company. These procedures were primarily those used by Joe's former employer and are no longer accomplishing economical, efficient, and effective manufacturing. Additional procedures, if any, have been implemented solely to address specific crisis-type situations. Accordingly, this method of operation has produced an operating environment characterized by individualized procedures that do not always efficiently meet manufacturing operating and reporting needs. In recognition of this need, Joe Sorry Company management engaged Reider Associates to assist in performing an operational review of its manufacturing procedures.

SCOPE OF OUR REVIEW

For the purpose of identifying areas for improvements, our review and analysis of present manufacturing procedures included the following work steps or tasks:

1. *Personnel Interviews.* We met with company and manufacturing management and operations personnel to analyze present operating procedures and associated areas for improvement, as well as to determine future requirements. These discussions and reviews provided us with a working knowledge of:
   - Present operating procedures
   - Timing and flow of current data
   - Problem areas, particularly the critical ones
   - Coordination and related reporting and communication networks between departments
   - Information requirements, present and future needs
2. *Functional Activities.* Review of systems and procedures presently required to perform such manufacturing related functions as:
   - Production Department organization structure and related functional job descriptions, including responsibility and authority relationships

---

EXHIBIT 6.1   CONTINUED

- Production Department planning systems, including the establishment of goals, objectives, and detail plans, and the integration of such plans with overall organizational planning systems
- Personnel practices, including employee hiring, orientation, training, evaluation, job expectations, monitoring and control
3. *Manufacturing Systems.* Observation and analysis of manufacturing operating and reporting systems, including:
    - Manufacturing plant layout
    - Manufacturing systems and procedures
    - Inventory control systems and procedures
    - Operational reporting: manual and computerized
    - Relationship to product lines: specialty, custom, defense, and basic boards

OBJECTIVES

The objectives of this operational review were to identify the work being performed by Manufacturing Department personnel in order to formulate future operational requirements, as well as to make observations and recommendations as to the manner in which immediate and short-term improvements could be realized. The principal focus of our efforts was toward developing operating procedures that would provide optimum efficiencies in meeting Joe Sorry Company requirements.

OUR APPROACH

Our approach to reviewing Manufacturing Department operating procedures involved an analysis of operations according to the existing organization structure. Accordingly, we divided our review into the Manufacturing Department functional activity areas as follows:

- Vice President of Production
- Manufacturing operations:
    - (6) Forepersons
    - (6) Production team leaders
    - (6) Production teams of six members each
- (5) Repairs and Maintenance

EXHIBIT 6.1   CONTINUED

- (4) Packers and Shippers
- (3) Receivers
- Inventory Control Manager
- Quality Control
  - Manager
  - (6) Inspectors
  - (2) Clerical Staff

REPORTING

At the conclusion of each of the five stages of analysis—manufacturing personnel, manufacturing systems, manufacturing facility and production procedures, inventory control, and the four business concepts—we prepared a review of findings and recommendations that were submitted to appropriate company management and operations personnel in oral presentations together with written documentation. Accordingly, these presentation materials are not being included in this report. Basically, our review of findings discussed present deficiencies, suggested methods of improvement, and identified areas where economies and efficiencies could be achieved immediately or as a result of additional work efforts.

In addition, we presented a conceptualized plan for an integrated manufacturing control operating and reporting computer system that was designed to meet Joe Sorry Company requirements as determined through our operational review and analysis. The proposed system would include all present manufacturing oriented manual and computer applications effectively integrated with:

- Manufacturing control systems, including such areas as sales forecasting, order entry, production scheduling and control, material requirements planning, capacity requirements planning, shop floor control, and inventory control procedures
- Cost accounting systems, including cost control (products, customers, and functions), cost-pricing-volume analysis, breakeven analysis, cost variance reporting, and job cost analysis.
- General ledger accounting system, particularly the sales forecast/expense budget/profit plan, purchasing, accounts payable, labor distribution and payroll, and accounts receivable modules

Such an integrated computer system would use common data sources, many of which exist presently, to efficiently update the system.

EXHIBIT 6.1   CONTINUED

SUMMARY OF FINDINGS AND RECOMMENDATIONS

We are summarizing our major findings below for your review. The details of each finding have been submitted under separate cover for your information. We believe that should you implement all of these recommendations, Joe Sorry Company could realize an estimated annual savings of $1,506,992, increase in sales of $1,935,000, and an increase in net income of $1,025,000, as well as increases in other economies, efficiencies, and effectiveness that cannot be qualified in dollars at this time. A summary of our major findings and recommendations, together with these dollar estimates, is shown as Attachment A of this report.

We are also attaching a list of other findings identified during the course of our review that we believe should be brought to your attention for remedial action to achieve increased economies, efficiencies, and effectiveness of results in the manufacturing-related areas.

    *   *   *   *   *   *

We appreciate the courtesies and cooperation extended to us by Joe Sorry Company personnel during the course of this operational review. We are, of course, prepared to discuss any aspects of this operational review or specific items mentioned in this report with you, should you so desire. In addition, we are available to provide further consultative assistance in the operational review of other functional areas, as well as work with you in the implementation of recommendations mentioned in this report. We appreciate the opportunity to assist Joe Sorry Company management in accomplishing the results of this operational review and look forward to continued good relations between Reider Associates and Joe Sorry Company.

Very truly yours,

_____

Rob Reider, President
REIDER ASSOCIATES

EXHIBIT 6.1   CONTINUED

JOE SORRY, INC.
MANUFACTURING DEPARTMENT OPERATIONAL REVIEW REPORT
TABLE OF CONTENTS

		Page
I.	MANUFACTURING PERSONNEL	I–1
	1. Vice President of Production	I–1
	2. Forepersons	I–1
	3. Production Team Leaders	I–1
	4. Production Teams	I–1
	5. Repairs and Maintenance	I–1
	6. Packing Operation	I–2
	7. Packing/Shipping and Receiving Areas	I–2
	8. Controlling Production by Product	I–2
	9. Short Small Quantities	I–2
	10. Receiving Function	I–3
	11. Inventory Control	I–3
	12. Quality Control	I–3
	13. Quality Control Manager	I–3
	14. Quality Control Clerical Staff	I–3
	Quantification of Findings	I–4
	Summary of Recommendations	I–4
II.	MANUFACTURING SYSTEMS	II–1
	1. Manufacturing Control Computer System	II–1
	2. Systems Specifications	II–1
	3. Computer Software Package Contents	II–1
	4. Modifications as to Product Lines	II–1
	5. Concentration on Specialty and Custom Boards	II–1
	6. Defense Business	II–2
	7. Basic Board Business	II–2
	8. Productivity Increases	II–2
	Quantification of Findings	II–2
	Summary of Recommendations	II–3

EXHIBIT 6.1   CONTINUED

III. MANUFACTURING FACILITY AND PRODUCTION
     PROCEDURES   III–1
     1. Uneven Distribution of Work   III–1
     2. Six-Member Work Teams Inefficient   III–1
     3. Present Plant Layout Concerns   III–1
     4. Quality Control Inefficiencies   III–1
     5. More Effective Use of Production Facilities   III–2
     6. More Efficient Production Methods   III–2
     7. Flexible Production Procedures   III–2
     8. Disbanding Defense Business   III–2
     9. Basic Board Business—Sales Distributorship   III–2
         Quantification of Findings   III–2
         Summary of Recommendations   III–4

IV. INVENTORY CONTROL SYSTEMS AND PROCEDURES   IV–1
     1. Misuse of Present Computer System   IV–1
     2. Excessive Inventory Levels   IV–1
     3. Ineffective Inventory Control Manager   IV–1
     4. Crisis Ordering of Raw Materials and Components   IV–1
     5. Customer Orders Not Being Shipped   IV–1
     6. Inadequate Storeroom Control Procedures   IV–1
     7. Chaotic Inventory Receiving Procedures   IV–1
     8. Inability to Locate Needed Materials   IV–2
     9. Uncontrolled Inventory Control Environment   IV–2
         Quantification of Findings   IV–2
         Summary of Recommendations   IV–3

V. FOUR BUSINESS CONCEPTS   V–1
     1. Specialty and Custom Boards—Main Businesses   V–1
     2. Convert Defense Business Space for Main Businesses   V–1
     3. Expand Basic Board Business   V–1
     4. Increase Competitiveness   V–1
     5. Convert Backlog into Sales   V–2
     6. Collect Accounts Receivable   V–2
     7. Uncontrollable Inventory Levels   V–2
     8. Service Major Customers—Increase Customer Base   V–2
     9. Revise Present Operations   V–2
         Quantification of Findings   V–3
         Summary of Recommendations   V–4

EXHIBIT 6.1   CONTINUED

VI. PROPOSED INTEGRATED COMPUTER SYSTEM   VI–1
    1. Proposed Computerization   VI–1
    2. Additional Personnel   VI–1
    3. Computer Processing Priorities   VI–1
    4. Computer Equipment Requirements   VI–2

ATTACHMENTS
A: Summary of Major Findings and Recommendations   A–1
B: Other Areas for Review   B–1

EXHIBIT 6.1   CONTINUED

I. MANUFACTURING PERSONNEL

We reviewed manufacturing personnel considerations to identify those areas of deficiency where positive improvements could be made in terms of economy, efficiency, and effectiveness. The following major areas for operational improvement were noted for your review:

1. *Vice President of Production.* Vice President of Production position at present is unnecessary. As plant operations are presently controlled by Joe, based on his priorities using a manual system, all that is needed is a plant manager or overseer. Ed Harrison should be used to get the MRP II system operational and improve operations per our review.
2. *Forepersons.* Foreperson positions are superfluous at present. All six positions could be eliminated with minimal impact to plant operations. They could be used to assist in implementing the MRP II system, and then retain at least three to function as database operators and analysts.
3. *Production Team Leaders.* Production team leaders (six) are really functioning as chief workers. Their emphasis is on controlling production and workers rather than helpers. With increased backlog and the need to increase productivity and satisfy customer demands, these personnel (probably three) could be used better as roving trainers, coaches, and work facilitators. The other three could be used better as production workers to improve productivity and meet production and delivery schedules.
4. *Production Teams.* Production teams (six teams of six members each) are divided by product type (one specialty, one custom, two defense, and two basic teams). This team concept needs to be reevaluated as the present methods of production are contrary to this concept. By developing more efficient production methods that are flexible and relate more to the product being produced, the company should be able to increase productivity with fewer employees and less cost, reduce backlogs, better control inventories, conserve production capacity, and increase profits.

EXHIBIT 6.1 CONTINUED

5. *Repairs and Maintenance.* The entire five-employee Repairs and Maintenance unit could be disbanded, with the possible exception of one person for regular tool maintenance and emergency repairs and auxiliary facility maintenance duties. Other tool repairs should be done on an outside vendor basis, or the tool replaced. Work area maintenance should be the responsibility of the work crews, with morning and evening maintenance jobbed to the outside.

6. *Packing Operation.* The packing operation should be moved online with production, so that the goods are counted and packed as they are produced and ready for shipment.

7. *Packing/Shipping and Receiving Areas.* Packing/shipping and receiving areas need to be unclogged and cleaned up so that materials and finished goods can be separated cleanly and the two operations function properly.

8. *Controlling Production by Product.* Consideration should be given to controlling production by product rather than by customer order. This should work cleanly for basic boards and to some extent for specialty boards. For custom boards, where there is a greater likelihood that another order for the same exact product is not in the system, production by customer order may have to continue. The defense (government) business needs to be reevaluated as to whether to remain in this business.

9. *Short Small Quantities.* For those customers requiring an exact quantity or more, there needs to be an integration with inventory and other customer orders to determine whether this quantity is in-house or needs to be produced. If it needs to be produced, a small work crew of two individuals should be set up, which would be more effective than holding the order in a wait state.

10. *Receiving Function.* Receiving needs to be recoordinated with the production system. Once this is done and conditions have been cleaned up, there is no need for more than one of the three receivers.

EXHIBIT 6.1   CONTINUED

---

11. *Inventory Control.* Inventory control has become uncontrollable, with the inventory control manager becoming a chaser rather than a controller. The inventory control portion of the MRP II system needs to be re-implemented so as to minimize the amount of raw materials and finished goods on hand. The present chaotic condition of these inventories needs to be cleaned up and the system put back in place to keep it that way.

12. *Quality Control.* Quality Control work stations should be brought in line with production by moving the six QC inspectors into the production area. This would create the maximum efficiency for work-in-process and finished goods inspections. QC personnel should be used based on work requirements per job rather than by the present assignment by production team.

    Raw material inspections should be set up close to the receiving area so that only acceptable raw materials are moved into production or temporary storage. Defective materials can be controlled and returned as soon as possible.

    The results of these two findings should result in reducing the number of QC inspectors from six to no more than four.

13. *Quality Control Manager.* The QC manager's job at present is unnecessary. Each QC inspector is managing his or her own area, and the MRP II system for QC is inoperable, leaving very little for the QC manager to do. This function could be handled by the recommended plant manager.

14. *Quality Control Clerical Staff.* The two clerical staff assigned to quality control have very little to do. They were hired for data entry, update, and inquiry of the MRP II system, which is not implemented. Present QC clerical requirements could be handled by a clerical pool operation. This whole area of clerical personnel assigned to all operating areas needs to be reviewed, as this appears to be a company-wide and costly problem.

EXHIBIT 6.1   CONTINUED

Quantification of Findings

The overuse of personnel in manufacturing operations has resulted in their being less than efficient and causing a number of functions and personnel to get in each other's way. In addition, the excess number of personnel are costing the company more than $500,000 as follows:

• Vice President of Operations	$ 74,000
• Forepersons (six @ $24,000)	144,000
• Repairs and Maintenance (four @ $24,000)	96,000
• Receivers (two @ $10,000)	20,000
• Quality Control inspectors (two @ $22,000)	44,000
• Quality Control manager	26,000
• Quality Control Clerical (two @ $16,000)	32,000
Total Cost of Personnel	$436,000
Less Cost of Plant Manager	36,000
Net Cost of Personnel	$400,000
Plus: Fringe Benefits @ 32%	128,000
Net Savings	$528,000

Summary of Recommendations

1. Eliminate Vice President of Production and six foreperson positions immediately, or use these personnel to assist in implementing MRP II system and procedures. You could also consider retaining at least three of the forepersons as database operators and analyzers or hire less expensive personnel once the MRP II system is operational. Hire a plant manager or use one of the present forepersons in this capacity.
2. Use present production team leaders (probably three) as roving trainers, coaches, and work facilitators. Use the other three as production workers to improve productivity, reduce the use of overtime, and meet production and delivery schedules.
3. Reevaluate the production team concept of assigning a six-member work team by product type. Consider a more flexible method based on the product being produced.

EXHIBIT 6.1   CONTINUED

4. Eliminate the repair and maintenance unit by using outside vendors for tool repairs or replacing the tool, and using an outside vendor for morning and evening maintenance. One individual could be considered for retention for regular tool maintenance, emergency repairs, and auxiliary maintenance.
5. Recoordinate receiving with the production system and clean up present conditions, reducing the need to only one receiver.
6. Bring QC workstations in line with production and use QC inspectors based on work requirements. Set up raw material inspections close to the receiving area. This will result in the ability to reduce present staff form six to four.
7. Eliminate the QC manager's position and have this function handled by the plant manager.
8. Eliminate the two QC clerical positions by using a clerical pool concept for this and other areas.

EXHIBIT 6.1   CONTINUED

II. MANUFACTURING SYSTEMS

As part of our operational review of manufacturing systems, functions, and activities, we found the following major findings and recommendations, summarized below:

1. *Manufacturing Control Computer System.* The JOBEASY MRP II software package is not being presently used. However, although this package is relatively complete for what it is intended to do, it is not compatible for this company.
2. *Systems Specifications.* The company needs to define its systems specifications for what it requires in a manufacturing control system, and then locate the software package that best fits the needs.
3. *Computer Software Package Contents.* The major elements to be considered in such a package include:

   - Sales forecasting
   - Production scheduling and control
   - Material requirements planning
   - Capacity requirements planning
   - Inventory control
   - Cost control
   - Integration with other systems modules (e.g., billing)
   - Operating reporting

4. *Modifications as to Product Lines.* Manufacturing systems and procedures need to be modified to fit the various product lines: specialty, custom, defense, and basic. Consideration should be given to customer order control, work center by product line, QC procedures, packing and shipping concepts, use of personnel (forepersons, production team leaders, six-member production teams), inventory storage, and control.
5. *Concentration on Specialty and Custom Boards.* Concentrate on main product strengths—specialty and custom boards—with manufacturing systems based on these product lines. Sales and engineering efforts should be directed toward more standardization among various customer needs, increasing the ability to more accurately forecast these sales.

EXHIBIT 6.1   CONTINUED

---

6. *Defense Business.* Determine whether the company should remain
   in the defense (government) business. It takes up an unequal
   amount of production space for its limited contribution to profits.
7. *Basic Board Business.* The basic board business, which is really
   that of a distributor, should become a business of buying and
   reselling (bypassing inventory and manufacturing processes).
8. *Productivity Increases.* Production capacity is being
   overextended while customer order backlog is increasing.
   Manufacturing systems and methods need to be streamlined so
   that productivity can be increased. Emphasis on specialty and
   custom boards, standardization, and manufacturing processes
   geared to individual products needs to be addressed.

Quantification of Findings

The defense business is taking up one-third of the company's
production capacity while contributing minimally to company sales and
net income. In addition, more profitable business segments (specialty,
custom, and basic boards) are building up customer orders in backlog.

   Based on disbanding the defense business, converting the basic board
business to a sales distribution business, adapting our other manufacturing
recommendations, and concentrating on the two core businesses of
specialty and custom boards, we estimate the company can:

- Increase production by over 50 percent (at less cost).
- Eliminate present specialty and custom backlog ($1,320,000).
- Increase sales of specialty and custom products by at least 20 percent
  or $860,000 (20 percent of $4,300,000).
- Increase overall annual sales by over $2,500,000.
- Provide additional net income of at least $625,000 (estimated at 25
  percent of $2,500,000).

   These figures do not include additional sales and net income to be
generated by converting the basic board business into a sales distribution
business.

EXHIBIT 6.1   CONTINUED

Summary of Recommendations

The company should determine whether it should remain in the defense and government contract business. In addition, it should be moving toward making the basic board business into a sales distribution business—that is, buying and reselling the products, with vendors direct shipping to customers whenever possible. We believe the company would become more efficient and increase overall productivity and resultant net income by disbanding the defense business, making the basic board business a sales distribution business, and allocating the resulting plant capacity to the other, more profitable, segments of the business: specialty and custom boards.

EXHIBIT 6.1   CONTINUED

III. MANUFACTURING FACILITY AND PRODUCTION PROCEDURES

As a result of our review of manufacturing facilities, including present plant layout, production operations and procedures, product line concerns, and proposed plant layout concepts, we identified the following major findings and recommendations:

1. *Uneven Distribution of Work.* Present plant layout and work flow based on six work centers by product line (one for specialty, one for custom, two for defense, two for basic boards) is causing uneven distribution of work and misuse of available space.
2. *Six-Member Work Teams Inefficient.* Six-member work teams are an efficient allocation of personnel and a negative factor in productivity. For almost all jobs, fewer personnel are required, normally two or three.
3. *Present Plant Layout Concerns.* The present plant layout and manufacturing methods have created the following adverse conditions:

   - Packing/shipping and receiving are becoming merged.
   - Inventory: raw materials, work-in-process, and finished goods are stored all over the production area, resulting in a lack of overall inventory control.
   - Quality Control performs offline inspection procedures, resulting in production delays.
   - Concept of six forepersons and six team leaders (one each for each work team) is counterproductive.

4. *Quality Control Inefficiencies.* Quality Control is housed in the office area and not readily available to production. Testing is done offline in a separate room at the back of production.
5. *More Effective Use of Production Facilities.* Main production facility should be devoted to specialty and custom board manufacturing. Production should be based on realistic sales forecasts and/or real customer orders. Standardization of parts and products should be maximized by the engineering and sales departments working together.
6. *More Efficient Production Methods.* Manufacturing processes should be analyzed so that each specialty and custom product uses the most efficient methods of production.

EXHIBIT 6.1   CONTINUED

---

7. *Flexible Production Procedures.* Production layout and procedures should be set up on a flexible basis considering the number of work steps and mix of products at any one time.
8. *Disbanding Defense Business.* Strong consideration should be given to getting out of the defense (government contracting) business.
9. *Basic Board Business—Sales Distributorship.* The basic board business should become that of a sales distribution business; with vendors storing and shipping as much of the product as possible.

Quantification of Findings

As a result of inefficient manufacturing procedures, the company has diminished its potential productivity, has inventory out of control, has production employees getting in each other's way, has increased the amount of rejected items and rework, is experiencing more than 20 percent overtime for production workers, and has a delivery on-time record of less than 40 percent. In addition, present manufacturing procedures are resulting in excess personnel and inefficient methods, which are costing the company over $1 million annually in unnecessary costs. We estimate that the company can (conservatively) save more than $900,000 in annual personnel costs just by implementing our proposed plant layout and related operating procedures as follows:

Present Condition			Proposed Condition			Savings	
No.	Position	Dollars	No.	Position	Dollars	No.	Dollars
1	VP-Production	$74,000	1	Plant Manager	$36,000	—	$38,000
6	Forepersons	144,000	—	—	—	6	144,000
6	Team Leaders	132,000	3	Trainer/Coach	66,000	3	66,000
36	Production	576,000	28	Production	448,000	8	128,000
5	Repair/Maint.	120,000	1	Repair/Maint	24,000	4	96,000
4	Packer/Shipper	52,000	4	Packer/Shipper	52,000	—	—
3	Receivers	30,000	1	Receiver	10,000	2	20,000
1	Inv. Cont. Mgr.	18,000	1	Inv. Cont. Mgr.	18,000	—	—
1	QC Manager	26,000	—	—	—	1	26,000
6	QC Inspectors	132,000	4	QC Inspectors	88,000	2	44,000
2	QC Clerical	32,000	—	—	—	2	32,000
71		$1,336,000	43		$742,000	28	$594,000

EXHIBIT 6.1   CONTINUED

Present Condition			Proposed Condition			Savings	
No.	Position	Dollars	No.	Position	Dollars	No.	Dollars
	Overtime 20% (Team Leaders & Production)	141,600			—		141,600
		$1,477,600			$742,000		$735,600
	Fringe Benefits @ 32%	472,832			237,440		235,392
	Totals	$1,950,432			$979,440		$970,992

These estimated savings do not include the additional amount of productivity to be accomplished through these recommendations—estimated to be at least 25 percent of present specialty and custom board production levels, or 25 percent of $4,300,000 = $1,075,000.

Summary of Recommendations

Implement our proposed plant layout and manufacturing procedural change recommendations, together with specific recommendations, features, and basic assumptions. Paramount to achieving the economy, efficiency, and effectiveness of these recommendations is implementation of the following specific recommendations:

- Disband the defense/government contracting business.
- Develop the basic board business into a sales distribution business.
- Stress specialty and custom boards as your main business.
- Do production scheduling by product or finished goods part number.
- Coordinate with materials vendors so that delivery schedules match your production schedule.
- Standardize specialty and custom parts, with the ability to separate out add-on options.
- Increase flexibility in production as to the type of processes and the number of work steps.
- Promote flexibility and interchangeability of production workers.
- Effectively use floating trainer/coaches.

EXHIBIT 6.1   CONTINUED

- Integrate QC inspection and packing/shipping into the online production process.
- Stress effectiveness in responding to periods of under or over plant capacity conditions and the ability to make effective decisions.
- Maintain effective control over work-in-process directed toward meeting customer delivery schedules.
- Institute effective inventory control procedures, resulting in lowering inventory levels over raw materials, components, work-in-process, and finished goods inventories.
- Change manufacturing attitude to one of increased productivity, working together and helping each other, fixing the problem and not the blame, and customer rather than crisis orientation.

EXHIBIT 6.1   CONTINUED

IV. INVENTORY CONTROL SYSTEMS AND PROCEDURES

Our review and analysis of present and proposed inventory control procedures identified the following major findings and recommendations:

1. *Misuse of Present Computer System.* The present JOBEASY computer system is not being properly maintained and kept up-to-date due to the volume of receipt and issue transactions.
2. *Excessive Inventory Levels.* Raw materials and components and finished goods inventories are not being kept to a minimum; present storeroom is beyond capacity, and materials are stored all over the production area
3. *Ineffective Inventory Control Manager.* The inventory control manager cannot effectively do his job, resulting in his chasing rather than controlling inventory.
4. *Crisis Ordering of Raw Materials and Components.* Raw materials and components are being ordered based on customer order crises rather than being integrated with a controlled production schedule.
5. *Customer Orders Not Being Shipped.* Finished goods inventory is not being shipped out as completed in production based on customer delivery schedules, due to short quantities, inability to ship, crises taking priority, and so on. This has resulted in finished goods being stored all over the plant facility.
6. *Inadequate Storeroom Control Procedures.* There are at present no adequate storeroom control procedures. Storeroom capacity is overextended, materials are sitting all over the production area, and items are located strictly on a search-and-find basis.
7. *Chaotic Inventory Receiving Procedures.* Inventory receiving procedures are chaotic because materials received for a customer order cannot be placed into production or the overcrowded storeroom, but most be placed somewhere in the production area.
8. *Inability to Locate Needed Materials.* When materials are needed to be issued into production, it becomes a search-and-find mission to locate the correct materials. Many times the materials cannot be found, the quantity is short, or additional different materials have been added.

EXHIBIT 6.1 CONTINUED

9. *Uncontrolled Inventory Control Environment.* Although the computerized JOBEASY inventory control system provides for effective inventory control reporting, it is not being used. Accordingly, proper inventory control reporting procedures are not present, which has resulted in an uncontrolled inventory control environment. All of the desired inventory control reporting features should be incorporated into the proposed computer system specifications.

Quantification of Findings

The result of inadequate inventory control procedures has been the storage of raw materials and components and finished goods all over the plant facility. Often, when materials are needed in production, the materials cannot be found (and may result in emergency reorders), quantities are short, other different materials have been added, and multiple quantities are found. This process of search and seek as materials are needed is also costly in the time required to locate items, as well as in inefficient production with these materials (and finished goods) in the way.

The related costs of having finished goods sitting in storage and not being shipped include the lost cost of shipping and collecting from the customer, the cost of carrying this inventory, the cost of not locating the order in whole or in part and having to redo production, the lost cost of the value of the money tied up in inventory, the cost to the company's cash position, the cost of customer dissatisfaction and loss of customers, and so on.

Although we cannot quantify many of these costs, such as the cost of locating inventory items, customer dissatisfaction and lost sales, and the cost of workers' being in an uncontrolled inventory control environment, we can estimate the cost of carrying inventory, based on the electronics industry standard of 20 percent of inventory value, to be approximately $536,000 (20 percent of present inventory of $2,680,000).

The present inventory condition has to be cleaned up and a controllable environment maintained, as it affects all aspects of manufacturing, as well as being costly in dollars and management of operations.

EXHIBIT 6.1   CONTINUED

Summary of Recommendations

1. Develop desired systems specifications for a proposed computerized inventory control system to include all necessary features to effectively control raw materials and components, and finished goods inventories.
2. Through the disbanding of the defense business, turn the present inventory of $340,000 into cash by using in specialty or custom board production, returning it to vendors, selling it to other customers, selling it to other manufacturers, and selling it for scrap. Finished goods inventory should be delivered and billed.
3. Basic board inventory of $600,000, which is mostly finished goods or close to it, should be reduced by turning it into sales and then concentrating on making this a sales distribution business, as previously discussed.
4. Raw materials and components inventories for specialty and custom boards needs to be controlled as to what exactly is on hand and which parts can still be used in production. This needs to be coordinated with customer orders in hand and in backlog so as to use these materials in production as soon as possible and not reorder them.
5. Raw materials and components that cannot be used (obsolete) or will not be used in production in the near term (within six months) should be disposed of (converted to cash) by returns to vendors, sales to others, modification for use in production, sale as scrap, and so on.
6. The remaining raw materials and components inventory needs to be physically controlled (hopefully, it will be minimum) and integrated with an adequate record keeping system.
7. Finished goods inventory of specialty and custom boards needs to be analyzed as to what orders are readily shippable, what orders need to be cleaned up or require additional production before they can be shipped, and what items are excess inventory. For these excess inventory items, efforts should be taken to convert them to cash through special sales efforts to present customers.

EXHIBIT 6.1   CONTINUED

V. FOUR BUSINESS CONCEPTS

Our review of the company's four product lines—specialty boards, custom boards, defense business, and basic boards—identified the following major findings and recommendations:

1. *Specialty and Custom Boards—Main Businesses.* The specialty board business creates the largest amount of annual sales ($2,950,000) with a respectable operating profit margin of 22.6 percent. The custom board business has grown in the three years to $1,350,000, with an operating profit margin of 24.4 percent for the past year. These numbers are with the many inefficiencies noted elsewhere in our review. These are the company's main businesses and should be expanded.

2. *Convert Defense Business Space for Main Businesses.* The defense business is operating at a marginal level (about 3 percent profit margin with underestimated costs) in a downward market. The company should disband these operations and devote its space and efforts to the specialty and custom businesses.

3. *Expand Basic Board Business.* The basic board business is a growth area of the company which should be expanded. It has almost doubled from last year ($600,000 in sales) to this year ($1,150,000 in sales) and has great potential. However, the present practice of bringing the finished product into the plant mainly to apply identifier materials should be discontinued. This should become a sales distribution business, with the company having the vendors direct ship to customers to the extent possible.

4. *Increase Competitiveness.* Sales prices have come down each of the three years the company has been in business. This is a result of more competition, the customer's push to lower their costs and prices, and an overall down economy. The company can probably expect further erosion of sales prices on their products. While there is still good potential for increased unit sales, this never makes up for loss of selling price. The company needs to become more competitive in engineering, manufacturing, and cost containment.

EXHIBIT 6.1   CONTINUED

---

5. *Convert Backlog into Sales.* Total customer order backlog is currently over 35 percent of last year's sales ($2,200 of $6,250); with 33.6 percent for specialty, 31.1 percent for custom, and 46.1 percent for basic boards. This is entirely too high, particularly in light of the company's current shaky cash position. This backlog needs to be converted into sales and collections before it disappears to the competition.

6. *Collect Accounts Receivable.* Accounts receivable is at an uncontrollable level. The collection period has gone over 100 days. This situation is mainly due to Joe's push to get sales, create production crises, and relax credit terms, and to customer complaints and held back payments for less than quality merchandise.

7. *Uncontrollable Inventory Levels.* Inventory levels have risen to uncontrollable proportions, with turnover ratios of about three times per year and the average age of inventory over 100 days. This situation is not only contributing to the poor cash position, but is clogging the plant facility.

8. *Service Major Customers—Increase Customer Base.* The company is dependent on a limited number of customers in each of the primary businesses—specialty, custom, and basic boards. While this is advantageous in working with these customers as to assisting them to define their needs, forecast their purchases, and more effectively service them, it leaves Joe Sorry Company open to possible quick losses of revenue and income should any one of these customers pull their orders and start to use one of the competition. This is particularly critical with the company's current large backlog, inability to meet delivery dates, large amount of customer complaints, amount of returned and defective merchandise, and so on. The company needs to better service these customers as well as look for an additional customer base.

9. *Revise Present Operations.* Operations need to be revised for the company to function more efficiently, provide better customer service, maximize production throughput, utilize plant capacity more effectively, minimize inventories, and so on. Areas that should be reviewed include:

   • Production control and scheduling by customer order rather than a combination of orders by product type.
   • Production scheduling by customer delivery date, ensuring on-time deliveries for all customer orders.

EXHIBIT 6.1 CONTINUED

- Sales staff, who are presently customer order takers, need to become more proactive with the customers to help them define their needs and forecast their purchases.
- Engineering presently looks at each customer order separately for product design. There is little coordination between previous orders or other customers' orders.
- Purchasing is primarily functioning as the processor of purchase orders for materials for each customer order. There is no coordination between customer orders or overall material requirements. This is costing the company considerably in higher prices for small amounts at a time.
- Purchasing is responsible for ordering materials for delivery at the time of planned production start for that customer order. However, this is not being effectively monitored or controlled, resulting in materials coming in and sitting in inventory all around the plant.
- The Customer Service unit, which was established to deal with customer after-sale concerns, is presently backed up over a month with such customer complaints. In addition, they are now spending almost as much of their time on preproduction customer calls.

Quantification of Findings

The buildup of customer backlog has resulted in reduced and canceled sales from some of the company's major customers. For instance, Apex Electronics accounted for $440,000 in specialty board sales in 20X2, but only $380,000 in 20X3. Discussions with this customer's representatives revealed that the drop in their business was attributed to Joe Sorry Company's inability to produce and deliver on time—otherwise Apex would have increased its business. Other major customers related the same story.

The total of $2,200,000 in present customer backlog could be converted to sales, producing an operating profit of approximately $400,000 (18 percent operating profit margin plus efficiencies).

EXHIBIT 6.1   CONTINUED

Summary of Recommendations

Adopt the proposed plant layout and related features and production method changes, as recommended previously, so as to increase throughput and productivity of specialty and custom board orders. At the same time, phase out of the defense business, and move toward making the basic board business into a sales distribution business.

EXHIBIT 6.1   CONTINUED

VI. PROPOSED INTEGRATED COMPUTER SYSTEM

The computerized integrated manufacturing control and management reporting system that we are proposing involves a communications process in which data are recorded initially, and revised as needed, in order to support management and staff decisions for planning, operating, and controlling manufacturing operations. Our conceptual design attempts to maximize the use of common data to satisfy the information requirements of Joe Sorry Company staff at various levels. It attempts to strike an economic balance between the values of the information to be carried and the cost of operating the system. Accordingly, our objective is not simply to mechanize, but to design an effective computerization plan that will provide Joe Sorry Company manufacturing personnel with the necessary data to manage and operate.

1. *Proposed Computerization.* Proposed computerization will also afford the opportunity for additional personnel cost savings in the purchasing, inventory control, and engineering functions. Accordingly, Joe Sorry Company management should review future departmental and personnel functions and responsibilities for possible elimination, combination, shifting, and downgrading. A personnel plan should be developed to coordinate procedural changes with personnel requirements on an ongoing basis as changes are implemented.
2. *Additional Personnel.* We believe that to successfully implement the proposed computer systems in a timely manner, in addition to simultaneously completing our other computer-related recommendations, one additional experienced manufacturing systems person will have to be hired or contracted with.
3. *Computer Processing Priorities.* We also believe that the most efficient and practical course of action for management to take in regard to computer processing is to establish the following priorities:

   - Implement our recommended manufacturing function improvements based on the priorities previously established.
   - Simultaneously implement the production and inventory control systems presently being designed.

EXHIBIT 6.1   CONTINUED

- Develop the system specifications with management and operations approval, determine the software package for your needs, implement modifications, and install the proposed integrated manufacturing control computer system as described.

4. *Computer Equipment Requirements.* We believe that the present computer systems are capable of performing the aforementioned processing. After the listed items have successfully been accomplished and are operational, Joe Sorry Company management should reappraise computer equipment needs with respect to total processing.

EXHIBIT 6.1   CONTINUED

Attachment A   Page A-1
JOE SORRY COMPANY
SUMMARY OF MAJOR FINDINGS AND RECOMMENDATIONS

Description	Estimated Annual Effect

1. *Manufacturing Personnel*
   a. Excess Personnel in Manufacturing — $ 528,000 *
   b. Packing Operations Online — **
   c. Packing/Shipping & Receiving Areas — ***
   d. Controlling Production by Product — **
   e. Quality Control In line with Production — **
2. *Manufacturing Systems*
   a. Manufacturing Control Computer System — **
   b. Modifications as to Product Lines — 50 % production increase
   c. Concentration on Specialty/Custom Boards — 860,000 sales
   d. Productivity Increases — 625,000 net income
3. *Manufacturing Facilities and Production Procedures*
   a. Uneven Distribution of Work — **
   b. Six-Member Work Teams Inefficient — **
   c. Plant Layout ($970,992–$528,000) — 442,992 *
   d. More Effective Use of Production Facilities — **
   e. Disband Defense Business & Convert Basic Board Business to Sales Distributorship — 1,075,000 Sales
4. *Inventory Control Systems and Procedures*
   a. Misuse of Present Computer System — ***
   b. Excessive Inventory Levels — ***
   c. Customer Orders Not Being Shipped — ***
   d. Uncontrolled Inventory Environment — 536,000 *
5. *Four Business Concepts*
   a. Specialty/Custom Boards—Main Business — ***
   b. Increase Competitiveness — ***
   c. Convert Backlog into Sales — 400,000 Net Income
   d. Service Major Customers—Increase Customer Base — ***
   e. Revise Present Operations — ***

EXHIBIT 6.1   CONTINUED

Description	Estimated Annual Effect
Summary:	
1. Annual Cost Savings:	$1,506,992
2. Increased Sales:	$1,935,000
3. Increased Net Income:	$1,025,000

* Estimated decreased costs. Annual savings should be greater.
** Improved productivity: cannot estimate effect.
*** Cannot be quantified.

EXHIBIT 6.1   CONTINUED

Attachment B   Page B-1
JOE SORRY, INC.
OTHER AREAS FOR REVIEW

Based on the work performed during our operational review of the
Manufacturing Department, we identified additional operational areas
that we believe should be brought to your attention for further review
and analysis. These additional areas include:

1. Organizational planning and related systems. We found that Joe
   Sorry Company operates on a reactive basis (i.e., in response to
   specific situations and crises). Steps should be taken to implement
   effective planning techniques, which encompass:

   • Sophisticated sales forecast procedures that allow management
     to determine related production requirements based on planned
     customer demand.
   • Effective production scheduling systems that provide for
     controlling manufacturing operations, based on planned
     customer orders rather than on inventory demands.
   • Formal planning procedures that include organizational and
     departmental goals, objectives, and detail plans, as well as an
     effective reporting and control system to ensure compliance with
     agreed-upon plans.
   • Development of departmental and work unit budgets that use
     established plans as their basis and report on a flexible basis as
     related to activity levels.

2. Organizational structure, in regard to making the organization
   more responsive to current demands. Areas to consider include
   reporting relationships, responsibility/authority relationships,
   management and supervisory assignments, workload distributions,
   and so on. For example, based on our review of the Manufacturing
   Department, we suggest you review the following areas:
   • Assistants to the President: functions, responsibilities, use, and
     authority of these staff positions.
   • Vice President of Operations (Flo Sorry): use and responsibilities
     of this position, as well as purpose for two assistants and a
     secretary.

EXHIBIT 6.1   CONTINUED

- Use of clerical staff, such as two Clerks for Personnel, three Clerks for Purchasing, four Clerks in Sales, three Clerks in Engineering, four Clerks in Accounting, and two Clerks in Customer Service.
- The specific functions for Personnel, Purchasing, Sales, Engineering, and Customer Service.

3. Personnel practices related to hiring, orientation, training, evaluation, promotion, and firing. We found no policies or procedures related to these personnel practices in existence. Accordingly, such practices are implemented by Joe and other managers/supervisors based on their own criteria and expertise. Procedures, therefore, are weak and inconsistent; resulting in employee confusion, improperly trained staff and management, and retention of undesirable employees.
4. Other operating systems and procedures, such as personnel, purchasing, sales, engineering, accounting, and customer service, in regard to performing necessary functions in the most economical and efficient manner without sacrificing expected results.
5. More efficient use and integration of computer techniques with actual operations. You have had your computer system operational for more than two years; however, you are still manually performing many functions which lend themselves to effective computerization. A major reason for this is the lack of direction of computer activities by top management. Computer hardware and software were originally implemented with the help of outside consultants at the time the computer system was installed. You are presently using these resources minimally (if at all). Our recommended integrated manufacturing control system is an excellent first step. However, other areas should be looked at as well, such as sales forecasting and reporting, personnel systems, purchasing, engineering, customer service statistics, billing, and collections.

REVIEW QUESTIONS

1. What are the principal objectives of the operational review report?
2. What are the four types of operational review reports?
3. What are some of the basic characteristics of good reporting?

SUGGESTED RESPONSES

1. What are the principal objectives of the operational review report?

Response

- Provide useful and timely information on significant matters.
- Recommend improvements in the conduct of operations.
- Get management's undivided attention.
- Show management the benefits of the operational review.
- Show management what the review team staff can accomplish.

2. What are the four types of operational review reports?

Response

- Formal
- Informal
- Oral
- Written

3. What are some of the basic characteristics of good reporting?

Response

- Significance: to justify reporting matter to management.
- Usefulness and timeliness: to meet the interests and needs of management in a timely manner for appropriate action to be taken.
- Accuracy and adequacy of support: no errors of act, logic, or reasoning.

- Convincingness: review findings presented in a convincing manner, and related conclusions and recommendations follow logically from the facts presented.
- Objectivity and perspective: presented in an objective unbiased
  manner.
- Clarity and simplicity: clear and simple as possible.
- Conciseness: no longer than necessary to communicate required
  information.
- Constructiveness of tone: to encourage favorable reaction to review
  findings and recommendations. Emphasize needed improvements
  rather than criticisms.